Star
Power

Star Power

Profiles of Today's Hottest Entertainers

Volume 4

Marie J. MacNee

Allison McNeill, Editor

AN IMPRINT OF THE GALE GROUP

DETROIT · SAN FRANCISCO · LONDON
BOSTON · WOODBRIDGE, CT

9855560

Star Power, Volume 4
Profiles of Today's Hottest Entertainers

Marie J. MacNee

Staff

Allison McNeill, *U•X•L Senior Editor*
Carol DeKane Nagel, *U•X•L Managing Editor*
Thomas L. Romig, *U•X•L Publisher*

Meggin Condino, *Senior Market Analyst–U•X•L*

Eric Johnson, *Art Director*
Cynthia Baldwin, *Product Design Manager*

Margaret Chamberlain, *Permissions Specialist (Pictures)*

Pamela Reed, *Imaging Coordinator*
Robert Duncan, *Senior Imaging Specialist*
Randy A. Bassett, *Image Database Supervisor*

Rita Wimberley, *Senior Buyer*
Evi Seoud, *Assistant Production Manager*
Dorothy Maki, *Manufacturing Manager*

Marco Di Vita, Graphix Group, *Typesetting*

Cover photographs: Jackie Chan (The Kobal Collection); Chris Tucker (AP/Wide World); Jennifer Love Hewitt (The Kobal Collection).

Copyright © 1999
U•X•L, an imprint of Gale Group
27500 Drake Rd.
Farmington Hills, MI 48331-3535

ISBN 0-7876-3940-0
ISSN 1524-7678
Printed in the United States of America

10 9 8 7 6 5 4 3 2 1

Contents of Volume 4

BIOGRAPHICAL LISTINGS

⭐**UPDATE** indicates update to original entry

Drew Barrymore (AP/Wide World).

Stars by Field of Endeavor

Boldface indicates main entries in *Star Power,* Volume 4, and their page numbers; *1–3* refers to entries in the three-volume *Performing Artists* base set. **UPDATE** indicates an update to the original entry.

Music

Reader's Guide

Awadagin Pratt (AP/Wide World)

S tar Power: Profiles of Today's Hottest Entertainers, Volume 4, features 40 biographies—30 new entries and 10 update entries—of actors, dancers, comedians, musicians, singers, television personalities, and writers and directors who have made an impact on the entertainment industry. Selected and written especially with students in mind, the entries focus on the performers' early lives and motivations as well as highlights (and lowlights) of their careers.

Format

Arranged alphabetically, the biographies open with the individual's birth date and place of birth—and, where applicable, the date and place of death. Each entry features a portrait of the subject, a 4- to 9-page essay on his or her life and career, and a list of sources for further reading. Additionally, sidebars containing interesting facts about or related to the star are sprinkled throughout the text, as are 70 movie stills and portrait shots. A cumulative index providing easy access to the people and works mentioned in *Star Power,* Volume 4, and *Performing Artists,* Volumes 1 to 3, concludes the volume.

From *Performing Artists* to *Star Power*

Star Power, Volume 4, is a continuation of U•X•L's 3-volume *Performing Artists* series. The title was changed to *Star Power* to more accurately reflect the content of the series as focusing on popular entertainers rather than those from the fine and performing arts. Readers will find references to *Performing Artists,* Volumes 1 to 3, throughout *Star Power,* Volume 4, specifically in the "Update" entries, which direct you back to the base set for the original entry, and in the cumulative field of endeavor index and general index.

Features

- "Update" entries keep readers current on stars profiled in the 3-volume *Performing Artists* base set who have remained active in their fields. Updates are clearly indicated on the first page of the entry next to the performer's photo as well as in the tables of contents. In addition, readers are directed back to the original essay on the performer, where they will find information on the performer's early life and early career. For example, the cross-reference "See original essay on Carrey in *Performing Artists,* Volume 1" appears in the beginning of the Jim Carrey update essay.

- The field of Writing and Directing has been added to *Star Power,* Volume 4, to profile those individuals who have made a behind-the-scenes impact on the entertainment industry.

- Sidebars provide cool supplemental information about or related to the star.

- Quotes—both by and about the stars—offer revealing insights into their lives.

- 70 portraits and movie stills showcase the stars and their recent works.

- Sources for further reading at the end of each entry list books, newspaper and magazine articles, and Internet addresses for additional information.

- A cumulative Field of Endeavor index lists stars by their entertainment fields—Comedy, Dance, Film and Television, Music, Writing and Directing—for easy access. The Field of Endeavor index includes stars from *Performing Artists,* Volumes 1 to 3, and *Star Power,* Volume 4.

- A cumulative general index covers the stars and their works found in *Performing Artists,* Volumes 1 to 3, and *Star Power,* Volume 4.

Acknowledgments

The editor would like to thank Bonnie Raasch, Media Specialist at Vernon Middle School in Marion, Iowa—and her students—for looking over the extensive inclusion list and helping narrow the scope to the 40 biographies profiled in *Star Power,* Volume 4.

Comments and Suggestions

We welcome your comments on this work as well as your suggestions for individuals to be featured in future editions of *Star Power: Profiles of Today's Hottest Entertainers.* Please write: Editor, *Star Power,* U•X•L, 27500 Drake Road, Farmington Hills, Michigan 48331; call toll-free: 1-800-877-4253; fax: 1-248-414-5043; or send e-mail via www.galegroup.com.

Drew Barrymore

Born February 22, 1975
Los Angeles, California

Actress, producer

Born into a show-business family, Drew Barrymore began acting at an age when most children still rely on stuffed animals and security blankets. After appearing in Steven Spielberg's blockbuster sensation, *E.T.*, she became a hot Hollywood commodity—a distinction she did not bear well. Living life in the fast lane, she fell prey to drug and alcohol addiction before reaching her teens. Having undergone years of therapy and rehabilitation, the young actress struggled to re-establish her career. Her wild child history behind her, she slowly built an impressive body of works consisting primarily of non-mainstream, character-driven roles. Looking back on her difficult past, she told *USA Today*, "I'm really a happy person. I think there were a lot of years of my life when I wasn't so happy because I was confused. . . . And when things come clear to you, no matter how you have to get there, as long as you grow and come out on the other side, then it's all worth it."

"She really is this sensitive, guileless [innocent], pure-artist Pisces person. But when you take it all away, Drew really does want to be a big, huge movie star."
—Courtney Love

(AP/Wide World Photos)

1

Born into the 'biz

Barrymore was born on February 22, 1975 in Los Angeles, California, just months after her parents separated. Her father, John Barrymore, Jr., a former B-movie actor and poet, was an abusive alcoholic who abandoned his family. Her mother, Ildiko Jaid Barrymore, a hard-partying former actress, took her young daughter with her as she made the rounds of Los Angeles's clubs and late-night parties. "People criticized her," Barrymore told *Mademoiselle*. ". . . taking me to nightclubs [when I was eight] isn't exactly a family value—but if it weren't for her, I wouldn't be sitting here."

The grand-niece of legendary actors Lionel and Ethel Barrymore—and granddaughter of Hollywood icon John Barrymore—Drew Barrymore was practically born into show business. She made her first screen appearance—in a Puppy Choice Dog Food commercial—when she was just eleven months old. When she was two years old, she landed her first movie role — as a boy—in *Suddenly Love,* a made-for-television drama.

Having made her feature-film debut as a five-year-old in *Altered States* (1980), Barrymore appeared two years later in the Steven Spielberg blockbuster, *E.T.,* the story of an extraterrestrial (alien) who lands on Earth and befriends a young boy and his sister. As the younger sister, Gertie, the young actress charmed critics. Almost overnight, Barrymore became a full-fledged star hotly pursued by both fans and studio executives.

Too much too soon

She didn't handle the pressure of sudden stardom well. "It was like an earthquake," she told a reporter from the *Chicago Tribune*. "People wanted so much from me and expected me to be much older. By the time I was eight I felt like I was this abnormal, crazy girl." Soon she began to experiment with alcohol and drugs. "I had my first drink at age nine, began smoking marijuana at ten, and at twelve took up cocaine," she later wrote in her autobiography *Little Girl Lost*. Having started drinking at a birthday party for actor Rob Lowe, Barrymore quickly found herself in the grip of alcohol dependency. "I would drink not to have fun—I would drink to get drunk," she told *People*. Drew was not the first Barrymore to experience substance abuse: her grandfather, John Barrymore, was reportedly an alcoholic by age fourteen and died prematurely due to his excessive drinking. Her father, too, has an extensive history of drug and alcohol abuse, and her aunt, Diana Barrymore, wrote about her chemical dependency in *Too Much, Too Soon,* a 1958 best-seller.

At first, Barrymore's mother was blind to her daughter's ordeal. "Like most parents, I had no idea what was going on," she told *Time*. ". . . .I felt I had to give her time and space. I began to lose perspective on what was going on with Drew." As the young actress's manager, Jaid Barrymore further distanced her daughter. "I had tried to be all things to Drew — mother, manager, drill sergeant, friend," she told *People*. "And when one assumes too many roles, none are done well." Her mother's attempts to intervene only angered the troubled young actress, whose life began to spin out of control. "We were always conflicting," she told *USA Today*. "She would try to be in my life and try and stop me from going out and put authority all over me all the time. But I just got to a point where I didn't care anymore. She really couldn't stop me."

Having become somewhat of a cult celebrity after starring as Charlie McGee in the 1984 Stephen King adaptation of *Firestarter,* Barrymore appeared in that year's *Irreconcilable Differences*. Her role as a young girl who sues her parents for emancipation [freedom from parental control] to find a more loving home earned her a Golden Globe nomination. Next she played Our Girl, who is rescued from a mischievous troll by her adopted cat, in *Cat's Eye,* a 1985 anthology (compilation) of three short stories by Stephen King.

Struggles with addiction

The actress's personal life, meantime, continued in its downward spiral. Too old for her years, the teenaged Barrymore was characterized by Steven Spielberg (who also happened to be her godfather), as being "13 going on 29." In June 1988, after a night of drinking, Barrymore exploded. She later told *People* that she shouted at her mother, "'What the hell are you doing here?'" She began to break dishes and glasses. "I wanted her out of the house," she explained to *People*. "It was my turn to

> ### A Barrymore Profile
>
> The Barrymore family has produced a number of notable performers. In the nineteenth century, Maurice Barrymore and his wife, Georgiana Drew, were both renowned actors. In the twentieth century, the names of Lionel and Ethel Barrymore were emblazoned on movie and theater marquees. Their brother, John Barrymore (Drew's grandfather) enjoyed tremendous popularity as an actor in the 1920s and 1930s, starring in such classic films as *Grand Hotel* and *Dinner at Eight*. A charismatic performer, he was dubbed "The Profile" for his classic good looks. Regarding her family's theatrical history, Drew Barrymore told *Mademoiselle,* "Anything I do, I put in the Barrymore bank and say, 'Here you go, another job done.'"

be Mom." Shortly after Barrymore's mother left the house, a friend of the actress arrived with her own mother. The two swept Barrymore into a car and drove her to ASAP Family Treatment Center, a rehabilitation clinic in Van Nuys, California.

Her stay in the clinic was brief. Less than three weeks after she entered the program, Barrymore flew to an acting job in Nevada and then to New York to audition for a play. Having been sober (drug and alcohol-free) for two months, she found herself in a nightclub where drugs were readily available. Thinking that a small amount of cocaine would not affect her recovery, she gave in to temptation. Next she took a credit card from her mother and hopped a plane to California. There she bought more cocaine and charged things on the credit card she had stolen. Captured by private investigators her mother had hired, Barrymore was taken back to the rehabilitation center in handcuffs.

The actress remained in the clinic for three months and celebrated her sobriety with a long and frank (open and honest) interview with *People* in the beginning of 1989. She also appeared in a television movie about teenage drug abuse. In March 1989, just months after her *People* confession was published, Barrymore went out with a friend to celebrate her six-month alcohol-free anniversary. This time, she gave in to the temptation to smoke marijuana, and gradually slid into a drug-addled depression. By mid-summer she hit rock-bottom: on July 4, 1989 she attempted to commit suicide. After a friend found her, Barrymore was rushed to a hospital. Next she was returned to ASAP, where she underwent three more months of rehabilitation.

A flower in the sidewalk

In October 1989, Barrymore was released into the custody of musician David Crosby (a former member of the band Crosby, Stills, Nash, and Young) and his wife, Jan Dance—both of whom were recovered drug addicts. One of the actress's counselors—a friend of Crosby and his wife—had arranged the situation in order to provide the teenager with a more understanding and supportive environment. At the same time, Barrymore's mother agreed to undergo therapy with the aim of creating a more positive relationship with her daughter. Having finally set her addictions aside, the fifteen-year-old actress successfully petitioned the State of California for emancipation from parental control—much as her character in *Irreconcilable Differences* had six years earlier.

Barrymore's struggle earned the actress a reputation for strength and courage. J. J. Harris, the agent who handled the actress from age 8 through 21, told *Premiere*, "I've always called Drew a flower coming up through the sidewalk—delicate, but indomitable [unconquerable]." Although the teenaged actress had managed to begin to put the pieces of her life back together, the Hollywood film industry turned a cold shoulder to her attempts to revive her career. She told a reporter for *USA Today* that casting agents were often cruel. "They looked at me like, 'Why are you even bothering?' They laughed at me when I walked into the room. I knew people could be mean, but I didn't realize how mean," she said. Joel Schumacher (who directed Barrymore in *Batman Forever*) told *Premiere* that Barrymore represents an inspirational survival story. "The industry needs someone like Drew. She's proof that this industry doesn't kill everybody, that it doesn't eat its young. Someone *can* go through the horror of too much, too soon, and really survive."

Rebuilding her career

In spite of resistance from producers and directors, Barrymore gradually worked her way back into Hollywood. She appeared in *No Place to Hide,* an unreleased Kris Kristofferson film, and *See You in the Morning,* a poorly received 1989 drama starring Jeff Bridges and Farrah Fawcett. Also in 1989, *Far From Home* hit the theaters. Filmed after her first rehab experience, the film—about a promiscuous teenager who is being stalked by a killer—did little to bolster the actress's reputation.

Gradually, Barrymore's career began to rebound. In 1992 she impressed critics as the lead in *Poison Ivy,* a lust-filled thriller. Also that year she played a street-wise messenger who witnesses a murder in *Sketch Artist,* produced by Showtime. The following year she appeared in *Guncrazy,* as a woman who embarks on a violent spree after running away from an abusive home. Later director Joel Schumacher cast her in a lead role in the prime-time television series, *2000 Malibu Road*. Barrymore played an aspiring actress in the short-lived CBS soap. Playing the lead role in the fact-based ABC movie, *The Amy Fisher Story*, Barrymore portrayed the Long Island, New York, teenager convicted in 1992 of shooting the wife of her married lover. Competing with NBC and CBS movies about the same subject, the ABC story proved to be the most successful. (The actress reportedly turned down roles in the CBS and NBC versions before agreeing to star in *The Amy Fisher Story*.)

Having appeared in the popular comedy *Wayne's World* (1993) as a Swedish receptionist and in *Bad Girls* (1994), an offbeat Western, Barrymore took part in the successful 1995 road movie *Boys on the Side*. Co-starring with Whoopi Goldberg and Mary Louise Parker, she played the former girlfriend of a drug dealer who travels cross-country with two other women. Barrymore's performance received positive reviews. *New York Times* film critic Janet Maslin, for instance, wrote that Barrymore "is so sharp, funny and wholehearted that this film creates an unexpected groundswell of emotion." (Shortly before beginning work on the movie, Barrymore married Jeremy Thomas, a Los Angeles bar owner. The ill-fated marriage lasted six weeks.) Adding to her growing resumé of popular and critical successes, Barrymore appeared in *Batman Forever*, a smashing box office success that reaped $53 million in its opening weekend.

When *Scream* (1996) producer Cary Woods was casting the lead role in the ground-breaking Kevin Williamson horror movie, he approached Barrymore first. Although she originally agreed to play the lead (the role of Sidney, played by Neve Campbell in the movie), the actress decided instead to play a smaller—yet memorable—role, which required her to die early on. "If you kill me at the beginning of the movie," she later told *Premiere*, "the audience will think *anything* can happen." Also that year she received positive reviews for her performance in Woody Allen's *Everyone Says I Love You*.

Barrymore launched 1998 by co-starring with Adam Sandler in *The Wedding Singer*. Although popular with audiences, the film received mixed critical reviews. Later that year she took the lead role in *Ever After*, a feminist retelling of the Cin-

"Love and laughter is, I'm convinced, what we live for. To love. And a day without laughter is a tough day, it really is."
–Barrymore, "Drew Barrymore Interview"

Drew Barrymore shares a scene with Dougray Scott in Ever After. (The Kobal Collection)

derella story. "I didn't want to portray a girl who sort of sat around and wished for what she wanted, and it magically came to her," she told *Seventeen*. "In this version, it's really her brains and the fact that she's well-read that make her win in the end." The actress told a Mr. Showbiz interviewer that she found the role to be personally inspiring. "This is the most inspirational character I've ever done in my life," she said. "She's a leader. That's what I aspire to be. . . ." *New York Times* critic Stephen Holden found Barrymore's performance inspirational, writing "Ms. Barrymore's buoyant [cheerful], unaffected [natural] performance is the best thing about the film." Barrymore won further critical raves for her appearance in the critically panned (unfavorably reviewed) *Home Fries,* a dark comedy about an unwed pregnant woman working as a waitress at a fast-food restaurant.

An Actress and A Spokeswoman

An actress with a social conscience, Barrymore uses her celebrity to help educate young people about the prevention of sexually transmitted disease and unintended pregnancy. As a spokeswoman for The Female Health Foundation (FHF), she visited colleges and universities in 1998 to join in panel discussions about safe sex with students, educators, and public health advocates. The FHF, formed in 1996, is a not-for-profit organization that is dedicated to improving women's health by elevating awareness of women's health issues and implementing education outreach programs to encourage healthier lifestyles.

Barrymore the businesswoman

Interested in the business end of filmmaking, Barrymore has managed her own production company, Flower Films, since 1994. Among the company's first projects are the movie *Never Been Kissed,* a comedy about a reporter who goes undercover in a high school, and *All She Wanted,* a fact-based account of a teenage runaway who disguises herself as a man and is eventually murdered. "I really enjoy sitting in meetings with people and really working and going through the script and writing and going through the business affairs with people," Barrymore told TNT Rough Cut reporter David Poland. "I find that exciting and I'm so fortunate to get to do that, because it's the greatest education. It's like an amazing college, and then there's grad school and you just keep going through it. So, I'm in this school of my choice, right now, which really works for me."

Sources

Barrymore, Drew, Todd Gold. *Little Girl Lost.* Pocket Books, 1991.

Chicago Tribune, June 21, 1992, TV Week, p. 3; August 2, 1992, Womanews section, p. 4.

"Drew Barrymore Interview." Mr. Showbiz. [Online] Available http://www.mrshowbiz.com/ (February 4, 1999).

"Drew Barrymore Star Bio." Celebsite. [Online] Available http://www.celebsite.com/people/drewbarrymore/index.html (February 4, 1999).

Holden, Stephen. "*Ever After:* No Helpless, Wimpy Waif Filling this Glass Slipper." *The New York Times,* July 31, 1998.

Maslin, Janet. "Another Buddy Story With a Twist or Two." *The New York Times,* February 3, 1995.

Millea, Holly. "Drew's Rules." *Premiere,* September 1998, pp. 72 ff.

People, January 16, 1989, p. 70; January 29, 1990, p. 56; April 11, 1994, p. 74.

"People Online Profiles Drew Barrymore." [Online] Available http://www.pathfinder.com/people/sp/halloween/hell/drew/drew2.html (February 4, 1999).

Poland, David. "Q&A with Drew Barrymore." TNT Rough Cut. [Online] Available http://www.roughcut.com/ (February 4, 1999).

Pyun, Jeanie. "Wild child to dream girl: Drew." *Mademoiselle,* February 1998, pp. 122 ff.

Rohrer, Trish Deitch. "True Drew." *In Style,* March 1999, pp. 295–300.

Schaefer, Stephen. "The l'il charmer who smooched an alien visitor in *E.T.* sets her cap for a prince in *Ever After*." Mr. Showbiz. [Online] Available www.mrshowbiz.com/ (February 4, 1999).

Shaw, Jessica. "Drew does Cinderella." *Seventeen,* August 1998, pp. 170–171.

Simanton, Keith. *"Home Fries is stale, lacks that special sauce." The Seattle Times.* [Online] Available www.seattletimes.com (February 4, 1999).

"Sobering Facts." Lycos Community Guide: Drug Abuse. [Online] Available http://www-spry.lycos.com/ (March 29, 1999).

USA Today, January 31, 1990, p. 1D; May 12, 1992, p. 6D; February 7, 1995, p. 8D.

Women's Health Foundation Home Page. [Online] Available http://www.femalehealth.com/ (March 29, 1999).

Brandy

Born February 11, 1979
McComb, Mississippi

Singer, actress

"I'm proud that little girls look up to me. Not to be boastful but I think I'm a pretty good girl to look up to."

"I didn't think my record company believed in me at first," singer and actress Brandy once said. "I didn't think the people on *Moesha* believed in me. I feel like my whole career has been a proving ground. But that's what I like. It makes things interesting, makes me work harder on my projects." Brandy's determination has paid off. As a singer, she has garnered an American Music Award, multiple Grammy nominations, and numerous Soul Train awards—including the Lady of Soul "Entertainer of the Year" Award. The leading player in a successful television series, she has won several National Association for the Advancement of Colored People (NAACP) image awards. "Brandy has relentless drive and love for what she does," explained Ron Shapiro, Atlantic Records Executive Vice President and General Manager. "More so than just about every other artist I've worked with, she's indefatigable [tireless], yet does everything with incredible grace and class. If I did an eighth of what she did, I'd wear myself out."

(The Kobal Collection)

Early singing career

Brandy—whose last name is Norwood but goes by her first name only professionally—was born in McComb, Mississippi, on February 11, 1979 to Willie, a church music director, and Sonja, a financial analyst. While they were still just toddlers, Brandy and her younger brother, Willie Norwood, Jr. (nicknamed Ray-J), became involved in the church choir in Brookhaven, Mississippi and, later, in California. Being the daughter of a church choir director had certain advantages. "My brother and I were always in the front as featured singers because our dad was the choir director," she told a *Rolling Stone* reporter. "Then I started being directress of younger choirs, and, well, I was just really hot in the church." Willie Norwood later told an *L.A. Times* reporter that leadership has always been one of his daughter's strong points: "Even back as a child, she was a leader," he explained. "She would get up on stage and direct kids much older than her and they would listen to what she said."

Having taken up singing before she was able to walk, Brandy set her sights on a vocal career at a very young age. The first time she heard Whitney Houston sing, she told her father that she wanted to sing like the popular vocalist. The Norwoods took their daughter's interest seriously. When Brandy was four years old, the family moved to Carson, California, near Los Angeles. The move was part of a non-stop business plan aimed at establishing careers for Brandy and Ray-J in the entertainment industry. Performing at talent shows and community and charity events, Brandy collected numerous awards. At the age of eleven, she met a producer who set up auditions at various recording studios. She signed her first recording contract—with Atlantic Records, the label that produced such world-famous singers as Ray Charles and Aretha Franklin—at the age of fourteen.

In 1993, three months after signing the contract, she was offered a part in the ABC sitcom, *Thea*. Brandy played Deneesha, the youngest daughter of the title character. No stranger to the camera, she had already appeared, in small parts, in the 1990 movie, *Arachnophobia,* and the 1993 Sylvester Stallone movie, *Demolition Man*. Her introduction to television acting, however, was not an experience she enjoyed. "I'm always smiling and happy," she later told *People*. "Other people on the set weren't. I was miserable. I couldn't wait for it to go off the air." Her wish came true: "Thea" was canceled after its first season. Her brother, in the meantime, had also landed a television part, as the foster son in the Fox network's successful sitcom, *The Sinbad Show.*

The next teenage big thing

When Brandy's first album, "Brandy," appeared in 1994, it became an instant success. Compiled with the artistic assistance of writer, producer, and programmer Keith Crousch, the album highlighted the vocal ability of the fifteen-year old alto. (An alto is a woman with a low voice.) The songs—one of which Brandy co-wrote—feature a soulful blend of rhythm and blues (R&B), pop, and gospel styles. Jeremy Helliger remarked in *People*: "Brandy's well-groomed blend of gently lilting hip hop and pop-soul has a more timeless appeal. With the poise and sassy confidence of a diva twice her age, Brandy mixes her love songs with tributes to her little brother ("Best Friend"), God ("Give Me You"), the perfect man ("Baby") and older crooners like Aretha [Franklin] and Whitney [Houston] ("I Dedicate"). While this isn't groundbreaking stuff, Brandy has the pipes to become more than the latest teenage next-big-thing." Brandy's debut album attracted a cross-over audience—appealing to lovers of many types of music, not just one specific type—and eventually became a quadruple-platinum hit, selling more than *4 million* copies. (An album achieves "platinum" status when it sells one million copies.)

When the album's first single—"I Wanna Be Down"—was issued, it quickly climbed to the top of the R&B charts. The single spent several weeks at the top of *Billboard* magazine's R&B chart, eventually earning "gold" status. (A single or an album achieves "gold" status when it reaches 500,000 units sold.) Heavily promoted on MTV, her second single, "Baby," also fared well on both R&B and pop charts. To help promote the release, Brandy toured high schools in thirteen U.S. cities, performing and talking about the importance of staying in school—and off drugs. She also embarked on a two-month stint as opening act for the popular group, Boyz II Men. "I prayed and I worked hard for [success]," Brandy told an *Ebony* reporter after "I Wanna Be Down" was released. "But I had no idea it was going to happen when I was fifteen. I really want a lot for fifteen. I want to be really big in singing because I want to share what God has given me with other people."

"I like [*Moesha*] because it's fresh, it's now, it's new. It's not like a lot of TV shows you see because it's really real. Other shows don't say what kids are really like, really going through, and I think we do. Most of the black shows on TV now are so unreal. There's no moral. There is a moral on *Moesha*."

—Brandy, *Jet*

Such early success was not without its pitfalls. Too busy to attend high school with other fifteen-year-olds, Brandy divided her time among promotional duties, vocal practice, and three-hour tutoring sessions. Friendships, she confided to a *People* reporter, were hard to maintain. The reason, she lamented, was simple: "They get jealous."

All In the Family

Brandy's brother, Willie Norwood, Jr.—known as Ray-J—is a singer in his own right. In 1997 he released his debut CD called "Everything You Want." "He sings like me," Brandy once told a *People* reporter, "but in a boyish way."

Moesha

When Ralph Farquhar (known for the TV series *South Central*), Sara Finney and Vida Spears (producers of *Family Matters*) first came up with the idea for an issue-oriented coming-of-age comedy that revolves around the life an African American girl, they envisioned a fourteen-year-old in the lead role. Brandy's unique qualifications, however, convinced them to re-cast the character as a slightly older girl. The decision to cast Brandy in the title role of Moesha was a sound one. Thanks, in part, to the singer's loyal following, the sitcom brought the UPN network record audiences when it premiered on January 23, 1996.

Set in the quiet neighborhood of Leimert Park, in south-central Los Angeles, *Moesha* focuses on the everyday life of the Mitchells, a middle class African American family. Loving and far from dysfunctional, the Mitchell family includes a hard-working car salesman father (played by William Allen Young), a new stepmother who teaches high school (Sheryl Lee Ralph), and a mischievous younger brother (Marcus T. Paulk). Playing Moesha Mitchell—a bright teenager who must cope with the normal pressures and complications of teen life—wasn't much of a stretch for Brandy, who shares many of her television character's traits. "[She is] very responsible," Brandy explained to a *Jet* reporter. "She's positive, and she likes boys. She goes to school. And I think she's the best person to play, because that's just the way I am." There is, however, one difference between Brandy and Moesha: Moesha will not sing on the program (although Brandy sings the show's theme song).

Critics praised *Moesha* for the normalcy of the Mitchell's family life, drawing comparisons to the acclaimed 1980's TV series *The Cosby Show*. Story lines deal with parental pressure, happy and sad times, sibling rivalry, and teen temptations. "We're not like any of those fluff shows," *Moesha* co-star

Sheryl Lee Ralph told *Jet* magazine. "We're a show about real folks dealing with real issues. Some of it is funny even when it's painful." William Allen Young agreed: "We're dealing with issues people need to talk about in family situations. We never try to answer all the questions. We try to stimulate so that people can discuss and come up with their own answers."

Portraying positive family values was part of *Moesha's* mission from the start. "Our collective goal," Farquhar, the show's executive producer, told *Jet*, "was to do a family show featuring an African American middle-class family, and do it with a great sense of humor but at the same time not shy away from the reality of what it is like grow up in America. . . ." The show's morality appealed to parents. Farquhar told *Jet*, "I get a lot of calls from parents saying 'Thank you. Finally a show I can sit down and watch with my children.'" Filled with up-to-date fashions and current slang, the show was equally popular among younger audiences. Rapper Busta Rhymes, for instance, called *Moesha* "the phattest show out there." Watched by more than four million viewers each week, it has received various nominations from the NAACP.

Back to the recording studio

Four years after her debut album was released, Brandy produced a second album, *Never Say Never*. During the time in between albums, she focused on her acting career and had returned to the studio only a couple of times—to record "Sittin' Up in My Room" and "Missing You" for soundtrack collections. Some people questioned the wisdom of putting her music career on hold for so long. "I was scared to sing again," Brandy told an *L.A. Times* reporter, "'cause I went through this phase of thinking people wouldn't accept me as a singer."

Her fears were misplaced. Older, more experienced, and a better-trained singer (thanks to voice coaching from her father), she had matured since her last album—both emotionally and vocally. *The L.A. Times* praised the album: "A defiant declaration of independence, "Never Say Never" is more reflective and emotionally complex than the first album. It's clearly the work

of an independent-minded artist who knows her own mind and doesn't suffer fools gladly. On songs such as "U Don't Know Me" and "Top of the World," it's almost as if Brandy is trying to debunk [reveal the falseness of] her own pristine [uncorrupted], Disney-fied image and smooth her own passage from child star to grown-up entertainer." Pleased with her effort, Brandy called the album her best performance as a vocalist.

Cinderella for a day

As tireless as she is versatile, Brandy starred as Cinderella in Disney's 1996 $12-million remake of the classic fairy tale. The made-for-television movie's multi-racial cast included Whitney Houston as the Fairy Godmother, Bernadette Peters as the stepmother, and Whoopi Goldberg as the queen. "I don't think the producers really believed in me on *Cinderella*," Brandy later admitted. "I thought maybe they cast me because of my name or because Whitney Houston wanted me in the part. I felt like I had to prove myself. There were dance rehearsals and music rehearsals, but on top of all that, I rehearsed by myself every day, an hour on every song. And you know what? By the time we got to the studio to record the score, they were shocked. I wasn't just the girl Whitney hand-picked. I was a real singer." *Cinderella* attracted sixty million viewers—bringing ABC its biggest ratings win in a decade.

Next Brandy appeared in the 1998 horror flick *I Still Know What You Did Last Summer,* her first starring role in a feature film. A sequel to the popular *I Know What You Did Last Summer,* the film was a critical flop. Even so, Brandy managed to stand out in her role as "Karla" and was praised by critics. In 1999, Brandy starred opposite singer Diana Ross in the TV movie "Double Platinum."

Fame and fortune haven't gotten in the way of Brandy's commitment to family and religion. Well-grounded and steadfast, she remains close to her parents and her younger brother. Although undeniably talented, she refuses to take for granted her success: "I think it's because of God that I am where I am today," she told a *Jet* reporter. "And I think He's the cause of all of us being here. I don't ever want to forget about Him."

Sources

"Brandy leads cast of 'Moesha' in fourth season." *Jet*, September 28, 1998, pp. 55-57.

"Brandy, Never Say Never." Atlantic Artists, June 1998. [Online] Available http://www.atlantic-records.com (December 11, 1998).

"Carson Citizens: Brandy." [Online] Available http://www.gjw.com/Fans/Brandy.htm (December 11, 1998).

Cooper, Carol. "Early Delivery." *Rolling Stone,* April 6, 1995, p. 32.

Corliss, Richard. "Swamp sweat." *Time*. [Online] Available time-webmaster@pathfinder.com (December 17, 1998).

Farley, Christopher John. "The Call of the Wild." *Time,* March 23, 1998.

Friedman, Linda. "Summer Time." *Teen People,* December 1998/January 1999, pp. 64–70.

Jones, Lisa C. "New teen sensations." *Ebony*, February 1995, pp. 128 ff.

Norment, Lynn. "Brandy: On her new movie, growing pains and dating in the spotlight." *Ebony*, August 1998, pp. 80-88.

Rice, Lynette. "ABC tries on 'Cinderella.'"*Broadcasting & Cable*, October 27, 1997, pp. 30-34.

Sharkey, Betsy. "Teen Angel." *Mediaweek*, February 19, 1996, pp. 20 ff.

Showalter, Elaine. "Tube." *People Weekly*, May 27, 1996, p. 15.

"Singer Brandy turns actress in new TV series 'Moesha.'" *Jet*, February 26, 1996, p. 58.

"TV's 'Moesha' gives positive view of Black family life." *Jet*, November 25, 1996, p.56.

Vejnoska, Jill. "I Still Know What You Did Last Summer," movie review. *Atlanta-Journal Constitution*. [Online] Available http://preview.access atlanta.cimedia.com/entertainment/movies/reviews/i_still_know.html (December 11, 1998).

Weingarten, Marc. "Diversified and then some." *L.A. Times*. [Online] Available http://latimes.com (December 11, 1998).

"When 'Down' is up." *People Weekly*, November 21, 1994, p. 99.

Neve Campbell

Born October 3, 1973
Guelph, Ontario, Canada

Actress, dancer

"My entire family is involved in the arts somehow. I've never assumed that I'd be anything but a performer."

"She's beautiful but accessible," said Peter Roth, president of the Fox Entertainment Group. "You feel she could be your friend." He was referring to Neve (pronounced like "Bev") Campbell, whose role in the popular Fox series *Party of Five* brought the young Canadian actress both critical recognition and the admiration of a large following of fans. Trained in dance and raised in a family of actors, Campbell has traded on her girl-next-door looks and demeanor (a person's attitude and behavior) to become a much-sought-after actress in both television and film—a medium in which she is perhaps best known for her role as Sidney Prescott, in *Scream* and *Scream 2*.

A show business family

Neve Campbell was born and raised in the Toronto suburb of Guelph, Ontario. Her father—Gerry Campbell, a high school drama and media teacher—and mother—Marnie Neve, a psychologist and manager of Campbell's fan club—divorced when she was young. Campbell's family has a history in show business: both her parents and grandparents were involved in the theater. At the age of nine, Campbell applied to be admitted to Canada's prestigious National Ballet School, and was accepted after a long and difficult tryout process. During the five years she spent with the company, she was trained in six different types of dance. By the time she was fourteen, however, her career in dance had come to an end. Due to numerous injuries—and arthritis in her toes—and what she referred to as a "nervous breakdown," she left the high-pressure environment of the National Ballet. "I basically cracked," she told *Twist* magazine. "But, no, I wasn't in an insane asylum."

A gifted and serious student, Campbell returned to school, this time at an alternative high school in Toronto, Canada. She dropped out at age sixteen, however, in order to take on a role with the Toronto theater production of *Phantom of the Opera.* Between 1989 and 1991, she appeared in 800 performances of that wildly successful production. Also during that period, Campbell met actor and songwriter Jeff Colt, who was then a bartender at the theater where *Phantom of the Opera* was playing. The two were later married, in England, in April 1995, while Campbell was filming *The Canterville Ghost,* a remake of the 1944 comedy. A little over two years later, in November 1997, they were divorced.

A party girl

During her time in the *Phantom of the Opera,* Campbell attracted the attention of a talent agent. She began to appear in television commercials—including a Tampax tampon advertisement—and became a familiar face on the Canadian program, *Catwalk.* Campbell's big break came in 1994, when she landed a part on the American television series *Party of Five* after competing with 300 other actresses for the role of Julia Salinger. "I read to them for two minutes," she recalled to Bernard Weinraub of *Cosmopolitan.* "Within two weeks, I was offered the role." Campbell looked at the new role as an important career move. She explained to *Twist* magazine: "The reason why I took *Party of Five* was not just because it was well-written, but also so I could get into the country from Canada and get my face seen."

An hour-long family drama series that airs on the Fox network, *Party of Five* concerns five children in San Francisco who struggle to keep their family together after their parents are killed in an automobile accident. Having first drawn poor ratings, the show eventually attracted a loyal base of ten million viewers. As Julia, a troubled and headstrong teenager, Campbell became somewhat of a teen idol, with a large following of dedicated fans. Weinraub described her character as "a smart and serious everygirl whose problems—including pregnancy — are far more realistic than those of [typical teenage characters on TV] on shows like *Beverly Hills 90210.*" *Time*'s Christopher John Farley also had praise for Campbell's portrayal of Julia: ". . . her character Julia is beset by such problems as a brother who may be dying and [a cheating] husband, but she's always glowingly empathetic [someone with whom you can identify], never simply tragic."

More screaming

Campbell's role in *Party of Five*—which won the 1996 Golden Globe award for Best Drama Series—also drew the attention of feature film makers. As Sidney Prescott in the 1996 horror movie *Scream* she received praise from critics and fans alike. Directed by Wes Craven, whose previous credits included *A Nightmare on Elm Street, Scream* was chosen as best movie of the year at the 1996 MTV film awards. Maintaining dual careers in television and film required Campbell to endure a grueling schedule. She told *Twist,* "I would finish at six in the morning on *Scream,* get home at 6:30, have 15 minutes to shower and get in the car for *Party of Five* and work all day."

Also in 1996 Campbell played Bonnie, a good witch, in *The Craft.* A black comedy (a comedy that contains dark—or morbid—humor), the movie did not receive enthusiastic raves from the critics. The following year, Campbell returned to the role of Sidney in *Scream 2,* which is constructed as a movie within a movie. As for the question whether she will play the role of Sidney in a second sequel, she told *Twist,* "I really want people to see a role where I'm not screaming, I'm not crying, and I'm not an orphan. People have to be getting tired of seeing me like that."

The Anatomy of A Scream

Movie-goers experience three stages of fear when watching a horror movie, according to Jeffrey Rosen, who is a professor of psychology at the University of Delaware. An expert in the fear response, Rosen says the first stage is anticipation—as tension builds, "all our senses are sharpened," Rosen told *USA Weekend.* "Heart rate slows. Muscles tense up." When the killer surprises his or her victim, the audience experiences a startle response. Our heart-rate skyrockets—and some of us may scream or jump out of our seats. Finally, viewers experience relief—accompanied by a slowing of the heart-rate and relaxation of tensed muscles—until the next surprise jolts us from our seats.

More movies

To avoid being typecast (being cast in the same types of roles) as a scream queen, Campbell accepted the role of Suzie Toller, a bisexual drug addict, in the 1998 erotic thriller *Wild Things.* The movie's website calls the picture a "tale of revenge, lust and murder played out in the Florida Everglades." The critics called it loathsome. In spite of the movie's failure, Campbell received positive notice for her performance. The role required a new look for the wholesome actress. "I had to punk up my hair, and work out to get a wiry look," she told *People,* "but I also liked looking healthy."

That same year Campbell appeared in *54*—a fictionalized account of the notorious 1970s New York nightclub, Studio 54—as Julie Black, a sullen soap opera diva. Following on the heels of two successful movies about the 1970s disco scene (*Boogie Nights* and *The Last Days of Disco*), *54,* directed by first-time feature director Mark Christopher, did not fare well among critics or theater-goers.

Campbell continued to take on projects that expanded her range of experience. She had a speaking role in *Lion King II: Simba's Pride,* as the voice of the adult Kiara. In partnership with her older brothers Christian and Matthew, her co-star in *Scream,* she formed her own production company, The Blue

The Prophet

Campbell told *Time* magazine reporter Christopher John Farley that *The Prophet*, by Kahlil Gibran, is her favorite book. "There's one passage about relationships," she said, "about two trees growing, and if they grow too close together they'll shade one another and won't be allowed to grow, but if they grow enough of a distance apart, they'll be able to grow and continue their love. I find that to be really beautiful."

Sphere Alliance, in Los Angeles. She starred in the company's first production, *Hairshirt*— a 1998 low-budget comedy about newcomers in L.A. In *Three to Tango*, a romantic comedy released in 1999, she played Amy, the object of Matthew Perry's affection. Under contract to appear in *Party of Five* until the year 2000, Campbell expresses the intention to concentrate on her film career once her six-year obligation is fulfilled. Because working in both television and film often requires her to work seven-day weeks, she has little time to devote to her personal life. "I need to have a life," she confessed to *Time* reporter Farley. "I don't have one right now." But her chosen profession has its benefits. Asked what she liked most about acting, she once replied, "Touching people's souls."

Sources

Corliss, Richard. "Swamp sweat." *Time,* March 23, 1998.

Cosmopolitan, January 1997, p. 80.

Dunn, Jancee. "Neve Campbell." *Rolling Stone,* September 18, 1997, pp. 56-60, 116.

Farley, Christopher John. "The call of the wild." *Time,* March 23, 1998.

54 film review. Movie Guru. [Online] Available MovieGuru.com (Accessed December 17, 1998).

54 movie preview. *Entertainment Weekly*. [Online] Available http://cgi.pathfinder.com/ew (Accessed December 17, 1998).

"The 50 most beautiful people in the world, 1998." *People*. [Online] Available www.pathfinder.com/people (Accessed December 17, 1998).

Goldman, Steven. "Full scream ahead!" *Interview,* January 1997, p. 60.

Jaret, Peter. "Why we love a good 'Scream.'" *The Detroit News and Free Press, USA Weekend,* October 23-25, 1998, p. 10.

Jewel, Dan. "Reigning Canadian." *People,* May 27, 1996.

McNeil, Alex. *Total Television,* 4th edition, Penguin Books, 1996, pp. 150, 643-44.

Min, Janice. "Party time." *People,* March 3, 1997.

"Neve Campbell." The Internet Movie Database Ltd. [Online] Available http://us.imdb.com (Accessed December 17, 1998).

"Neve of the North." *Twist*. [Online] Available http://www.dubbie.com/neve/twist/ (Accessed December 17, 1998).

The Phantom of the Opera. [Online] Available http://phantom.skywalk.com/ (March 30, 1999).

"*Wild Things*." SPE! Movies [Online] Available www.spe.sony.com/movies/wildthings/intro.html (March 19, 1998).

Jim Carrey

Born January 17, 1962
Newmarket, Ontario, Canada

Actor, comedian

UPDATE

"For years I used to drive up to Mulholland Drive every night and look at the city and sit and imagine myself with all this money and being sought after," actor Jim Carrey recalled in *The New York Times*. The Canadian-born comic soon saw his wish fulfilled. Blessed with a natural gift for physical comedy, Carrey started out as a stand-up comedian when he was just a teenager. Soon came a role in *In Living Color*, the popular Fox variety show that helped launch the careers of numerous other stars. Carrey's over-the-top characterizations of such characters as Fire Marshal Bill—a badly burned fireman—and Vera de Milo—a steroid-taking female bodybuilder—won the elastic-faced comedian legions of fans. It was not until 1994, however, that Carrey gained widespread fame, starring in the lead role in the blockbuster comedy, *Ace Ventura: Pet Detective*. Soon followed starring roles in two other box-office bonanzas, *The Mask* and *Dumb and Dumber*. In less than two years' time, his asking price skyrocketed from $350,000 to an astonishing $20 million for a leading appearance in a feature film, making him, according to *Scholastic Ac-*

"I'm not an expert on anything but laughs. I just know how to make people feel good."

(Corbis Corporation)

tion, the highest-paid actor in Hollywood. **(See original entry on Carrey in *Performing Artists,* Volume 1.)**

A villain, a pet detective, and a cable guy

Following on the heels of the spectacular success of *The Mask* (1994) and *Dumb and Dumber* (1995), Carrey put his talent for physical humor to the test in the role of The Riddler in *Batman Forever.* While the 1995 summer release was criticized as an overblown Hollywood extravaganza, Carrey was widely praised for stealing the show with his antics as the witty villain. The third installment in the Batman series, the movie earned $53 million during its opening weekend—breaking the record *Jurassic Park* had set in 1993.

The former *In Living Color* cast member impressed *Batman* director Joel Schumacher with his serious approach to acting—even in hilarious roles. "Fame is really secondary," Schumacher told *Esquire.* "I've never seen anybody work harder than Jim. And everything that appears spontaneous [unplanned] is the result of hours and hours of preparation." Carrey, who received $7 million for his supporting role, received a 1996 MTV Movie Award for Best Villain.

Next the comedian produced a sequel to the wildly successful 1993 comedy, *Ace Ventura, Pet Detective. Ace Ventura: When Nature Calls* was, as predicted, a tremendous hit at the box office—even though it was widely disliked by critics. *People* critic Ralph Novak, for one, accused Carrey of being "two Stooges shy of a load—slow, clumsy and as subtle as an eye gouge," and complained that "[he] blurts or blares every line and over plays every expression and gesture." Nevertheless, Carrey's performance garnered numerous awards, including the 1996 MTV Movie Award for Best Male Performance and that year's Blockbuster Entertainment Award for Comedy Actor.

Less successful was Carrey's turn in the dark comedy, *The Cable Guy.* Originally planned as a vehicle for comedian Chris Farley, the movie was roundly dismissed by critics. Audiences, who were used to Carrey's usual goofy roles, were unaccepting of his performance as the demented cable repair guy. Wrote *Rolling Stone* critic Peter Travers, "Carrey knocks himself out trying to make *The Cable Guy* different, then neglects the quiet, telling moments that would make it real."

Equally unreal was Carrey's salary for that picture. Sony's $20 million paycheck represented what was then the largest straight sum ever paid to an actor for a single movie. Criticized as an overpaid Hollywood ego, Carrey defended his claim to a multi-million-dollar jackpot. "The money just happened, and it's great," he explained to *Esquire*. "And now everybody's . . . moaning about it—about my $20 million. Unions are [upset] because they don't get paid enough. But, basically, it's up to the movie company. If they are going to pay me $20 million, then they need to pay everybody what they deserve. But why shouldn't I get $20 million when they make a half a billion? It's ridiculous, but it's fair."

The Cable Guy turned out to be a box-office disappointment. But *Liar, Liar,* also released in 1996, proved that Carrey had not lost his box office appeal. The film—about a compulsive liar who is magically forced to tell the truth for 24 hours—earned nearly $200 million during its theatrical release. Carrey's performance in that film also earned him a Golden Globe nomination.

The television guy: Truman Burbank

Next Carrey took on his first leading role in a serious dramatic film in the 1998 mega-hit, *The Truman Show*. The film represented a departure from the comedian's earlier cartoon-like characterizations. "I'm gonna lose some people on this and gain some people," he told *Entertainment Weekly,* "but that's the way you've gotta go." As Truman Burbank, Carrey portrayed a 30-year-old man who realizes that he has been the unwitting star of a television show that has recorded every moment of his life since he was born. The actor told *Scholastic Action* that he sees similarities between himself and his character. "[He's] a man who will not be beaten," he explained. "Presented with a challenge, he becomes the explorer he always wanted to be. I want to turn out to be Truman Burbank. I want to be the guy who won't be caged, but still has hope and faith in people, and in life."

Although not unanimous in their praise, many critics applauded Carrey's first foray into serious drama. "Carrey triumphs in a hilarious and heartfelt performance that reveals an uncommon sensitivity and grace," wrote *Rolling Stone* critic Peter Travers. "The question is: Can audiences stand the shock?" While *The Truman Show* garnered three Academy

"I've never had any trouble being in front of a camera. . . . There are many things I could do before a camera that I can't do before my family. When the camera goes on, hey, desperation steps in. You better do something interesting." –Carrey, *The New York Times*

Jim Carrey as the fanciful Truman Burbank in **The Truman Show.** *(The Kobal Collection)*

Award nominations, Carrey was not among the nominees for Best Actor. He did, however, collect a 1999 Golden Globe award — for Best Actor in a Dramatic Motion Picture.

Carrey followed *Truman* with an interesting assortment of projects, including the role actor Danny Kaye (1913–87) made famous in *The Secret Life of Walter Mitty,* and a leading part in the children's movie, *How the Grinch Stole Christmas,* directed by Ron Howard. In *Man on the Moon,* directed by Milos Forman, he took on the role of controversial comedian Andy Kaufman (1949–84), who died from cancer at the age of thirty-five. Carrey — who had to shave his head bald for the final scenes in which Kaufman suffers from cancer — won the role over a number of other actors, including Nicholas Cage, John Cusack, Edward Norton, and Kevin Spacey.

Above all, Carrey, whose take-home pay still hovers around the $20 million-mark per movie, remains confident about his talent. "Even if something should happen to me," he once told *TV Guide,* "and—heaven forbid—all I could move was my baby finger, a few months later people would be saying, 'Hey, you gotta go down to the club to see what Carrey is doing with his finger, man. It's weird!'"

Sources

"71st Annual Academy Awards nominations announced." Jim Carrey Online. [Online] Available http://www.jimcarreyonline.com/ (March 8, 1999).

Byrne, Bridget. "*In Living Color's* funny face plays it straight." *TV Guide,* March 14, 1992.

"Jim Carrey Biography." Mr. Showbiz. [Online] Available http://mrshowbiz. go.com/ (March 8, 1999).

Morreale, Marie. "Jim Carrey: Class clown makes good." *Scholastic Action,* October 5, 1998, pp. 2-3.

Novak, Ralph. "Picks & pans —*Ace Ventura: When Nature Calls.*" *People Weekly,* November 27, 1995, p. 19.

Sherrill, Martha. "Renaissance Man." *Esquire,* December 1995, pp. 98 ff.

Travers, Peter. "Movies: Freaks of comedy." *Rolling Stone,* July 11-25, 1996, pp. 95 ff.

Travers, Peter. "The Truman Show." *Rolling Stone,* June 25, 1998, pp. 99-100.

Weinraub, Bernard. "A comic on the edge at $7 million a movie." *The New York Times,* August 1, 1994.

Jackie Chan

Born April 7, 1954
Hong Kong, China

Actor, director, stunt coordinator

"Everybody says, 'Ah, you are one of the action stars.' No, I am different. I am [Sylvester] Stallone, Dustin Hoffman, Donald Duck and Gene Kelly."

(AP/Wide World)

"He's the greatest action star alive! No one can move like him!" enthused Chris Tucker, after co-starring with Chan in the 1998 action blockbuster, *Rush Hour*. Having enjoyed mega-star status throughout Asia since the late 1970s, Chan found breaking into the American market to be one of the most difficult stunts of his career—a career that has been built around difficult stunts. Chan's signature action films—such as *Project A, Police Story*, and *Armour of God*—feature death-defying stunts performed without body doubles or trick photography. Willie Chan (no relation), Chan's longtime business manager, explained in *Forbes*, "Jackie's philosophy is that the audience pays money to see him, not a double." Chan entered the Hong Kong film industry at a time when formulaic (predictable) kung-fu films—featuring strong, handsome, and unbeatable heroes—dominated the market. Raised with strict physical discipline and self-taught in the silent film classics, Chan forged a new kind of action hero — one who doesn't always win and doesn't necessarily even like to fight. "In most action movies," Chan explains in his autobiography (co-written with Jeff Yang), "the hero is usually a perfect fighting machine—a killer who never loses a battle and who hardly ever gets hurt. In my movies, I get beaten up all the time. It's not that I like looking like a loser; it's just that that's the way life is. You lose, and lose, and lose, and then, with any kind of luck, you eventually find a way to win. Life isn't about winning every battle; it's about winning the ones that count."

Not a scholarly child

Jackie Chan's parents, Charles and Lee-lee Chan, fled from China to Hong Kong (a then-British-owned colony within the boundaries of China; returned to Chinese ownership in 1997) during the Japanese invasion of mainland China (1938). The couple met in Charles' native Shandong province (territory), an area noted for legendary warriors and martial artists. Married shortly after their arrival in Hong Kong, they soon had a child: Chan Kong-sang—which means "born in Hong Kong."

For six years Chan lived with his parents in the home of the French ambassador to Hong Kong, where Charles worked as a cook and Lee-lee as the family's housekeeper. The Chans shared none of the luxury that other residents of the exclusive Victoria Park neighborhood enjoyed: they shared a tiny, sparsely furnished room which, Chan later recalled, could be crossed in four long steps. Charles Chan believed firmly that suffering and discipline were critical to his son's development as a man. Rousing his son from bed at dawn, he put him through a difficult daily routine that included running, weightlifting (using bags of sand rather than expensive equipment), push-ups—and hours of martial arts training. Kung fu, which translates loosely as "skill," was the cornerstone of Chan's athletic training, even as a five-year-old. Looking back at his rigorous upbringing, he explained in his autobiography: "Now, the techniques of kung fu are practiced everywhere by those who realize that it builds the character traits that lead to greatness: strength, patience, courage, and subtlety. My father believed this more than anyone. To him, learning kung fu was the same as learning how to be a man."

Chan—who was nicknamed Pao-pao, or "cannonball," because of his hearty size—was an energetic child and soon learned to enjoy fighting. But he was also undisciplined and difficult to manage. Frequently punished for misbehaving in

Chan was born in 1954, the Year of the Horse, according to the Chinese calendar. The Horse, in Chinese lore, represents ambition, energy, and success.

the classroom, he attended only one year of school before his parents, who had been informed he would have to repeat the first grade, decided to keep him home. Since he considered it torture to sit still in class, Chan was thrilled to be excused from school. But his freedom was short-lived. Soon, his father accepted an offer to work as a cook in Australia. Convinced that Lee-lee could not care for their unruly seven-year-old son alone, he enrolled his boy in the China Drama Academy—a preparatory school where boys and girls learned the fundamentals of Peking Opera.

A decade at the opera

A uniquely Chinese form of entertainment, Peking Opera combines song and dance with awe-inspiring acrobatic feats, gymnastic stunts, sword fighting and martial arts displays. Drama academies—where students were taught to perform—were notoriously brutal training grounds. The China Drama Academy, run by master Yu Jim-Yuen, was no exception. Training began at five o'clock in the morning, on an empty stomach. Breakfast, which consisted of a bowl of thin rice porridge, came only after the students had finished their morning run. A bathroom break was not allowed until lunchtime. Most of the remainder of the day was devoted to strenuous and often painful training. Flips and somersaults were done with no safety harness or net. Students were expected to perform complete leg splits no matter how much it hurt. Martial arts training often involved balancing in difficult positions for long periods of time.

Disobedience was not taken lightly. Chan's parents—like the parents of other students at the academy—had signed an agreement that permitted the master to use physical punishment. In fact, the contract gave the master the right to 'discipline the boy, even to death.' Severe beatings, often with wicker canes, were common, and provided a painful incentive to follow the master's orders. Now outlawed in China, the physical discipline that was common among drama academies at that time would be considered child abuse in the United States.

Lessons at the academy focused on physical training, and academics were given low priority. Students received classroom instruction after dinner, but lessons were very basic and teachers were often chased out of class. (As a result, by the time Chan left the academy at the age of seventeen, he was barely able to read or write his native language.)

In order to prepare the students to put their skills in action, Master Yu sometimes took his students to opera performances. Chan was thrilled by his first visit to the opera. In his autobiography, he recalls: *"It's all worth it,* I thought, looking at the rapt faces of the other audience members. I realized that, more than anything else, I wanted that to be *me* up there on that stage; I wanted to hear a crowd clapping and cheering and screaming for me."

Kong-sang becomes Jackie

By 1971, when Chan left the drama academy, the Peking Opera had become a dying art. With few opportunities to perform in the Opera, many former drama students turned to stunt work in the rapidly growing Hong Kong film industry. Having first appeared in a movie at the age of eight (*Big and Little Wong Tin Bar,* in 1962), Chan was no stranger to the film world. Starting as a junior stuntman, he took whatever work was available, playing extras in the crowd or corpses—which sometimes required him to lie on the ground for hours at a time. Soon, however, Chan made a name for himself, taking on death-defying stunts that others deemed impossible. His role in *Fist of Fury,* starring the legendary martial artist Bruce Lee (1941–73), was one such example. In the final fight scene, Chan is kicked through a wall and falls fifteen feet before hitting the ground—the furthest a Hong Kong stuntman had been thrown without a safety device at that time.

Chan's first starring role in a film came in 1971, with *The Little Tiger of Canton.* Shot in seven days on a very small budget, the film was an embarrassment to Chan, who refused to use his real name in the credits. *Little Tiger* was a disaster, and Chan was never paid for his appearance. Destitute (penniless) and discouraged, he eventually decided to accept his parents' offer of a plane ticket to Australia, where they had settled. Within six months, however, he returned to Hong Kong to try his luck again as a stuntman. And again his luck was poor. Using borrowed money, he returned to Australia, where he found work as a brick layer at a construction site. His boss, an

Australian named Jack, realized that Kong-sang was not a name his fellow workers could easily pronounce. He introduced Chan as "Jack"—which soon turned to "Jackie" to avoid confusing the two Jacks. Chan—whose nickname at the academy had been "Big Nose"—took a liking to the name. From then on, he called himself Jackie Chan.

Having all but given up hope of working in his chosen profession, Chan worked exhausting hours, taking on a second job as a kitchen worker in a Chinese restaurant. One day, however, he returned home to find a telegram that would resurrect his hopes: Willie Chan, a Hong Kong film executive who had seen his stunt work, wanted him to play the lead role in a film his studio was planning to shoot. The film—*New Fist of Fury*—would be a sequel to the Bruce Lee blockbuster, *Fist of Fury*. And Chan, in the starring role, was to be the film world's next Bruce Lee.

In the shadow of the dragon

When Bruce Lee (nicknamed "the Dragon") died unexpectedly at the peak of his career in 1973 (from swelling of the brain, during the filming of his sixth film), the Hong Kong film industry scrambled to find someone to fill "the Dragon's" fighting shoes. Willie Chan and director Lo Wei—the millionaire owner of Lo Wei Productions—decided that Chan was their man. Eager to jump back into the film business, Chan returned to Hong Kong and signed an eight-year contract with Lo Wei Productions—for something less than a superstar's salary. Chan was to work for Lo—and Lo only—on whatever projects the studio saw fit to produce.

The studio's attempt to make Chan into the new Bruce Lee proved to be disastrous. Slight of build and far from menacing, Chan could match neither Lee's physical presence nor his on-screen attitude. *New Fist of Fury* and the flurry of films that followed were flops. In no time, Chan had become box-office poison. Chan later told *Hong Kong Film Connection:* "Nobody can imitate Bruce Lee. [Lo] wants me to do the same kick, the same punch. I think even now nobody can do better than Bruce Lee. . . . In the movie he wants every girl to love me. I'm not a handsome boy, not [1950's film star] James Dean. I'm just not this kind of person. It's totally wrong, and none of [the films] are a success."

A kung fu comic

Disappointed in his leading man's box-office appeal, Lo decided to lend Chan to another studio. Seasonal Films, an independent studio headed by Ng See-yuen, opted not to cast him as a Bruce Lee imitator. Instead, Chan was given free reign to develop his own screen personality. A devoted fan of silent film stars, Chan incorporated slapstick comedy into his martial arts displays. In place of the tough-as-nails superhero, he played an underdog. In short, he was everything that Bruce Lee was not. "I look at Bruce Lee film," Chan later explained in the *New York Times*. "When he kick high, I kick low. When he not smiling, always smiling. He can one-punch break the wall; after I break the wall, I hurt. I do the funny face."

The first true Jackie Chan movie—*Snake in Eagle's Shadow* (1978)—was an instant success in Asian markets. A groundbreaking example of comic kung fu, it features fight scenes in which Chan's character incorporates the moves of his pet cat into his fighting style. Next came *Drunken Master* (1978), which surprised audiences with its irreverent (disrespectful) treatment of the Chinese folk hero Wong Fei Hong. In it, Chan displays a humorous fighting style based on the movements of a drunken man. Even more successful than Chan's first kung fu comedy, *Drunken Master* earned $8 million (Hong Kong funds) at the box office. Chan had become a star. "So successful was he," the *South China Post* reported in a tribute, "that Chan can be said to have revitalized [gave new life to] the entire Asian film business. Many producers and their stars tried to imitate Jackie's new genre of comedy kung fu, but all came to realize that Jackie Chan—like Bruce Lee before him—was one of a kind . . . " With success came increased artistic freedom: Chan was given increasing responsibility behind the camera, as director or stunt coordinator—or both.

Marriage—to Taiwanese actress Lin Feng-jiao—and fatherhood—to a son named Jackson—did nothing to slow Chan's daredevil approach to filmmaking. Turning to action films in the 1980s, he introduced death-defying stunts the likes of which no one had ever seen. *Project A* (1984)—in which Chan plays a coast guard officer—features the first in a long series

School Ties

Many of Chan's former classmates at the China Drama Academy became involved in the Hong Kong film industry. Yuen Lung, who had been Chan's "big brother" in school, helped his former classmate find work as a stuntman. Eventually, the two worked together—both on-camera and behind the scenes. Yuen Lung, now known as Sammo Hung, directed Chan in *Mr. Niceguy* (1997) and later starred in his own CBS television series, *Martial Law*.

of what would become trademark superstunts. In a scene that
pays tribute to silent screen comedian Harold Lloyd, Chan falls
from a tall tower, crashing through two awnings into a head-
first landing. This stunt—like all Jackie Chan stunts—was
performed without stunt doubles, without trick photography—and without insurance. So risky are Chan's superstunts
that insurance companies are afraid to insure his films. (Chan
pays his hospital costs, and those of the stunt men and

women in his films, out of his own pocket.) Recounted Richard Corliss in *Time:* "Jackie takes a licking and keeps on ticking."

America loves Jackie Chan

Easily the biggest star in Asia, Chan was still unfamiliar to the vast majority of American movie-goers—outside of a small but devoted cult following. His brief attempt at breaking into Hollywood in the early 1980s had done nothing to further his reputation in the U.S.. In *Cannonball Run* and *Cannonball Run 2,* filmed while he was still under contract to Lo Wei, Chan played an incompetent *Japanese* racecar driver. Although successful in the United States, the films bombed in Hong Kong—as did Chan with American audiences. The American media didn't know what to make of him. After flying cross-country to appear on the *Today* show, Chan was informed that instead of an interview (because he didn't speak English well), he was to demonstrate kung fu moves. "I was aghast," Chan recalled in his autobiography. "Here I was, the biggest star in Asia, and the host was asking me to perform like a trained dog!"

By the mid-1990s, however, the tide had begun to turn. Presenting Chan with a Lifetime Achievement Award at the 1995 MTV Movie Awards, *Pulp Fiction* director Quentin Tarantino gushed, "It's one of the achievements of my lifetime to honor one of my heroes of all time. . . . When you watch a Jackie Chan movie, you want to be Jackie Chan. You want to run through the glass the way only he can. You want to fight twenty-five guys, lose only until the last moment, and then take them all on the way only he can. He is one of the best filmmakers the world has ever known. He is one of the greatest physical comedians since sound came into films." Mobbed by fans throughout Asia, Chan was met by a small crowd of two-dozen people when he arrived in Los Angeles to attend the awards. One held a sign that read: "All Americans love Jackie. Some just don't know it yet."

By the time *Rush Hour,* co-starring Chris Tucker, opened in the United States in 1998, Chan had become a familiar face to American movie-goers. *Rumble in the Bronx,* released in 1996, earned $10 million in its first week—good enough to take first place among films released in North America that week. *Rush Hour,* which had been tailored to American tastes, was even more successful. At one point in the movie, Chan dangles from a Hollywood Boulevard street sign, drops onto a truck, slides in and out of a small bus, skids over the top of a taxi, and in through a rear window. The actor explained the significance of that 15-second sequence to *Time* reporter Corliss: "The director had me hanging off a Sunset Boulevard sign, and I asked him if I could hang from a Hollywood sign. That sign has meaning to the Chinese. It's like I grab Hollywood. If the movie opened at only $1 million in the U.S., I would have let go. But now I'm happy. It says: Hollywood, I've come back." *Rush Hour* raked in $33 million in its first week—as much as *Rumble* had during its entire theatrical run.

Chan followed up *Rush Hour* with 1999's *Twin Dragon*. Clearly, American audiences had begun to realize that they loved Jackie Chan.

Sources

Cerio, Gregory. "Feat of the Feet." *People,* March 11, 1996, p. 57.

Chan, Jackie. "How to make a real impact." *Men's Health,* April 1997, p. 184.

Chan, Jackie and Jeff Yang. *I Am Jackie Chan, My Life in Action.* New York, 1998.

Corliss, Richard. "Jackie Can!" *Time,* February 13, 1995.

Jackie Chan's Home Page. [Online] Available http://www.web-vue.com (November 31, 1998).

Johnson, Brian D. "Lethal laughter." *Maclean's,* March 4, 1996, p. 74.

Server, Lee. "Chan the Man." *Gallery.* [Online] Available http://www.web-vue.com/articles.htm (November 31, 1998).

Tanzer, Andrew. "See Jackie break his neck." *Forbes,* April 22, 1996, p. 229.

Wolf, Jaime. "Jackie Chan, American action hero?" *The New York Times Magazine,* January 21, 1996, pp. 22 ff.

Matt Damon

Born October 8, 1970
Cambridge, Massachusetts

Actor, screenwriter

Three months before Matt Damon was nominated for two Oscars, few people had ever heard of the young actor and screenwriter. Although his success seemed to arrive overnight, it was preceded by years of hard work and frustration. Together with childhood buddy Ben Affleck, he spent years writing and revising the screenplay for *Good Will Hunting.* "A lot of things were important to us writing this script," Damon told People Online, "just treating people nice, not having regrets in the world, being responsible in your relationships and the way you treat other people. That's our philosophy, basically the Golden Rule." What proved to be most difficult, however, was the job of convincing a Hollywood studio to gamble on casting the two screenwriters—who had written the screenplay in an effort to produce a work that would highlight their acting skills.

Making up stories

Born in Cambridge, Massachusetts in 1970, Matthew Paige Damon was the second son of Kent Damon, a stock broker, and

"For as long as I can remember, I've wanted to be an actor . . ." (from the introduction to Damon's application to Harvard University)

(AP/Wide World)

Nancy Carlsson-Paige, a professor of early childhood education at nearby Lesley College. (His brother, Kyle, born in 1967, is now a sculptor.) Damon's parents divorced when the future actor was two years old. "My dad had this *Leave It to Beaver* idea of how life should be, and it just didn't work out," Damon told an E! Online interviewer.

Raised by their mother in a cooperative near their father's home [a cooperative is a residence owned jointly by those who use its services] the Damon boys were not allowed to watch cartoons or play with war toys."We didn't rebel much," Kyle told *People*. "We didn't do drugs, stay out late, or bad-mouth our parents." Encouraged to use his imagination to entertain himself, Damon play-acted as a young child. "I was always making up stories and acting out plays; that's just the way I was raised," the actor told *Interview*. Involved with children's theater groups by the age of eight, Matt acted while older brother, Kyle, provided costumes. Acting, however, had not been Damon's first career aspiration. A basketball hopeful, he soon realized that his height would limit his future in the game. (As an adult, Damon, who has a stocky wrestler's build, stands five feet ten inches tall.)

At the age of eight, Damon struck a binding friendship that would last into adulthood and help steer the course of his career. He met Ben Affleck, who lived just blocks away, through his mother (who was friends with Affleck's mother.) "We did everything together, from Little League to chasing girls," Damon told a *Washington Times* reporter.

School days

As a student at Cambridge Rindge and Latin School, a public high school near Harvard University, Damon took English and drama courses in which he was required to help write dialogue. He learned to use improvisation [making things up at the spur of the moment] as a creative tool—a technique he and Affleck would later employ in writing the screenplay for *Good Will Hunting*. After graduating from high school in 1988, Damon enrolled in Harvard University as an English major. Having applied to eleven colleges, he settled on Harvard because it was close to home. Planning later to attend Yale's graduate school of drama, the aspiring actor wrote in his Harvard application, "For as long as I can remember, I've wanted to be an actor. . . ."

While a student at Harvard, Damon took a play-writing course with Anthony Kubiak. Required to produce a one-act play, he turned in an unfinished draft and apologized for not being able to write an ending to his 40-page manuscript. Kubiak liked the unfinished play, and urged his student not to dismiss it. That writing assignment would later be transformed into the Academy Award-winning script for *Good Will Hunting*.

Bit parts and writer's block

Damon took his first film acting role straight out of high school. As Steamer in the 1988 sleeper (surprise hit) *Mystic Pizza*, his screen time was limited: the role required the young actor to utter just one line (*Mystic Pizza* also marked the debut of the then-unknown Julia Roberts). During his first year at Harvard, Damon auditioned for a part in the Mickey Mouse Fan Club—a role for which he later rejoiced in having been turned down. In the years that followed, he took small roles in a number of films, including *The Good Mother,* as an uncredited extra (1988), *Rising Son,* as Charlie Robinson (television, 1990), *School Ties,* as Charlie Dillon (1992—with pal Affleck), *Geronimo: An American Legend,* as Lt. Britton Davis (1993), and *The Good Old Boys,* as Cotton Calloway (television, 1995). Damon's primary focus, however, had turned to writing—in specific, to transforming his abandoned 40-page draft into a showpiece for his—and Affleck's—acting abilities.

When the twenty-two year old Damon asked Affleck for help on his script, the younger actor read the unfinished work and liked it. But he didn't have any ideas about how to tie the piece together into a coherent—and completed—script. "I had written forty pages for a class and I didn't know what to do with them," Damon told a Film Scouts interviewer. "Didn't know where to go, didn't have the discipline to sit in front of the computer and wait for something to happen. I showed it to Ben who, I think, is one of the brightest guys that I know, we have similar sensibilities—and he had the same reaction: He liked it but didn't know where to go with it. We sat on it for a year. And then it started coming. And it was through

Good Tim Affleck

Ben Affleck's father provided the screenwriting duo with inspiration for the script for *Good Will Hunting,* the story of a mathematical genius who works as a janitor for MIT (Massachusetts Institute of Technology). The younger Affleck explained to *Premiere* how his father, Tim—a onetime bartender, Harvard janitor, and actor at Boston's prestigious Theater Company—influenced the story of a brilliant young janitor. "He was the inspiration for a lot of stuff in the movie: The perspective on class, intelligence, snobbery. Being around a bunch of punk kids who went to Harvard, I used to always think they looked down on him as the janitor, when he was really an extremely smart guy."

Weighty Roles

Damon went on a crash diet to lose forty pounds from his solid build to play a drug-addicted Gulf War veteran in *Courage Under Fire.* His health was devastated by the severe diet, and the young actor was forced to take medication to heal damage done to his adrenal glands. When director Steven Spielberg saw Damon in *Courage,* he considered him for the lead role in *Saving Private Ryan.* He decided against Damon, however, because the actor was *too thin* for the part. It was not until Spielberg was introduced to Damon (through actor Robin Williams) during the filming of *Good Will Hunting* that he decided to cast the robust actor in the role of Private Ryan.

Damon and Affleck spent five years revising the draft for what would become the Academy Award-winning screenplay for *Good Will Hunting.* At one point, the script grew to 1,500 pages, which would have produced a *ten hour movie.*

conversation that the movie kind of came out. Had I written it alone, it would have never gone beyond the forty pages." Using hours of improvisation to come up with a few words of dialogue, they read their work-in-progress at theater workshops to solicit feedback from other actors and directors. "It was five years of a lot of struggling," Damon later told *People,* "with very low lows and very high highs."

Fire and rain

As the script for *Good Will Hunting* was being passed over (rejected) by Hollywood studios, Damon's career as an actor began to simmer. Having landed a breakthrough role as Specialist Ilario, a Gulf War (1991) veteran-turned heroin addict, in the 1996 drama *Courage Under Fire* (starring Meg Ryan and Denzel Washington), he attracted the notice of both critics and Hollywood directors. The following year director Francis Ford Coppola chose him for the leading role in *The Rainmaker,* a screen adaptation of a novel by popular author John Grisham. Damon was widely praised for his compelling performance as Rudy Baylor, an idealistic young lawyer who is pitted against a dishonest insurance company. Barbara Shulgasser wrote in the *San Francisco Examiner,* "Damon reveals a storehouse of deep emotion and considerable poise for someone so young. He brings a gravity [seriousness] to Rudy that makes it possible for us to believe he could go up against the legal team of a major insurance company and not be crushed at the first deposition [testimony given under oath]."

Oscar hunting

Having been rejected by numerous studios, the script for *Good Will Hunting* finally made its way to Miramax chief Harvey Weinstein, thanks to the intervention of Kevin Smith, who had worked with both Damon and Affleck as the director of *Chasing Amy* (1997). At Smith's urging, Weinstein looked at the script. After Miramax paid $1 million for the script (a huge amount of money for first-time writers), Weinstein was pressured to cast well-known actors in the leading roles. "We stuck with Ben and Matt when nobody wanted them," he told *USA*

Today. "Other studios wouldn't make the movie with them. Even once I had agreed to make the movie, everyone kept saying, 'Look, I can get you big stars.' Some big-name directors turned it down because we went with those actors."

Weinstein's decision was justified. The film was a critical and commercial success, and Damon, in particular, won raves from film critics in the lead role as an MIT (Massachusetts Institute of Technology) janitor who has a genius IQ. Damon was nominated for a 1998 Academy Award (nicknamed the Oscar award) for Best Actor. Had he won, he would have become the youngest Oscar recipient in that category. (He did, however, win that year's ShoWest award for the Male Star of the Year.) Nominated for a total of nine Academy Awards, *Good Will Hunting* won an Oscar and a Golden Globe Award for Best Screenplay, which went to its writers Damon and Affleck.

Perseverance Pays Off

Although Damon seemed to have become a success overnight, he struggled for years as an actor before deciding to write a screenplay that would provide good roles for him and for his longtime friend, Ben Affleck. After collaborating on the script, the two actors had a difficult time finding a studio that would produce the movie. "The writing nomination [for Academy Award for Best Screenplay for *Good Will Hunting*] is the most amazing kind of accomplishment," Damon later told *USA Today*. "It took five years out of my life and [Ben Affleck's]. We were told 'no' by so many people in so many rooms. Every studio had a chance. We were told, 'You can't do this,' 'The script isn't good enough,' over and over.

Much ado about something

Suddenly an actor in much demand, Damon was cast as paratrooper James Ryan in Steven Spielberg's highly acclaimed World War II (1939–45) drama, *Saving Private Ryan* (1998). A hit among critics and movie-goers, the film was hailed as an exemplary war film and earned an Academy Award nomination for Best Film. Also that year, Damon portrayed law student Mike McDermott, an ace card player, in the drama *Rounders*. Directed by John Dahl (whose previous credits included *The Last Seduction* and *Red Rock West*), the film co-starred Ed Norton as McDermott's low-life friend, Worm. *Premiere* reporter Glenn Kenny described Damon's McDermott as "a bit like Will Hunting, truth be told, only more well-mannered and clearly conscience-stricken."

Damon's next projects included *Dogma* (1999), in which he plays the angel of death; *The Talented Mr. Ripley* (1999), based on the classic French noir thriller, *Purple Noon;* and *Planet Ice* (1999), a futuristic animated story. A hot commodity in Hollywood since *Good Will Hunting* ignited his career, Damon remains unfazed by fame. "Success is not something I've

Matt Damon as poker ace Mike McDermott in Rounders. *(The Kobal Collection)*

wrapped my brain around," Damon once told a Mr. Showbiz interviewer. "If people go to these movies, then yes, that's big-time success. If not, it's much ado about nothing."

Sources

Brodie, John. "Boston Uncommon." *Premiere,* January 1998. [Online] Available http://www.premiere.com/goodwill/index.html.

Busch, Kristen. *Golden Boy: The Matt Damon Story.* New York: Ballantine, 1998.

Diamond, Maxine and Harriet Hemmings. *Matt Damon: A Biography.* New York: Pocket Books, 1998.

Kenny, Glenn. "Gamespotting." *Premiere,* October 1998, pp. 51-54.

Maslin, Janet. *"Good Will Hunting:* Logorhythms and Biorhythms Test a Young Janitor." *The New York Times,* December 5, 1997.

Maslin, Janet. *"Rounders:* knowing when to hold 'em and fold 'em but just not when to run." *The New York Times,* September 11, 1998.

Maslin, Janet. "*Saving Private Ryan*, A Soberly Magnificent New War Film." *The New York Times,* July 24, 1998.

"Matt Damon." People Online. [Online] Available http://www.pathfinder. com/people/sp/damon/damon2.html (February 4, 1999).

"Matt Damon is one of Hollywood's up-and-comers." People Online, February 23, 1998. [Online] Available http://www.pathfinder.com/people/ 980223/features/damon2.html. (February 4, 1999).

Neville, Ken. "ShoWest Wraps with Damon, Driver." E! Online, March 13, 1998. [Online] Available http://www.eonline.com/News/Items/ 0,1,2684,00.html. (February 4, 1999).

"Profiles: Matt Damon." People Online. [Online] Available http://www. casenet.com/people/mattdamona.htm (February 4, 1999).

Puig, Claudia. "Damon's 'Good Will' glory was hard-won." *USA Today,* February 12, 1998.

Schaefer, Stephen. "Rain Man." Mr. Showbiz. [Online] Available http:// www.mrshowbiz.com/interviews/384_1.html (February 4, 1999).

Spines, Christine. "Going All the Way." *Premiere,* August 1998, pp. 56 ff.

Cameron Diaz

Born August 30, 1972
San Diego, California

Actress

> "I have a plan, and this business definitely has a plan for you. You have to have an idea of what you want for yourself, or else you just end up getting used up in their plan."

A self-described "heavy metal chick," Cameron Diaz began modeling as a teenager, thanks to a chance meeting with a photographer. Her acting career began by chance as well, after she answered a casting call for models. Starring in films such as *She's the One* and *There's Something About Mary,* she soon found her niche in independent films that feature ensemble (group) casts. While she professes not to be interested in the box-office potential of a movie (how much money a movie will make), Diaz looks carefully at roles to determine whether they fit into her career plan. The actress explained her career philosophy to *Premiere* contributor Robert Hofler: "I just look for roles that will be fun for me."

A Southern California girl

Cameron Diaz was born in San Diego, California, on August 30, 1972. The second child of Emilio and Billie Diaz, she has an older sister, Chimene. Blonde-haired and blue-eyed, Diaz has a diverse cultural background: her father, a foreman for a large oil company, is a second-generation Cuban American, while her mother, an import-export agent, is part English, part German, and part Native American. "I grew up with Cuban food and with the music," Diaz told an Internet Archive interviewer. "I grew up with the hospitality, passion and warmth of the Latin family." Although close to her older sister, she often fought with her sibling. "I adore and love her like nobody ever," she explained. "But we fought like crazy when we were kids. We were maniacal [crazed]—everybody in the neighborhood knew that when we started fighting, to step back. We were like two Tasmanian devils." In spite of the fighting, Chimene Diaz looked out for her younger sister. "I was a total terror to her, and she was patient with me," Diaz concluded. "She took care of me, looked out for me, was the perfect big sister."

Raised in a two-story stucco house in suburban Long Beach, California, Diaz liked to take care of animals and dreamed of becoming a zoologist [a scientist who studies animals]. "I've always loved animals," she said. "When I was growing up I had two snakes. The bigger one was about six-and-a-half feet, and I raised mice for them to eat. I also had three dogs, three cats, and five birds."

A onetime cheerleader who hung out with the skateboarding crowd, Diaz developed a passion for heavy metal music by her early teens. A die-hard Van Halen fan by the age of thirteen, she attended concerts by Metallica, Ozzy Osbourne, Ratt, and other bands that performed at the Long Beach Arena. Somewhat of a tomboy, she wore the uniform of a heavy metal teen—blue jeans (with a comb in the pocket), flannel shirts, and feathered hair. As a teenager Diaz also started to hang out with a hard-partying nightlife crowd in Los Angeles. At one such Hollywood party, she met photographer Jeff Dunas, who expressed interest in helping her break into modeling. Dunas, she explained, had the ability to spot a diamond in the rough. "I looked hideous," she told Internet Archive. "I was wearing, like, a jump-suit with heels." It was not the first time Diaz had been approached by someone claiming to be a photographer. She recalled the parties where "[a] bunch of sleazy guys were coming up and saying, 'Hey, baby, wanna be a model? I'm a photographer.'" Dunas, however, gave her a business card, and turned out to be a professional fashion photographer who was genuinely interested in jump-starting her modeling career.

"It" Girls Don't Wear Plaid

A member of the heavy-metal skateboarding crowd in high school, Diaz typically wore jeans and flannel shirts. After she began modeling, she traveled around the United States, to Japan, and throughout Europe to shoot commercials, magazine ads, and catalogs. Soon after venturing beyond the confines of southern California, she began to develop her own style. "Until I started traveling, I didn't know what my options were," she told Chris Mundy. "I didn't want the [style] I used to have, which was the stoner girl, the metal chick. I had to learn to become girlie. Girlie's a recent thing."

A model teen

After signing a contract with the Elite Modeling Agency, the sixteen-year-old aspiring model told none of her friends, for fear that nothing would come of the agreement. Several months passed before she was given an assignment—an "advertorial" for *Teen* magazine. Earning far less than super-model wages, she took home $125 for the job. After graduating from Polytechnic High School in Long Beach, Diaz traveled to Japan to find modeling work. Returning to California, she worked as a model for catalogs. "I was successful in L.A. doing catalog," she told *Harper's Bazaar* reporter Chris Mundy. "Not because I was the prettiest girl. I had a good relationship with the people I was working with. That was it. They wanted to know that they'd have a good time and not be stuck with some prima-donna [vain] model."

Magazine and catalog work took Diaz to Europe, as well. Although she earned as much as $2,000 a day, Diaz was never—despite popular rumors—a teenage supermodel. "I was a working model," she told *Premiere* contributor Robert Hofler. "I was doing junior ads for newspapers every single day of the week. I never got the work I wanted. I had to become an actress to get the cover of *Vogue*. I worked *twice* when I was in Paris, and I lived there for nine months. From the age of sixteen, I'd been working my ass off. That was my suffering. I was trying to get over that hump of trying to make something of myself."

A less ordinary life

When a Hollywood casting agent put out a call for models, Diaz auditioned for a role in the movie—even though she had never had a burning desire to become an actress. After surviving twelve call-back auditions for the part, she won the role of night-club singer Tina Carlyle in *The Mask,* a 1995 action-comedy starring Jim Carrey. (Although Anna Nicole Smith had been brought in to audition, Diaz won the part because the infamous actress had recently been offered a part in the feature *Naked Gun 33 1/3.*) Suddenly thrust into the limelight, Diaz won the 1996 ShoWest Award for the "Female Star of Tomorrow."

Following her success in *The Mask,* Diaz hired a movie agent (Nick Styne, of the ICM agency) and a manager (Rick Yorn). Inexperienced in the movie industry, she pondered how best to avoid becoming yesterday's next big thing—a trap in to which she'd witnessed too many young performers fall. The actress explained her reasoning to Hofler: "I don't have any experience. I don't want to go straight into leading roles. I have too much to learn." Turning down parts in mega-budget mainstream films, she decided to take on small—yet deep— roles in low-budget independent films. First in line was *The Last Supper* (directed by Stacy Title), the story of a group of young liberals who decide to poison conservative foes. (Diaz played the wife of Harvey Keitel.) Although she was originally offered the pretty-girl part of Paulie, she opted to play the more gutsy role of Jude. Next came a string of roles in small movies, including *She's the One*—a film by Edward Burns, the director, writer, and star of *The Brothers McMullen*—and *Feeling Minnesota,* co-starring Keanu Reeves and Vincent D'Onofrio. The story of a bride who realizes—at her wedding — that she is about to marry the wrong man, *Minnesota* was neither a critical nor box-office hit. Other independent film credits included parts in *Head Above Water* and *The Keys to Tulsa*—in which Diaz appears in just one scene as a flighty southern belle. "When you look at the parts I've taken," Diaz told Internet Archive, "they've actually been quite different from one another. My character in *The Last Supper* is a million miles away from the girl in *The Mask,* or the girl in *She's the One.* It's not like I'm really trying to avoid playing pretty girl roles either. . . . You've just got to find different ways of playing each role."

Working without a break for the first two years of her film career, Diaz stored her possessions and lived in a friend's guest house. Starring opposite Julia Roberts in the 1997 mainstream blockbuster *My Best Friend's Wedding,* she found Hollywood increasingly receptive to her. "It's always good to be in a film that does well," she explained in a Mr. Showbiz interview. "So [*My Best Friend's Wedding*] made it better for me, it opened a few more doors." After spending five months filming *Wedding,* Diaz went straight to work on *A Life Less Ordinary.* Exhausted following her three-month shoot on that movie, she took a long break from work. "I pretty much slept for ten months," she later told *Harper's Bazaar.*

"It's not like I'm really trying to avoid playing pretty girl roles either.. . . . You've just got to find different ways of playing each role."

There Was Something About *Mary*

There's Something About Mary—the 1998 romantic comedy that features Cameron Diaz as a young woman who unintentionally drives men crazy—became a surprise blockbuster whose success few if any box office analysts anticipated. Directed by Peter and Bobby Farrelly—who also wrote the screenplay for the successful 1994 comedy *Dumb and Dumber*—*Mary* earned more than $100 million at the box office before the end of its summer run. Even more surprisingly, it climbed to first place at the box office for the first time on Labor Day weekend, *eight weeks* after its release, earning about $11.6 million in that weekend alone.

There's something about Cameron

Diaz's starring role in the surprise blockbuster, *There's Something About Mary*, earned the actress *Entertainment Weekly*'s "It Girl" approval. Directed by brothers Peter and Bobby Farrelly (the directors of the lowbrow comedy *Dumb and Dumber*), the movie follows Mary Jenson, whose unlucky high school prom date (played by Ben Stiller) hires a private investigator (Diaz's then boyfriend, Matt Dillon) to track her down. A critical success, *Mary* boosted the actress's resumé and garnered her a 1999 Golden Globe nomination for Best Actress in a Musical or Comedy. *New York Times* critic Janet Maslin praised Diaz's portrayal as having "a blithe [cheerful] comic style that makes her as funny as she is dazzling." Director Bobby Farrelly shared the public's enthusiasm over Diaz. "Mary is kind of the perfect woman," he told *Harper's Bazaar*. "We rank Cameron in that category. To me there are only a couple other actresses who have that quality where they're luminous [full of light]. It's hard to describe. She's like one of the guys except she's a gorgeous babe."

Diaz followed her success in *Mary* with a characteristically quirky selection of films, including *Being John Malkovich*; *Very Bad Things,* a black comedy (a comedy that employs dark, or morbid, humor) about a bachelor party gone wrong; and *Any Given Sunday*, directed by Hollywood heavyweight Oliver Stone, whose previous credits include *Platoon* (1986) and *Born on the Fourth of July* (1989). Diaz found the prospect of working with the legendary director intimidating: "I'm so excited," she told *Premiere*. "I'm terrified at the same time. Terrified that I won't be able to deliver, but I'll take the chance, because, why not. If I fall flat on my face, I'd feel horrible. I'd be doing a disservice to Oliver." On the other hand, she admitted, "I'd be an idiot not to do it."

Having gotten into acting almost by accident, Diaz is aware that other opportunities are available to her. "Just because I'm an actor now," she told *Harper's Bazaar*, "doesn't mean I have to do it for the rest of my life." She has no imme-

diate plans to abandon her career, however. "I'm not just going to drop out. The more I learn about acting, the more I like it."

Cameron Diaz in a memorable scene from the hit film There's Something About Mary. *(The Kobal Collection)*

Sources

"Cameron Diaz Cyber Profile." People Online, August 3, 1998. [Online] Available http://www.pathfinder.com/people/profiles/diaz/index.html (February 4, 1999).

"Cameron Diaz Internet Archive." [Online] Available http://www.geocities.com/~cameron-diaz/archive.html (February 4, 1999).

"Cameron Diaz." Mr. Showbiz. [Online] Available http://www.mrshowbiz.com (February 4, 1999).

Hofler, Robert. "A Year of Living Famously." *Premiere,* December 1998, pp. 98-104.

Maslin, Janet. "'Feeling Minnesota': Attitude Posing for Substance." *The New York Times,* September 13, 1996.

Maslin, Janet. "'She's the One': Light, Sardonic Comedy." *The New York Times,* August 23, 1996.

Maslin, Janet. "'There's Something About Mary': Slapstick Pursuit of an Old Flame." *The New York Times,* July 15, 1998.

Mundy, Chris. "A Fine Romance." *Harper's Bazaar,* August 1998, pp. 114-121.

Wolf, Jeanne. "Q & A with Matt Dillon & Cameron Diaz." E! Online. [Online] Available http://www.eonline.com/Hot/Qa/Diaz98/index.html (February 4, 1999).

Leonardo DiCaprio

Born November 11, 1974
Los Angeles, California

Actor

A well-respected actor in independent films, Leonardo ("Leo") Wilhelm DiCaprio reportedly had no designs on becoming a mainstream movie star. Thanks to his role as the romantic leading man in James Cameron's *Titanic,* however, he has become just that. (He later confessed to *Vanity Fair* that his *Titanic* stint was not his "cup of tea.") Now commanding $20 million for a leading appearance in a movie, the actor carefully reviews scripts with his father before committing to take on a role. Favoring interesting, character-driven roles, DiCaprio has turned down numerous plum parts—such as the role of Robin in 1995's *Batman Forever.* "I want to take my time with each role," he explained, "and that's how you plan a long career rather than doing it all at once in a big explosion."

"You definitely want to be remembered for your work rather than being sort of the hunk-of-the month type of deal. That's what I've always aimed for. . . .What you want is your work to speak for itself."

A Hollywood hippie family

Leonardo DiCaprio was born in Los Angeles, California, on November 11, 1974. Although his parents separated before his first birthday, they remained on good terms. George, his Italian American father, worked as a performance artist and distributed

(AP/Wide World)

51

underground comic books from his garage. His German-born mother, Irmalin, worked as a legal secretary. An only child, DiCaprio has an older stepbrother, Adam Farrar.

Both of DiCaprio's parents were former hippies who held liberal views and raised their son in a non-traditional environment. "We're not the hippie family who only eats organic [natural or home-grown foods] and the children meditate and go to a school of the arts," the actor is quoted in the DiCaprio Home Page. "But we're not apple-pie and Republican, either." Household guests included renegade comic-book artist Robert Crumb (the subject of the documentary, *Crumb*), novelist Hubert Selby, Jr., and writer Charles Bukowski. The actor regards his unusual upbringing as an asset. He told Jamie Diamond of *Mademoiselle:* "I've grown up with the fact that I wasn't normal—the strangest people I've ever met were at my parents' houses. It was odd to visit friends who lived in all-white houses and didn't have bizarre artwork on the wall!"

Raised in a rough neighborhood in Hollywood, DiCaprio attended the Center for Enriched Studies and John Marshall High School in Los Angeles. Never an enthusiastic student, he spent much of his time in school socializing and entertaining classmates. "I cheated a lot because I just could not sit and do homework," he told *Interview.* "Most of the stuff that I got from school was from hanging out with friends and meeting kids."

From *Romper Room* to *Growing Pains*

DiCaprio had his first television experience at the age of five, when he made a guest appearance on the children's program *Romper Room.* The role was brief, however: DiCaprio was kicked off the set because of his uncontrollable behavior. Untrained in drama, he had little interest in acting until his stepbrother, Adam, brought home a handsome paycheck for his appearance in a Golden Grahams cereal commercial. At the age of ten, DiCaprio started auditioning for television commercials. Slow in finding work at first, he was told that he should think about changing his name to something less ethnic-sounding, such as "Lenny Williams." Eventually, he earned spots in more than thirty commercials, including one for Matchbox cars. He also appeared in "Open Your Heart," a 1986 video by popular singer Madonna. Later came small roles on television series such as *Roseanne, Santa Barbara, The Outsiders,* and *The New Lassie.* He also appeared in educational films, including *How to Deal with a Parent Who Takes Drugs* and *Mickey's Safety Club.* Equally unmemorable was his small part in the feature film *Critters 3*—a poorly rated 1991 horror comedy.

Having won a part on the short-lived television series *Parenthood,* DiCaprio soon landed a regular role on the ABC family sitcom, *Growing Pains,* starring Alan Thicke, Joanna Kerns, and Kirk Cameron. Sixteen years old at the time, he left the eleventh grade to join the cast of *Growing Pains* and finished high school through home study. Joining the long-running show in its last season, 1991–92, DiCaprio's tenure as Luke Brower—a character *People Online* described as "a sanitized street urchin"—was brief. "I got to know what I don't want to do," the actor told *People.* "I had these lame lines. I couldn't bear it, actually. Everyone was bright and chipper." All griping aside, the series brought DiCaprio considerable visibility—and enough cash to purchase a new house for his mother. (He lived with his mother in her new Los Angeles home until he was 21, at which time he moved into his own place nearby.)

Troubled teens

Shortly before the end of his stint on *Growing Pains,* DiCaprio won his first major role in a feature film—for which he competed with four hundred other young actors. Playing a confused teenager in *This Boy's Life*—based on Tobias Wolff's autobiographical story of a boy who comes of age in the Pacific Northwest during the 1950s—he shared the screen with Ellen Barkin as his fun-loving but unpredictable mother and Robert DeNiro as his abusive and controlling stepfather. "It was kind of hard not to get frightened," DiCaprio told *Premiere* about his experience acting with DeNiro, who is noted for his on-screen intensity. "But I liked it when he scared me. It helped me react." Although the film, released in the spring of 1993, fared poorly at the box office, critics noted DiCaprio's powerful performance. *Newsweek's* David Ansen, for example, raved that the young actor was "astonishingly talented." DiCaprio clearly displayed natural acting ability. Director Michael Caton-Jones explained to *Newsweek,* "[he] has this amazing ability to convey quite complex emotions. All I wanted him to do was be a kid. He did that magnificently."

Attracted to offbeat roles, DiCaprio next played a mentally challenged teenager in Lasse Halstrom's independent feature, *What's Eating Gilbert Grape?* Set in a small town in Iowa, the film features Johnny Depp—who also gravitates toward unconventional characters—in the title role. Cast as Arnie (a role he almost lost because he was considered to be too handsome to play the troubled and untidy teen), DiCaprio approached his character intuitively. "I didn't even know what I did in *Gilbert Grape*," he told *Interview.* "I just went off with whatever I felt instinctively without a second thought." The actor's instincts proved to be dead-on: widely praised for his honest and open performance, he was nominated for an Academy Award as Best Supporting Actor—a rare honor for such a young person.

DiCaprio's next movie, *The Quick and the Dead,* contributed to his reputation as a promising young actor. "Leonardo DiCaprio proves that he's got a star's charisma and a precocious [mature] talent," raved Hal Hinson in the *Washington Post,* "he's more impressive with each movie he makes." A satire of macho Westerns, *The Quick and the Dead* was directed by Sam Raimi, whose previous movies included *Darkman* and *Evil Dead.* Playing a character known simply as "The Kid"—who is gunned down by his father, played by Gene Hackman—DiCaprio impressed co-star Sharon Stone. "[He was] so good, it's scary," the actress told *Entertainment Weekly.* "I would have carried the boy on my back to the set every day if that's what it would have taken. Luckily, Leonardo is down-to-earth and walked by himself."

Self-destructive characters

Next DiCaprio took on the lead role in *The Basketball Diaries,* a wrenching, factual account of a young New York basketball player's harrowing experience with heroin addiction. Based on James Carroll's 1978 book, *The Basketball Diaries* was shelved several times before it was finally produced in 1994. First-time feature director Scott Kalvert chose DiCaprio to play the drug-addicted teenager after a number of other actors expressed interest in the role, including Matt Dillon, Anthony Michael Hall, the late River Phoenix, Rick Schroeder, and Eric Stolz.

While the film proved to be a disappointment, DiCaprio stunned the critics with his raw portrayal of heroin addiction. "You leave *The Basketball Diaries* believing that Leonardo DiCaprio can do anything," wrote Peter Travers in *Rolling Stone.*

"The best thing about acting is that I get to lose myself in another character and actually get paid for it. It's a great outlet. As for myself, I'm not sure who I am. It seems that I change every day."–DiCaprio, Leonardo DiCaprio Home Page

Janet Maslin said in *The New York Times,* "What saves the film from self-destructing entirely is Mr. DiCaprio's terrifying performance." Noted for his ability to immerse himself in troubled roles, the actor spent weeks preparing for the movie's drug-withdrawal scene. DiCaprio reported (cited in the Celebsite online biography) that it required "a primal state of being—I had to turn into an animal almost." Noting his sensitive portrayals in *What's Eating Gilbert Grape?* and *This Boy's Life,* Maslin praised the actor's natural ability. "Mr. DiCaprio may harden into a practiced Hollywood actor someday," she continued, "but for the moment he's a stunning natural performer who hides nothing. . . . "

Critics were less impressed by DiCaprio's portrayal of the nineteenth-century French poet Arthur Rimbaud in *Total Eclipse,* directed by Polish filmmaker Agnieszka Holland. "[He] conveys all of Rimbaud's arrogance with little of his all-important acuity [keen mind] and charisma," Maslin complained in *The New York Times.*

A star of titanic proportions

DiCaprio's portrayal of a star-crossed lover—opposite Claire Danes in a modern update of William Shakespeare's *Romeo and Juliet*—garnered more praise for the young actor. The film's casting director, too, noticed the actor's intuitive ability. "He has an innate ability to get under the skin of a character that I believe even he himself doesn't quite understand," David Rubin told *People.* "He's one of the most instinctual young actors today." Even more of a hit abroad than in the United States, *Romeo and Juliet* was the actor's first introduction to international celebrity.

Interested in expanding his repertory (body of work), DiCaprio next took a secondary role as a rebellious teenager in *Marvin's Room* (1996). Based on a 1991 play by Scott McPherson, the gut-wrenching drama stars Diane Keaton as a woman stricken by leukemia and Meryl Streep as her estranged (alienated) sister. Of DiCaprio's performance as Hank, Streep's troubled son, the actress told *People,* "He's always compelling. You can't watch anything else when he's acting."

Next came the $200 million budgeted *Titanic,* which catapulted the young actor into international super-stardom. The story of the infamous ocean-liner disaster that took place on April 15, 1912, *Titanic* "made DiCaprio a virtually unsinkable

Leonardo DiCaprio (with Gretchen
Mol) feels the pressure of being a
Celebrity in the 1998 Woody
Allen film. (The Kobal Collection)

superstar," according to *People*. As Jack Dawson, a carefree
young man who wins a third-class ticket for the ocean liner in
a poker game, DiCaprio played his first role as a romantic leading man, opposite Kate Winslet. "I was interested [in the
part] because I've traditionally played characters that have
been tortured in some aspect, whether it be by love, or drugs,
or whatever," he told Joel Siegel on *Good Morning America*.
"But this guy was an open book. He was an open-hearted guy
with no demons, and it was more of a challenge than I ever
thought it would be." Although the movie was nominated for
fourteen awards at the 1998 Academy Awards, DiCaprio was
overlooked (although he did receive a Golden Globe nomination for Best Actor in a Drama). While some critics complained
that the actor had been cheated out of a Best Actor Award
that he deserved, many others noted that his role in the

mega-budget blockbuster did not represent his best work.

DiCaprio next took on the challenge of a dual role in *The Man in the Iron Mask,* an adaptation of the swashbuckling classic Alexandre Dumas novel. Playing the part of twin heirs to the French throne—one of whom is good, the other evil—DiCaprio performed alongside veteran actors, including Gabriel Byrne, Jeremy Irons, and John Malkovich. He followed that performance with a small role as a spoiled and self-indulgent young star in Woody Allen's *Celebrity.* Next, after much consideration, DiCaprio signed a $20 million contract to star in *The Beach.* Based on a novel by Alex Garland, the story concerns a man who is given a map to paradise by a mysterious stranger.

Noted for his deliberate approach to acting and to choosing his roles, DiCaprio is thoughtful about his approach to a long-lasting career. "Just because you did a good performance once doesn't mean you're always going to be good," he told the *Chicago Sun Times.* "I guess I just never want to be in that 'Whatever happened? You used to love me' situation."

Unsinkable

Time magazine reported that five weeks into *Titanic's* theater run, 20th Century Fox (the studio that produced the movie) estimated that seven percent of all U.S. teenage girls had already seen the movie twice.

Sources

Busch, Anita M. "Wuz he robbed?" *Time,* March 23, 1998. [Online] Available www.time.com (January 19, 1999).

Celebsite: Leonardo DiCaprio Star Bio. [Online] Available http://celebsite.com/people/leonardodicaprio/content/bio.html (January 19, 1999).

Diamond, Jamie. "Leo rising." *Mademoiselle,* April 1995, p. 98.

Entertainment Weekly, March 24, 1995, pp. 6-7; May 5, 1995, pp. 34-37.

"Good Morning America." Mr. Showbiz. [Online] Available http://mrshowbiz.go.com/interviews/389_1.html (January 19, 1999).

Kirkland, Bruce. "Reconstructing Woody in Celebrity." *The Toronto Sun,* November 20, 1998. [Online] Available http://www.canoe.ca/JamMoviesReviewsC/celebrity_kirkland.html (January 19, 1999).

Leonardo DiCaprio Home Page. [Online] Available http://www.dicaprio.com/biographical_info.html (January 19, 1999).

"Leonardo DiCaprio is getting more gold and glory than he imagined," "Leonardo DiCaprio, troubled son or cheeky geek?," "Young Hollywood." People Online. [Online] Available http://www.pathfinder.com/people (January 19, 1999).

New York Times, February 12, 1995, sect. 6, p.28; April 21, 1995, p. C12; November 3, 1995, p. C14; November 1, 1996, p. C1; November 5, 1996, p. C13; November 12, 1996, p. C11; November 18, 1996, p. C 15; December 19, 1997.

Premiere, January 1994, p. 30; October 1996, pp. 89-96, 137-138.

Rolling Stone, March 23, 1995, pp. 127-128.

Sischy, Ingrid. "Leonardo DiCaprio interview." *Interview,* June 1994, p. 62.

Washington Post, April 21, 1995, p. D1; November 3, 1995, p. F6; November 1, 1996, p. D1; November 8, 1996, p. D1.

"Web Celeb—Leonardo DiCaprio." Yahooligans! [Online] Available http://www.yahooligans.com/content/webceleb/dicaprio/ (January 19, 1999).

Michael Flatley

Born July 16, 1958
Chicago, Illinois

Dancer, choreographer

"Who would have predicted that Irish dance would graduate from St. Patrick's Day parades to sold-out arenas. Michael Flatley may have. . . . [he] has gone from one of the best performers in a seldom seen art form to an internationally known celebrity," Christina Barron wrote in *Europe*. Born and raised in the United States, Michael Ryan Flatley mastered the traditional Irish style of dancing as a youngster, and soon transformed the discipline with his swaggering and adrenalized style. A chess master, boxing champ, and respected flutist, the former championship dancer has received honors and awards nationally and abroad. The youngest-ever recipient of the U.S. National Heritage Fellowship (awarded to him by former President Ronald Reagan), he has been recognized by the National Endowment for the Arts as one of the country's greatest performers. In 1991, the National Geographic Society declared him a Living Treasure. Having risen quickly from humble beginnings, Flatley once told *Time:* "I flew to Ireland in 1994 with a standby ticket on Aer Lingus and I came back on the Concorde. Not bad for a kid from Chicago who does the jig."

"What we do transcends dance. It's all about energy. We're making people feel things."

(AP/Wide World)

Raised in the Windy City

Born in Chicago, Illinois, on July 16, 1958, Michael Flatley was the second of five children born to Michael and Eilish Flatley. His parents immigrated to the United States from Ireland in 1947. His father, the owner of a construction company, hailed from County Sligo, while his mother was a native of County Carol. Raised on the tough south side of Chicago, Flatley learned to value hard work from his father, who devoted long hours to the family's construction firm. Teased by other children, he took boxing lessons, which eventually led to first-place honors in the Chicago Golden Gloves Amateur Boxing Championship.

Encouraged by his maternal (on his mother's side) grandmother, Hannah Ryan—who had once been the dance champion of Leinster province in Ireland—Flatley took up Irish step dancing. Although he learned his first steps as a four-year-old, he did not begin taking formal lessons until the age of eleven, when his mother—also a former Irish dance champion—enrolled him and his four siblings in dance school. Flatley was told that he was too old to begin training to become a world-class dancer. Never one to be discouraged, he worked hard to learn the routines his fellow classmates had been studying for years. "If you can dream it, you can have it," Flatley once told *People* with typical bravado. "That's what I thought even as a boy."

The young dancer—who frequently traveled with his parents to their native Ireland—displayed a natural gift for Irish dancing. "It came to me so easy what they were doing because it was in me—I got good at it fast. . . . I was learning at such a fast rate compared to the other dancers, that when I got to class I was bored to tears working at that speed," Flatley once explained through his publicists, PMK Public Relations. Honing his skills through private lessons, Flatley spent hour after hour in his parents' garage practicing steps. At the age of sixteen—after just five years of formal instruction—he entered the world championship of Irish dancing. His win there made him the first American ever to earn that title. Following his success at the world championship, Flatley became a dominant figure in the Irish dance circuit, winning more than 100 titles in 13 countries.

Chieftain for a day

After graduating from Brother Rice High School in 1977, Flatley left the competitive circuit to dance professionally. Having danced with a number of companies, he joined The Chieftains in the early 1980s. His tenure with the popular Irish music group was brief. Chieftains leader Paddy Moloney told *People:* "From the start what Michael was doing was brilliant. I could see he was not going to settle down with us."

While touring with The Chieftains, Flatley met Beata Dziaba, a Polish makeup artist who was working as a hotel receptionist in London. The two were married in 1986, but were divorced eleven years later. (Flatley later explained in an online Teletext interview, "As to the break-up of my relationships, I have no regrets. I don't look back. What matters most is the integrity of the art.")

Seven minutes that shook Ireland

Flatley struggled to survive during his first years as a professional performer and was forced to take other work—as a bartender, laborer, plumber, and travel agent—to support himself. His first big break came in early 1994 when an Irish television producer decided to cast him in a seven-minute filler piece for a pop-song contest. Moya Doherty—who had seen the Irish-American perform the previous year in County Mayo, Ireland—decided to create a show based on the unconventional dancing style of Flatley and another dancer, Jean Butler. (Butler, too, was an American-born Irish dance champion.) "I wanted to show a modern image of Ireland, not the old green pastures," she told *Time* reporter Martha Duffy. "Irish dance is frozen in tradition, and I thought it's time to thaw it out."

Flatley, who was living in California, flew to Dublin (on an inexpensive stand-by ticket) after Doherty contacted him about the dance segment. The two Irish American dancers, Doherty, choreographer Mavis Ascott, and composer Bill Whelan worked together to produce a daring and innovative seven-minute dance number. The music added a contemporary New-Age edge to traditional Irish reels and jigs. Going against tradi-

---

Traditional Irish Dance

While traditional Irish dance demands lightening-quick foot moves, it does not allow upper body movement. Dancers maintain rigid posture; they hold their arms tightly against their sides, and do not raise their legs above the waist. A serious expression is mandatory.

Flatley mastered the traditional style, even though he found it stifling. "You go to Ireland and people have such pride and passion and personality," he told *Irish Voice,* "and they're oozing with character, and it's such a contradiction that they dance like this."

---

tion, Flatley and Butler incorporated expressive arm movements—even daring to exchange fiery looks. *Riverdance*—broadcast at intermission of the April 1994 Eurovision Song Contest—was a spectacular success. Dubbed "The Seven Minutes That Shook Ireland," the act was broadcast to a global audience of millions. Released as a single, the music from the act reached the top of Irish charts, and a video of the performance sold 100,000 copies (a staggering sales figure in a country of four million people).

Riverdance rocks

Convinced that they had a hit on their hands, Doherty and her husband, John McCoglan, also a producer, turned the intermission act into a full-length production. Flatley—who was again featured as principal dancer—devised the choreography (the arrangement of the dance). The show, also called *Riverdance*, played to full houses when it opened in Dublin, Ireland, early in 1995. Not just a popular success, the showy dance extravaganza was a hit among dance critics as well. As Septime Webre, artistic director of the American Repertory Ballet Company, explained in *Time*: "The precision and uniformity with which these dancers execute their steps is on par with the great ballet companies of the world."

Truly a variety show, *Riverdance* combined traditional Irish and non-Irish elements—such as a gospel choir and a flamenco dancer. Doherty explained to the *Wall Street Journal*: "The first half examines our Irish roots, who we are, our heritage as Celts and our spirituality, while the second half is the journey out, the embracing by the Irish diaspora [settlements far from the homeland] of other cultures and how we, as Irish, are changed culturally when we return to our homeland." Months after opening in Dublin, *Riverdance* played to enthusiastic crowds throughout Great Britain. After a second stint in Ireland, it set out for a repeat tour of Britain. The production returned to England, however, without its star performer.

Breaking up is hard to do

In October 1995, after just six months as lead dancer, Flatley split from *Riverdance*. The dancer—who had already been accused by the British press of attempting to take more than his share of credit for the success of the show—demanded full artistic control on top of copyright for his choreographic contributions. The show's producers refused. *Time* magazine reported: "Flatley was dismissed from the company following stymied [blocked] contract negotiations during which producers refused to accede [give in] to his demands for full artistic control of the show." For his part, Flatley claimed that firing him from the show was "like a car firing the driver." The dancer filed suit against *Riverdance* for copyright credit and a two-percent share of the show's multi-million dollar ticket revenues.

Flatley took his dismissal from *Riverdance* personally. He explained in material provided by PMK Public Relations: "I felt like I was terribly betrayed. For someone to take your work is not an easy thing for an artist to live with. It was heartbreaking. I was devastated."

He got over it. "In the end I just decided I was either going to roll over and die or come out fighting," he told the *London Daily Express*. "And I realized all of a sudden that, whatever happened, they could never take my clogs—dance shoes—anyway. They could take my ideas and my steps, but not what was in my heart. I knew I could always come up with more ideas." Eleven days after he left Riverdance, Flatley later reported, the idea for *Lord of the Dance* came to him.

A self-appointed Lord

After opening in Dublin on July 2, 1996, Flatley's *Lord of the Dance* traveled to London, New Zealand, and Australia. The following spring, a stint in Manhattan, New York, launched the show's American debut. Each of the show's thirteen performances at Radio City Music Hall—which boasts nearly 6,000

The Name's Familiar

Most Americans associate the name of Michael Flatley with the spectacularly popular dance show *Riverdance*. But Flatley, who split from the production after only six months, never danced with the show in front of a U.S. audience. It is with the show *Lord of the Dance* that Flatley came before U.S. audiences.

seats—was sold out. *Billboard* reporter Susan Nunziata explained the show's appeal: *Lord of the Dance* takes the unique art of Irish step-dancing introduced so well in *Riverdance* to another level. This new spectacle, replete [filled] with pyrotechnics [spectacular displays], two huge video screens, and some saucy dance numbers, is equal parts Las Vegas and Ireland."

Flatley created his Irish vision of Vegas with the help of light and set designers who had experience with pop music acts. He also enlisted the assistance of John Reid, singer Elton John's manager, and choreographer Arlene Philips, who had previously collaborated with the pop acts Duran Duran, The Pet Shop Boys, and Tina Turner. In spite of the impressive credentials of his collaborators, he insisted on total artistic control. "I just wanted people who would go away and do what I showed them to do," he explained to *Midweek Magazine*. "Because I have to be in control."

Few critics questioned the outstanding dancing ability of Flatley and his crew of dancers, but reviews of the show—and of Flatley himself—were mixed. Some found *Lord of the Dance* merely to be a copy of *Riverdance* and a showcase for Flatley, while others found the show to be unique and breathtaking. Flatley, who claims to devour self-help and motivational books, took criticism in stride. He told *Time*, "When there are 7,000 people in an audience cheerin' and there's one guy who doesn't like what I'm doin', what does it matter?"

While Flatley does not foresee an end to his dancing days in the near future, the physical demands of his profession will eventually force him to retire from the stage. He doesn't, however, intend to retire from the limelight. Intent on a film career, he developed a movie idea, tentatively called *Dream Dancer*. The storyline is familiar: a young artist struggles to reach the top of his chosen profession. The similarities to the dancer's life are no coincidence: Flatley's life story is the stuff that movies are made of. "If you do what you love," he once told *the Sydney Morning Herald,* "money will follow. Who would have thought that the kid from Chicago who does the jig would be the highest paid dancer in the world?"

Sources

Barron, Christina. "Sites of the month: 'Dance' fever." *Europe,* November 1997, p. 7.

Bellafante, Ginia. "Mr. Big of the new jig." *Time,* March 31, 1997, pp. 76-78.

Duffy, Martha. "Not your father's jig." *Time,* March 18, 1996, p. 92.

Hitchner, Earle. "Riverdance, traditional Irish dance liberated." *Wall Street Journal,* March 12, 1996, p. A16.

Jackson, George. "Stomping on Irish tradition." *Washington Post,* April 22, 1997.

London Daily Express, June 15, 1996, Saturday section, pp. 9-11.

"Lord of the Dance, Fast-footed facts." [Online] Available http://www.lordofthedance.com/fastfacts.html (Accessed January 11, 1999).

McColdrick, Debbie. "Fabulous Flatley comes back home." *Irish Voice,* February 19-25, 1997, p. 20.

"Michael Flatley." [Online] Available http://farady.ucd.ie/~joseph/lordofthedance/flatley.html (Accessed January 11, 1999).

Midweek Magazine (London), August 12, 1996, p. 20.

Nunziata, Susan. Review of *Lord of the Dance. Billboard,* March 29, 1997, p. 76.

"Star Interview: Flatley dances solo" October 27, 1997. [Online] Available http://www.teletext.co.uk/total/celeb/flatley.htm (Accessed January 11, 1999).

Sydney Morning Herald, November 5, 1996.

Tresniowski, Alex, et al. "Gael force." *People,* April 14, 1997, pp. 135-136.

Additional material obtained from PMK Public Relations.

Jamie Foxx

Born December 13, 1967
Terrell, Texas

Comedian, actor, singer

"As a comedian, as an actor, you've got to make things happen. You've got to have a lot of things in the air."

A classically trained musician, Jamie Foxx—born Eric Bishop—did not set out to become a comedian or actor. Having performed his first stand-up routine on a dare, he discovered a love—and a talent—for making people laugh. As a career move, he changed his name to Jamie Foxx, and soon found himself involved in a steady stream of projects for television, cable, recording and film studios. *Jet* magazine wrote, "Foxx . . . found that after he changed his name, he has become one of the busiest and most sought-after entertainers in show business." The comedian landed his first television gig in 1991, when he took his place beside Damon Wayans, Jim Carrey, and Tommy Davidson in the popular Fox network variety show, *In Living Color.* Already a favorite among local comedy lovers, he developed a large and devoted following. He later told *Jet* magazine, "After [*In Living Color*] my life changed, my life literally changed forever."

No Beaver Cleaver

Jamie Foxx was born Eric Bishop on December 13, 1967 in Terrell, Texas, a small town (population: 14,000) 31 miles east of

Dallas. His parents, Shaheed Abdullah, a stockbroker, and Louise Annette Talley (now Dixon), a homemaker, were unable to care for their young son. "When my mom had me . . . she wasn't ready for responsibility," Foxx told *People*. "I'm not saying my parents were bad people." When Foxx was seven months old, he was adopted by his maternal grandparents, Mark and Esther Talley. Mark, a yardman (who died in 1985), and Esther, a retired maid and nursery operator, were, in fact, Louise Talley's adoptive parents. Foxx revealed in a *Jet* interview, "Legally my mother is my sister because the lady who adopted her in turn adopted me. It's a unique situation." Raised with two half sisters and a stepbrother, Foxx rarely saw his biological parents, who divorced when he was about six years old. "Sometimes," Foxx told *People,* "Things don't work out as they do at the Cleavers [referring to the family from the 1950s TV show *Leave it to Beaver*]."

Raised by his grandparents, Foxx spent afternoons at the New Hope Baptist Church. In spite of financial hardship, the Talleys provided a happy family life for their adoptive son. "Though we were broke, I had a great childhood," Foxx told *Texas Monthly*. "No killing, none of that. Just good fun. It wasn't a 'hood back then. It was a neighborhood." From an early age, Foxx was interested in music. At the age of five he started taking piano lessons, and by his mid-teens he had become the choir leader and music director at New Hope Baptist. He played the piano during services every Sunday—for which he earned a paycheck. Foxx recalled his youthful impression of the experience in *Texas Monthly:* "I was making seventy-five dollars a Sunday: Church is big time!" Together with some friends, Foxx started a rhythm and blues (R&B) band called Leather & Lace—a group he would later characterize as "terrible." When he entered a youth talent competition at the age of fifteen, Foxx already exhibited star quality. His childhood friend Chris Barron told *People:* "He was singing, and the women just moved to the front to be near him. He had that magnetism." An excellent student, Foxx earned good grades at Terrell High School and was quarterback on the school's football team. Already a comedian, he amused his teammates with comic impressions of the coaches.

Dare to be funny

After graduating from high school, Foxx accepted a scholarship at U.S. International University in San Diego, California, where he studied classical music. As a student, he often spent weekends in Los Angeles, where he started to frequent comedy clubs. One evening, on a dare from his girlfriend, Foxx entered an open-mike competition. His impressions of comedian/actor Bill Cosby, former president Ronald Reagan, and boxer Mike Tyson left the audience howling with laughter. The comedian, who received a standing ovation for his performance, later told *Texas Monthly,* "It was the most incredible feeling. It was, 'Okay, I think I know what I want to be right now.'"

Dropping out of school, Foxx moved to Los Angeles in 1990 hoping to make a name for himself as a stand-up comic. To support himself, he took a job at Thom McAn selling shoes, but soon found that it left him no time to perform. "I didn't come all the way to L.A. to sell shoes," he later told *People.* After six months on the job, Foxx quit—and started performing comedy seven days a week. A gifted impressionist, Foxx was extremely popular with audiences. Envious of his popularity, fellow comedians who were responsible for selecting performers in comedy clubs began to refuse to put him on stage. In an effort to ensure regular work, Foxx—who was still known as Eric Bishop—began to consider changing his name.

> Other comedians began to refer to him as "the stand-up kid"—not because he was a stand-up comic, but because of the standing ovations he received every night.

The comedian realized that it would be to his advantage to choose a name that was not gender-specific (not distinctly male or female). He confessed to *Jet* magazine, "[t]hree girls would show up and 22 guys would show up [at auditions]. They had to put all the girls on who were on the list to break up the monotony." Foxx began to sign audition lists using unisex names. "So when they look up and they see Tracey Green, Tracey Brown, all these unisex names I had written on the list, they picked Jamie Foxx," he explained. Permanently changing his name to Jamie Foxx, he set the Los Angeles comedy circuit on fire. Within a year of his debut as a comedian, he won the Bay Area Black Comedy Competition in Oakland, California. During that period he traveled frequently to Atlanta, Georgia, a popular spot for stand-up comedy at the time. There he performed at the Comedy Act Theater, entertaining packed houses with his impersonations of celebrities and a cast of characters he had developed—including "Wanda the Ugly Woman." Foxx told *Texas Monthly* that other comedians began to refer to him as "the stand-up kid"—not because he was a stand-up comic, but because of the standing ovations he received every night.

Wanda rocks the world

Sometime after winning the Bay Area competition, Foxx signed with an agent and manager and soon auditioned for a part on the Fox network's *In Living Color*. Competing with 100 other comics, Foxx was selected to join the talented *Living Color* cast, which included Damon Wayons, Tommy Davidson, and Jim Carrey. Foxx recalled in *Texas Monthly*, "I went from going to college on a music scholarship and playing modern jazz for the dance class, where I was making sixteen dollars an hour, to Los Angeles doing jokes. And the next thing you know, I was making thousands of dollars a week." Performing hilarious and dead-on accurate impressions—including Bill Cosby as a gangster, and absurd caricatures of reverend Jesse Jackson, Nation of Islam leader Louis Farrakhan, and rapper Biggie Smalls—and signature characters he had developed during his stand-up routines—such as "Wanda the Ugly Woman" (whose most memorable line was "I'll rock your world")—Foxx attracted an enthusiastic national following. "Without *In Living Color,* I don't think I would exist now," he explained to *People*. "People got to know me because of that show." During the three years Foxx appeared in the Fox network's variety show, he also made recurring appearances as Crazy George on the sitcom *Roc* (starring Charles S. Dutton). He also created a one-man show for HBO: *Jamie Foxx, Straight From the Foxx-hole*. Aired on uncensored cable television, the special allowed the comedian to return to the raw style of his earlier material.

Shortly after *In Living Color* was canceled in 1994, Foxx recorded his first album, *Peep This*. Released in 1995, the full-length album features twelve R&B songs written, produced, and performed by the versatile comedian. Well received by music critics, the album climbed to the twelfth spot on *Billboard* magazine's R&B sales charts. Foxx also began touring the country as a stand-up comic. Even though he did not have a firm contract to star in a television series, he told his audiences to watch for his upcoming show. He later told *Texas Monthly*, "I told everybody I was working on *The Jamie Foxx Show,* and that when it came out, I wanted them to tune in." When the WB (Warner Brothers) network first aired the family-oriented situation comedy in January 1995, it became clear that Foxx's strategy had worked. The comedian's fans tuned in—and in large numbers. *The Jamie Foxx Show* became one of the network's highest rated shows, scoring especially well with young audiences and women.

The series—which Foxx co-created with Bentley Kyle Evans—also features model Garcelle Beauvais, former *Saturday Night Live* comic Garrett Morris, Ellia English, and Christopher B. Duncan. Based loosely on the comedian's own experiences, it follows the life of Jamie King, an aspiring performer who leaves Terrell, Texas, to make his mark in Hollywood. Unlike Foxx, however, King struggles to make his way in show business. Creating a show for a family-oriented network provided a creative challenge for Foxx, who has drawn some criticism for resorting to objectionable material. He told *Mediaweek,* "It makes you say, 'How can I be funny without [swearing]?' Like *I Love Lucy* or *The Dick Van Dyke Show*. They were clean and still funny. If you try to be on the edge, you cut lots of people out." Further, he explained, the show owes its universal appeal to the fact that it does not rely on gimmicks or stereotypes. Considered a "crossover" success, the show attracts an audience that is not limited by race, gender, or age.

> "How can I be funny without [swearing]? Like *I Love Lucy* or *The Dick Van Dyke Show*. They were clean and still funny."

Superman

In 1997, Foxx took his first starring role in a feature film, playing Bunz in the sexy comedy *Booty Call*. His previous film experience included supporting roles in *Toys,* with Robin Williams, *The Truth About Cats and Dogs,* and *The Great White Hype*— for which he received warm reviews for his portrayal of a small-time boxing manager. Foxx told *Entertainment Weekly* that he decided to play the part of Bunz because it allowed him to impersonate various celebrities, including Jesse Jackson and Bill Cosby, in some funny situations. *Booty Call,* however,—which reunited Foxx with fellow *In Living Color* player Tommy Davidson—did not fare well with film critics.

Still involved in his successful self-titled series, Foxx attracted additional young fans by providing voices for the animated children's program, *C Bear and Jamal*. He also landed another movie role in Oliver Stone's *Any Given Sunday,* alternatively known as *The League*. Foxx won the part of backup quarterback Willie Beaman after recording artist Sean "Puffy" Combs withdrew from consideration due to scheduling conflicts. He stars opposite Al Pacino, who plays the team coach, Cameron Diaz, the team owner, and Dennis Quaid, the injured star quarterback his character replaces. Also in the works are plans to release a follow-up to his debut album, *Peep This*.

Foxx launched 1998 with an eleven-month tour to perform his stand-up material nation-wide. A smashing success, the tour grossed nearly $5 million. Only one African American comic has earned more on a single road tour: actor-comedian Eddie Murphy. Having performed his first comedy routine less than ten years earlier, Foxx's amazing shot to stardom seemed downright super-human. "I loved my old name," he once told *People*. "but Eric Bishop was Clark Kent. And Jamie Foxx is Superman."

Sources

Glieberman, Owen. "Fever Pitched, in two overheated comedies, scoring doesn't come easy." Entertainment Weekly Online. [Online] Available http://cgi.pathfinder.com/ew. (January 11, 1999).

Holden, Stephen. "Booty Call, Michael Jackson as potent aphrodisiac." *The New York Times*, February 26, 1997.

"Jamie Foxx replaces Puff Daddy in Oliver Stone flick." MTV News Gallery. [Online] Available http://mtv.com (December 29, 1998).

"Jamie Foxx tells how he became Jamie Foxx." *Jet*, March 24, 1997, pp. 32-35.

Lang, Steven. "Crazy like a Foxx." *People Weekly*, January 13, 1997, pp. 81-82.

Stanley, T.L., "Foxx has WB popping cork." *Mediaweek*, October 21, 1996, p. 9.

True, Cynthia. "Foxx, whole." *Texas Monthly*, November 1998, pp. 88-114.

James Galway

Born December 8, 1939
Belfast, Northern Ireland

Flutist

"I've set the standard. . . . I think I've inspired a lot of kids to really try to do something better with the flute."

A charismatic showman who displays exceptional technique and improvisational genius in his playing, James Galway has been credited with turning the flute into a center-stage instrument. As Philip Kennicott noted, "His image as the laughing Irishman has served him especially well in entertaining new audiences, and breaking down some of the barriers between classical and crossover." Thoughtful in his interpretation of music, Galway has sought to expand the repertoire (body of works) for flute—and to build a new audience for the instrument. Named a member of the Order of the British Empire—a commendation by Queen Elizabeth II that recognizes his musical contribution to society—the flutist (who plays a 14-karat gold instrument) is not shy about his gift. "I know who has the best chops," he once boasted, "—me."

Penny whistle days

James Galway was born on December 8, 1939 in Belfast, Northern Ireland. His parents—James, a shipyard riveter, and Ethel, a textile mill worker—were both musical. His mother was a self-taught pianist and his father played flute and accordion in a local band. Raised in a working-class neighborhood, Galway expressed an interest in music at a very young age. As a small child he took to the violin and harmonica. He also experimented with the penny whistle (a small, flute-like instrument) before moving on to the flute, an instrument he immediately liked.

Flouting the Rules

Galway insists on being called a flutist (FLOO-tist)—and not a flautist (FLOU-tist), as many in the classical music establishment prefer. His reason, he explained to Philip Kennicott in an online interview, is simple: "I haven't got a flaut."

While the leader of the local flute band taught Galway to read music, the young musician's father and grandfather tutored him with informal flute lessons. Just ten years old when he entered the Irish Flute Championship contest, he won each of the three solo contests he entered. Galway, who had been playing the flute for only two years, decided that he had found his calling.

As a student at Mountcollyer Secondary Modern School, Galway met two people who would help him develop as a musician. Muriel Dawn, who was a flutist with the British Broadcasting Corporation's (BBC) Northern Ireland Symphony Orchestra, tutored him in the fundamental skills of flute playing. Her husband, Douglas Dawn, secured Galway work as a piano-tuner's apprentice (assistant in training). He also made arrangements for the young musician to perform with orchestras around Belfast, and helped to convince the Belfast Education Committee to provide scholarship money that would enable Galway to study at the prestigious Royal Academy of Music in London, England.

After three years at the Royal Academy of Music, where he studied with John Francis, Galway entered the Guildhall School for Music. He learned many of the intricacies of technique as a student of Geoffrey Gilbert, whom he later acknowledged as one of the primary technical influences in his career. By the early 1960s, Galway moved to Paris, France, to study at the Conservatoire National Superieur de Musique, under the teachings of Gaston Crunelle and Jean-Pierre Rampal (see box p. 76).

A brief orchestral career

When Galway returned to the United Kingdom, he had no trouble finding work with orchestras and ensembles—even though he had never graduated from any of the music academies he attended. He took his first professional job as an orchestral player with the Wind Band of the Royal Shakespeare Theatre at Stratford-upon-Avon. Next he took a post with the Sadler's Wells Opera Orchestra, playing both flute and piccolo. At the Royal Opera House Orchestra, too, he played both wind instruments. He then served as principal flutist of the London Symphony Orchestra. After winning the Birmingham International Competition in 1966, he became principal flute in the Royal Philharmonic, also in London. After two seasons with that orchestra, he resigned in order to accept a position as principal solo flutist for the Berlin Philharmonic Orchestra.

Galway's six years with the Berlin Philharmonic, beginning in 1969, were not entirely fulfilling. Under the baton of Maestro Herbert von Karajan, he felt under-appreciated and lacking in artistic direction. Further, as Philip Kennicott noted in an online summary of an interview with Galway, "It's also possible that the flutist's independent temperament rankled [became irritated] at the authoritarian Karajan." During his time with the Berlin Philharmonic, Galway sought out opportunities to perform apart from the orchestra, often renting halls to stage private performances with other musicians. The concerts sold out. Encouraged by Michael Emmerson, a former talent scout who was eager to manage the promising young flutist, Galway resigned from his post at the Berlin Philharmonic. "When I decided to leave I did it very quickly," he told Kennicott. ". . . . I didn't want to end my days in an orchestra."

Going it alone

Galway—who had risen to the highest position as an orchestral performer before reaching his thirtieth birthday—was immediately successful as a full-time solo instrumentalist. During his first year as a soloist, he performed with each of the four major orchestras in England and appeared in more than 120 concerts world-wide. Within one year of his departure from Berlin, he also recorded four albums for RCA.

During the decades that followed, Galway continued to perform all over the world, staging chamber music and concerto performances, recitals, and popular music concerts. He also sought out opportunities to broaden the appeal of the flute. Through master classes, he shared his technical gift with other students of the instrument. He commissioned new works in an effort to expand the repertoire of works for the flute—an in-

"Music has to be what you want to do, something which makes you and everybody listening feel they are in touch with the extra-special." –James Galway, *Flute*

strument for which only a limited number of works have been written—and often featured contemporary music in his performances. During his career, Galway has commissioned works from Malcom Arnold, John Corigliano, David Heath, Loren Maazel, John Mayer, Thea Musgrave, Joaquin Rodrigo, and Lowell Liebermann, among others. Sometimes, he has recorded performances of new works. One such recording, *James Galway Plays Lowell Liebermann,* was warmly received by music critics. Terry Teachout, for example, wrote in *Time*: "If you stopped paying attention to new classical music after [Benjamin] Britten and [Dmitri] Shostakovich died, it's time to tune in again. The famous flutist has put his weight behind one of America's most gifted "new tonalist" composers, with electrifying results."

Waiting to Inhale

Some of Galway's flute adaptations have managed to amaze critics. For instance, Donald Vroon wrote in his review of Galway's adaptation of Franck's 'Sonata in A' in *American Record Guide:* "The Franck sonata was written for violin but is played on viola and cello as well. Mr. Galway was one of the first to record it played on the flute. The concept seems unlikely. How can the flute play those long lines and sustain the legato [smooth and even] writing? . . . one is left wondering how Mr. Galway can possibly sustain his tone for so long, over and over again, without seeming to breath. In fact, in the last movement I almost missed the beauty of his playing because I was trying to figure out where he breathed."

Galway has also attempted to broaden the repertoire of flute music by transcribing [adapting] a wide variety of pieces written for other instruments. Among his arrangements for the flute are transcriptions of classical pieces such as Antonio Vivaldi's symphony, *The Four Seasons,* and Aram Khachaturian's concerto for violin. He has also popularized new arrangements of popular contemporary tunes, ranging from country music to show tunes, jazz, and folk music—from the melodies of his native Ireland (including performances with the popular Celtic music group, the Chieftains) to the traditional music of Japan (recorded on the CD *Enchanted Forest*).

Galway's interpretation of folksinger John Denver's "Annie's Song" proved to be one of the innovative flutist's most successful arrangements. Following the song's release in 1978, Galway saw his popularity soar among crossover audiences (audiences whose tastes are not limited to classical works but who like other types of music, too). Encouraged by his crossover success, he began to collaborate with a number of other popular performers, including composer Henry Mancini and singer Cleo Laine. By the time he released his *Greatest Hits Volume 3* in 1998, Galway was firmly established as one of the era's top crossover artists. *People* reviewer Ralph Novak observed: "Classical musicians who dabble in pop music inevitably have to counteract the stiffness that carries over from their usual formal approach. In this collection of mostly pop songs [*Greatest Hits Volume 3*], Galway, a spirited Irish flutist, combines extraordinary technique with warmth and ease and manages to seem at home with popular material without turning it into Muzak [the electronic rendering of music, commonly known as "elevator music"]." Further, Novak concludes, "Crossover attempts by classical artists can be discomfiting, but Galway seems as at home with [John] Lennon and [Paul] McCartney as he does with Mozart and Bach. He manages to communicate the joy of music in both domains."

A popular Irishman

Not everyone, however, has appreciated Galway's efforts to popularize the flute. Many music-lovers feel that pieces not originally written for the flute should remain that way. Kennicott noted, "Galway argues that musical practice of the time included a great deal of shifting about among instruments, and that composers such as Bach regularly re-worked material for different instruments. He's right of course, but the popularity of his crossover and transcription discs doesn't rest on any such historical premise. They're popular because Galway is performing them, and flute lovers are grateful for almost anything he performs."

Television has also contributed to Galway's popularity with wide-ranging audiences. In addition to having been featured in numerous specials and music videos, he has made frequent guest appearances on *The Tonight Show, The Today Show, Live from Lincoln Center,* as well as the critically acclaimed children's program, *Sesame Street.*

In the recording studio, Galway has earned a reputation as a perfectionist who will not release a product until it satisfies his high standards. His passion for detail has paid off handsomely. The recipient of several gold and platinum records (for selling records by the thousands), he was awarded the Grand

Prix du Disque for his recordings of Mozart's concertos. Both *Billboard* and *Cashbox* magazines conferred on him record of the year awards. Named Musical America's musician of the year in 1997, he received the honorary degree of Doctor of Music the following year from the University of St. Andrews in Scotland.

Having earned both critical acclaim and commercial success, Galway enjoys a reputation as the premiere flutist of his generation. "I've set the standard, a standard set for me by [Vladimir] Horowitz and [Jascha] Heifetz," he explained to Kennicott. "Whether you like them or not, you could never say they play their instrument badly."

Sources

Contemporary Musicians, Volume 3, Gale, 1990, pp. 87-89.

Galway, James. *Autobiography,* enlarged edition, Chivers, 1980.

Galway, James. *Flute.* New York: Schirmer Books, 1982, p.193.

"James Galway." [Online] Available http://www.futurenet.com/classicalnet/ artitsts/galway/interview. html (January 10, 1999).

"James Galway." [Online] Available http://www.dj-records.com/aboutjam.html (January 10, 1999).

"The James Galway Flute Page." [Online] Available http://www.bmgclassics. com/classics/jamesgal way/bio.html (January 10, 1999).

Novak, Ralph. Review of *Greatest Hits, Volume 3. People Weekly,* February 23, 1998, p. 25.

Teachout, Terry. Review of *James Galway Plays Lowell Liebermann. Time,* November 30, 1998, p. 124.

Vroon, Donald R. Review of Franck: Sonata in A; Prokofieff: Flute Sonata; Reinecke: Undine Sonata. *American Record Guide,* July/August 1997, pp. 109-110.

Janeane Garofalo

Born September 28, 1964
Newton, New Jersey

Actress, comedian

> "I consider myself a person who has throughout my entire life stood up for myself. It's never been my ambition to be someone who takes a backseat to anything."

(AP/Wide World)

A class comedian turned stand-up comic, Janeane Garofalo found her way to Hollywood after a chance late-night meeting with actor Ben Stiller. After a brief stint on Stiller's short-lived television series, she landed a role on the popular cable series, *The Larry Sanders Show,* starring Garry Shandling. "If it hadn't been for Ben and Garry, I don't know *what* I'd be doing now," the actress once said. Soon came a number of film roles, including a role in the comedy *Reality Bites,* which earned Garofalo the dubious (questionable) reputation as poster-girl for Generation-X. Vocal in her opinions about feminist issues in Hollywood, she has built a career around her sharp comic personality.

A class clown

Janeane Garofalo was born September 28, 1964 in Newton, New Jersey. The youngest of three children, she is the daughter of Carmine, an executive for the Exxon corporation, and Joan, a homemaker. In spite of her average childhood in suburban New Jersey, she looked to comedy as a way to escape from the anxiety she experienced as an adolescent. "I thought people in show business are never unhappy," she told *Vogue* reporter David Handleman. "Look how able they are to talk to the camera. They probably laugh all day and get paid for it."

Voted Class Clown in her New Jersey high school yearbook, Garofalo was forced to complete her last year of high school among unfamiliar faces when her father was transferred to Houston, Texas. She found the move unsettling. "I had no friends and I thought I was so fat," she told Michael Lipton and Craig Tomashoff in *People*. "I went through this pit of despair. All I did was eat and sleep, eat and sleep." In spite of being ill at ease in her new surroundings, she managed, in just one year at Houston's James E. Taylor High School, to recapture the title of Class Clown.

Garofalo returned to the East Coast to attend Providence College, in Rhode Island. While majoring in history and American studies, she started to dabble in stand-up comedy. She explained her evolution as a comic in a *People* Online interview: "It's not like as a kid I dreamed of the Oscars. I wanted to be a secretary; my mom was a secretary. Then when I was a senior in high school, [*Late Night* host David] Letterman came on, and that changed my life. And I thought, I wanna write for David Letterman. Then when I was a senior in college I thought no, I wanna be a standup comic." In November 1985—two months after she turned twenty-one—she entered a Showtime contest for the funniest person in Rhode Island. It was her first performance as a stand-up comedian. Drawing on her college studies, she threw in clever references to history. Afraid that she might forget her lines, she wrote the entire routine on her arm—and checked it periodically during her act. The audience laughed every time she consulted her arm for cues, thinking it was part of the comedian's act. Garofalo graduated from two-time Class Clown to Showtime's "funniest person in Rhode Island."

After graduating in 1986 with a degree in history and American studies, Garofalo focused on developing a career in stand-up comedy. She moved to Boston, Massachusetts, where she worked unglamorous day-jobs as a bike messenger and health club receptionist to support her evening assault on comedy clubs. Garofalo later explained her unique qualifications as a stand-up comedian to *Esquire* reporter David Noonan: "Actually, it takes a huge ego combined with self-loathing. It's a nice combination. It works."

A fateful night at Carter's deli

Deciding to venture further into the comic club circuit, Garofalo moved to Los Angeles, California, in 1990 (after a brief stop in Houston, Texas, where she had relatives). She recalls the move to Los Angeles as her most difficult experience as a comic. In the midst of hard times, however, came a lucky break. While eating a bagel at Carter's deli at three o'clock one morning, she met a young actor who would help change the course of her career. Ben Stiller, who was familiar with the 27-year-old comic's stand-up routine, offered Garofalo a part in the new Fox series, *The Ben Stiller Show*. Garofalo later told Tori Galore, in an Internet *Bust* interview, "He believed in me, for whatever reason. All he knew of me was as a stand-up; he didn't know if I could act or anything. And I didn't know if I could, either."

Although *The Ben Stiller Show* was canceled after its first season, the Emmy-award winning series silenced any questions about Garofalo's acting ability and provided a stepping-stone to another role. The show's pilot episode featured a guest appearance by actor/comedian Garry Shandling. The experience convinced Shandling, who was at that time putting together *The Larry Sanders Show*, that Garofalo was a comedic talent. He told *People*, "I called our casting director right after I met her and said we had to get her." Without skipping a beat, Garofalo joined the cast of the popular cable series after Stiller's show was canceled. As Paula, an efficient but slightly neurotic talent-booker, she received enthusiastic reviews and was nominated for Best Supporting Actress in a Comedy Series by the Cable Ace Awards.

Reality bites—and other weighty issues

Next Garofalo made her film debut in the 1994 romantic comedy, *Reality Bites*—thanks, again, to the intervention of her friend, Stiller, who directed the picture. As Vickie, a cool and always-tidying Gap employee, she stood out in a cast that included Stiller, Winona Ryder, and Ethan Hawk. (In one memorable scene, Garofalo asks a convenience store clerk to turn up the 80s anthem "My Sharona"—sung by The Knack—so that she and her friends can dance to it.) Reviewing the movie in

> "I'm trying to be one of the few people in [acting] who don't make teenage girls feel bad about themselves." –Garofalo

New York, John Powers called Vickie "the movie's most compelling character," and credited Garofalo with turning a good part into a great one.

Garofalo's first film role had not come without compromise. A staunch feminist who believes that Hollywood presents harmful and unrealistic images of women's bodies, she was told to lose weight—or lose the part. "I was contractually forced to lose weight for *Reality Bites,* against my will," she told *Vogue* reporter David Handleman. "They hired me a trainer and a nutritionist, and I lost 12 pounds; they wanted me to lose 26. I fought it every step, because I thought it was important that I make my movie debut as a person with some heft—as a normal-looking person. I'm trying to be one of the few people in my job who don't make teenage girls feel bad about themselves."

Glass Ceilings and Double Standards

"If you are a character actor, like I am, and a woman, there is a glass ceiling. ['Glass ceiling' is an expression used to describe the invisible limits imposed on minorities in the work force.] You are not cast as the lead. And if you are the lead, it's about the fact that you are not gorgeous—that you are the offbeat person. Whereas male leads can be anyone from Danny De Vito to John Goodman. They can work and work and work, and get the girl, and be successful, but females are not afforded that same luxury." —Janeane Garofalo, "Hi. I'm Janeane Garofalo, & all I got was this lousy interview."

Saturday Night Live bites

Although it received lukewarm critical reviews, *Reality Bites* had turned Garofalo (unwillingly) into a representative of the so-called Generation X (a term generally applied to those people born between 1965 and 1980)—in spite of the fact that she was somewhat older than the majority of Gen X'ers. Suddenly, the producers of *Saturday Night Live* wanted her to join the show's ensemble (group) cast. It was not the first time, however, that SNL had offered her a position. When Garofalo was 25, Lorne Michaels, the producer of *Saturday Night Live,* had visited New York's Catch a Rising Star comedy club to see her stand-up act. "I was really nervous!," Garofalo later told Jen Heck in an online interview. "And ordinarily I had done really well at Catch a Rising Star—it was a club that was really good to me. Well, I bombed that night. I had performed there a hundred times, but I just couldn't buy a laugh." Even so, SNL offered her a writing position, which she turned down because she wanted to perform. When she was offered the opportunity to perform with the SNL cast in 1994, she accepted, although she had developed serious doubts concerning the quality of the struggling show. Enlisted for the 1994–95 sea-

Weight and See

Garofalo—who feels strongly about presenting powerful female characters (who are not impossibly thin)—found that her weight (normal for her height) was limiting the kind of roles she was offered. At one point, her agent told her told her she needed to lose weight. Reluctantly, she decided to lose weight as an experiment. She explained to Tori Galore of *Bust* magazine that she decided, "'OK, let's see if I get more talented.' And what has changed [after losing 30 pounds] is I am now auditioning for different types of parts. I always used to audition for the friend, and now I'm actually going to read for people's wives and girlfriends, and I'm like, 'Oh, I see, I am now more talented somehow. Talented enough to play the wife rather than the roommate.' And no one has said anything outright, but it's just changed. I get different offers now."

son, she was given the dressing room that once belonged to famed SNL funny-woman Gilda Radner (1946–89).

In an interview with Jonathan Storm, for the *Knight-Ridder Tribune,* Garofalo expressed confusion over finally being hired to perform on SNL. Asked why Lorne Michaels hired her, she responded, "I have no idea"; to the question whether she had any hilarious characters in mind, she said, "None at all"; and to an inquiry as to how she was going to fit in with the cast, she replied, "I don't know. We'll see." It was soon evident that Garofalo didn't fit in at SNL. Outspoken about her opinions, she ruffled the feathers of a number of SNL cast members and producers when she described the show's previous seasons as "unwatchable" in a newspaper interview. She did little to improve the situation when she called Adam Sandler's characters "childish" in another interview. Soon, she found herself sidelined for much of the show's weekly one-and-a-half hour run.

Garofalo later recalled her stint on SNL as a painful experience. In an online interview for *Bust* magazine, she called that season "One of the worst experiences I've ever had. One of the worst things for my ego, for my self-esteem, for my person. I have yet to figure out what the gain in that was."

The truth about life after SNL

Having appeared in her final episode of *Saturday Night Live* on February 25, 1995, Garofalo continued to build a solid film career. In 1995 she played the part of Randy Quaid's neurotic girlfriend in *Bye Bye Love,* a comedy about divorced dads, in addition to small parts in *Now and Then,* and *Cold Blooded,* featuring Jason Priestly (best known for his role in *Beverly Hills 90210.*) The following year she garnered even more screen time, including small roles in *Kids In the Hall: Brain Candy,* and *Larger Than Life,* with her comic idol—and also a former SNL'er—Bill Murray. As a high school graduate who made good in *Romy and Michele's High School Reunion*—featuring *Friends* star Lisa Kudrow and Academy Award-winner Mira Sorvino—Garofalo

won kudos (praise) from the critics, including a *People* magazine reviewer who called her "an acerbic [bitter] delight."

Also in 1996, Garofalo landed her first lead role, co-starring with Uma Thurman in *The Truth About Cats and Dogs*. While critics had little positive to say about the film, most had nothing but good words for Garofalo. In spite of positive notice from film critics, Garofalo later admitted that filming *The Truth About Cats and Dogs* "was a horrible experience, absolutely unrelentingly horrible." She explained why to *Bust* reporter Tori Galore: "The script changed constantly for the worse and I had no control. I was not allowed to put my two cents in at all."

The fact that Mark Joffe, the director of *Matchmaker,* welcomed Garofalo's input, was one of the factors contributing to

Janeane Garofalo strikes a pose with **Romy and Michele's High School Reunion** *co-stars* **Lisa Kudrow and Mira Sorvino.** *(The Kobal Collection)*

her decision to take a part in that movie. (That, and the fact that the movie was filmed in Ireland.) She told *People*, "He was fun and funny and said, 'The female part isn't well-written. I'd like your notes.' That's unheard of, especially for someone at my level of show business."

When Garofalo read the script for *Clay Pigeons* (written by first-time screenwriter Matt Healy and directed by commercial director David Dobkin), the gender of one of the characters — an FBI agent who is sent to a small town in Montana to investigate the deaths of two women—had not been decided. The actress told *Entertainment Weekly*: "I said, 'It's gotta be a girl, and it's gotta be me. . . . If there's a guy in this FBI part, it'll make me mad.'" She won both the part and the praise of critics who trashed the movie. *People* critic Tom Gliatto wrote that "Garofalo, working as usual from a palette of blackest cynicism, is effortlessly, endlessly funny," while an EW Online reviewer stated that *Clay Pigeons* "is worthwhile for one reason: the unceasingly interesting Garofalo. Once again, she's the real McCoy in a phony premise . . . ."

In spite of her successes and growing popularity, Garofalo has expressed some doubts about her acting ability. She told a *People* reporter, however, that she has been gaining confidence. She said, "I actually am confident that I can do a few things well as an actor. I am confident that I can look natural in front of the camera and do a deadpan line fairly well." She added, "There's no evidence that I'm a good actor, so I can't even say that I'm good at what I do. But I've been able to survive to this point without being bashed."

Sources

Chang, Yahlin. "Uncategorically comic." *Newsweek,* April 29, 1996, p. 82.

Galore, Tori. "I Dream of Janeane." *Bust,* Spring 1996. [Online] Available http://www.cs.buffalo.edu~negrin/bustarticle.html (January 7, 1998).

Gliatto, Tom. Review of *Clay Pigeons*. *People Weekly,* October 12, 1998, p. 42.

Handleman, David. "honestly, janeane!" *Vogue,* April 1995, p. 204.

Heck, Jen. "Hi. I'm Janeane Garofalo, & all I got was this lousy interview." [Online] Available http://www.tumyeto.com/tydu/foxy/garofalo.html (January 7, 1999).

Lipton, M.A. "Calamity Janeane." *People Weekly,* August 1, 1994, pp. 63-64.

Noonan, David. "Riotous grrrl." *Esquire,* October 1994, p. 42.

"Q & A with Janeane Garofalo"; review of *Romy and Michele's High School Reunion. People.* [Online] Available http://www.pathfinder.com/people/sp/garofalo/garofalo2.html (January 7, 1999).

Review of *Clay Pigeons* (September 25 1998); "Weighing In" (September 22, 1998), *Entertainment Weekly* [Online] Available http://cgi.pathfinder. com/ew/daily/ (January 7, 1999).

Rozen, Leah. Review of *The Truth About Cats & Dogs. People Weekly,* April 29, 1996, p. 19.

Smith, Chris. "Comedy isn't funny: *Saturday Night Live* at twenty." *New York,* March 13, 1995, pp. 31-41.

Stone, Laurie. "Reality bites Janeane Garofalo." *The Village Voice,* October 3, 1995, p. 49.

Storm, Jonathon. "Reality doesn't bite for new SNL cast member Janeane Garofalo." *Knight-Ridder Tribune,* August 31, 1994. [Online] Available http://www.cs.buffalo.edu/~negrin/knight.html (January 7, 1999).

Thompson, Malissa. "Janeane Garofalo: 17 questions." *Seventeen,* November 1994, pp. 98-100.

Travers, Peter. Review of *The Truth About Cats & Dogs. Rolling Stone,* May 16, 1996, p. 74.

Sarah Michelle Gellar

Born April 19, 1977
New York, New York

Actress

"She's turned most skeptics around who would want to dismiss *Buffy* out of hand. Take a look at how she brings the character of Buffy to life in a very funny and smart and sexy way. You realize there's a star there." —Matt Roush, *TV Guide*

(Archive Photos)

Having fallen into acting as a young child, Sarah Michelle Gellar made her first major impression in the role of Kendall Hart during a two-and-a-half year stint on the popular ABC soap opera *All My Children*. Next came a leading role on the WB network's cult favorite, *Buffy the Vampire Slayer*. Dubbed "the coolest teen on TV by far" by *Fortune* magazine's "Field Guide to Your Daughter's Heroes," Gellar sees her vampire-slaying character as a hero. "[W]e are showing real situations, real people," she told *Dungeon of Darkness* interviewer Sean Decker. "Buffy is not the prettiest girl in school, she's not the most popular and she's not the smartest. She makes mistakes; she makes good decisions and bad decisions, and [she is a character] that people can look up to."

A well-employed child actor

Born in New York City in 1977, Sarah Michelle Gellar started acting at the age of four, after a talent scout spotted her at a local restaurant. Three weeks after that meeting, she landed her first movie role in *An Invasion of Privacy*. More than one hundred appearances in commercials followed, including a spot on a Burger King ad.

Raised by her single mother (her parents divorced when she was young), Gellar started carrying a pager when she was in the seventh grade—so that her mother could keep track of her busy schedule. "Elementary school was very difficult for me," she told *YM*. "On the weekends I had to decide whether to go out with all the kids or go to auditions." She chose auditions. But spending so much time away from school and social functions was difficult. "The second you start missing school, you stop getting invited to parties and people stop talking to you."

High school was no better. "I was a nerd," she confessed to *YM*. After she transferred to the Professional Children's School in New York, however, things improved. Surrounded by fellow performers, the young actress was able to schedule classes around her work calendar.

Soap opera stardom

Gellar's persistence paid off. A well-employed actress, she hosted *Girl Talk,* a teen talk show, and appeared on numerous television series, including *Spenser: For Hire* and *Love, Sidney,* and *Swan's Crossing*. She also starred as young Jacqueline Bouvier (the wife of President John F. Kennedy) in the NBC miniseries *A Woman Named Jackie* and appeared on stage with Matthew Broderick and Eric Stoltz in *The Window Claire*.

Gellar's first major breakthrough came at the age of fifteen, when she landed a part on the long-running ABC soap opera *All My Children*. Joining the cast on February 24, 1993, she assumed the role of Kendall Hart, the long-lost daughter of soap diva Erica Kane (played by Susan Lucci). In the role of a manipulative and self-centered trouble-maker, Gellar found herself involved in a far-fetched story line. "[M]y character tried to seduce my stepfather, then my mother turned around and stabbed him with a letter opener, then I told my mother that he raped me," she told *Seventeen*. One year after joining the cast of the popular soap, Gellar was nominated for Outstanding Younger Actress at the 1994 Daytime Emmy Awards.

Don't Call Her Beautiful

Being included on *People* magazine's 1998 "50 Most Beautiful People" list is not at the top of Gellar's resumé of career achievements. "I think of myself as smart before I would ever think of myself as beautiful," she told *USA Today*. "It's annoying because sometimes you meet people and they think, 'Look! Another cute little blond actress.' That's not who I am."

"I had to decide between going to my junior prom and the Emmys," she told *YM*. Opting to attend the award ceremony, Gellar did not win. Nominated again the following year, she pocketed the award at the age of seventeen, during her final season on *All My Children*.

Buffy, the vampire phenomenon

Having informed the show's producers that she would be leaving AMC, Gellar moved from New York to California. Familiar with the actress's portrayal of Kendall Hart, the casting director for the WB television series *Buffy the Vampire Slayer* considered her for the part of a popular and snobbish high school student. Although Gellar auditioned for the part of Cordelia, she had her sights set on playing the role of the teenaged vampire slayer. It took four auditions and five screen tests to convince the show's producers that she had the makings of a teen vamp whose job it is to eliminate the Undead.

Buffy the Vampire Slayer debuted in 1997 as a mid-season replacement with the WB network's highest-ever ratings for a Monday night (at 4.8 million viewers) and garnered positive critical reviews. Although the show's ratings eventually dropped, *Buffy* remained the network's highest-ranked program, thanks to a devoted cult following (as evidenced by more than three hundred web sites devoted to everything Buffy).

The story of the trials of four teens, *Buffy the Vampire Slayer* is the brainchild of Joss Whedon—creator of the 1992 *Buffy* movie, former writer for the *Roseanne* television series, and screenwriter of *Toy Story* and *Alien Resurrection*. Whedon struck on the *Buffy* concept after watching countless horror movies in which "bubblehead blondes wandered into dark alleys and got murdered by some creature," he told *Time*. He decided: "I would love to see a movie in which a blond wanders into a dark alley, takes care of herself and deploys her powers."

As a tough, smart, and self-reliant teen, Buffy has been labeled a feminist heroine. "Feminism [the concept of equal rights for women and men] sort of has a negative connotation [suggested meaning]," Gellar told *USA Weekend* reporter Jen-

The cast of Buffy the Vampire Slayer. *(Del Valle Gallery)*

nifer Mendelsohn. "It makes you think of women that don't shave their legs. But feminism is not just about being weak. It's about being able to take care of yourself. Just because you might care about what you look like or what the opposite sex thinks of you, it doesn't make you not a feminist." The show's subtle feminism is probably responsible for attracting a viewership that is not narrowly defined by age or gender. "If [*Buffy* and programs like it] have managed to grab the attention of 13-year-olds and thirtysomethings alike, it is because they have avoided coming off as dramatized infomercials for the National Organization for Women [a well-known feminist organization]," wrote *Time* reporter Ginia Bellafante. "Most of these characters [such as Buffy] are the product of a . . . feminism that embraces the very pragmatic [practical] idea that women can be smart and successful and still care about shoes, *Vogue* and, of course, the charms of the opposite sex." Series creator Whedon acknowledges that *Buffy's* soft-sell approach to feminism doesn't alienate boys. "If I can make teenage boys comfortable with a girl who takes charge of a situation without their knowing that's what's happening, it's better than sitting down and selling them on feminism," he told Bellafante.

Buffy owes much of its success to its realistic depiction of teen problems. "[W]e take real situations and we put them on a fantasy level," Gellar told *Dungeon of Darkness* interviewer Sean Decker. "I mean, everyone has either felt or known someone who felt invisible in school. Well, on one show we had a character who actually became invisible. Buffy is really dealing with, 'Well, am I an adult? Am I a child? I don't know what I want.'" Actor David Boreanz, who plays Buffy's boyfriend, Angel, expressed similar sentiments. "I think that [*Buffy*] is appealing because it's an hour of fun," he told *Cinescape,* "not-too-heavy-thinking with a bit of humor and drama mixed in. It taps into people's adolescence and [they], in turn, can identify with the characters." While every episode of *Buffy* carries a message, the show's creators insist on keeping the tone light-hearted and fun. "We're always very strict about what we have learned from a given episode," Whedon told *New York Times* reporter Thomas Hine. "We're not very strict about feeding it to the viewer. The characters have experiences from which they learn. If people in the audience don't get it, that's OK, they probably had fun."

One fascinating person

Selected as one of the "TV's 40 Most Fascinating People" and "A Breakthrough of '97" by *People* magazine, Gellar soon found herself cast to appear on the silver screen. "I believe [*Buffy*] had a lot to do with me getting the movies," she told *Entertainment Weekly*. "It got my name out in a different circle than soap fans. Now when people look at me they scream 'Buffy!' instead of 'Kendall!'"

Having auditioned for a part in Kevin Williamson's film *I Know What You Did Last Summer*, she was cast in the role of Helen. A fan of Williamson's tongue-in-cheek brand of horror, Gellar approved of his changes from the 1973 Lois Duncan book on which the movie is based. "The Helen in the book is not a character I would have ever played," she told Sean Decker. "This would not have been a role I wanted to take, and the thing about Helen in the script and Kevin's characters in general is that he writes three dimensional characters for young people. It is very rare when you play the age that I play to see well-written, strongly developed characters." Although well-written and strongly developed, Gellar's character dies an ugly death before the movie's end.

The day she finished filming *I Know What You Did Last Summer*, Gellar flew from North Carolina to Atlanta, Georgia, to begin work on Williamson's *Scream 2*. Again, her character expired before the movie's final sequence: she appears as a co-ed who is brutally killed in a sorority house. "For such a kick-butt TV heroine, I can't seem to stay alive in the movies," she told *Calgary Sun* reporter Louis B. Hobson. With three consecutive horror projects to her credit, she did not worry about being typecast. "It's random that I worked these three jobs in a row," she told Decker. "The reason that I have is because of all of the offers that have come to me and the scripts that I have read, these were the three that were the most interesting and diverse roles. . . . And if I get stuck doing work like this, I mean God help me, I should be so lucky!"

As it turned out, Gellar soon shed her horror-chick persona. In 1999 she appeared in *Simply Irresistible*, a poorly received romantic story about a young woman who inherits her mother's ailing New York restaurant. Also that year Gellar co-starred with Ryan Phillippe in *Cruel Intentions*, a retelling of the 18th-century French novel, *Les Liasions Dangereuses*, by

"Characters grappling with the dark side are likely to be complex. Right now, some of the best work for girls my age is in [the horror] genre."
–Gellar, *Dungeon of Darkness*

Choderlos de Laclos (also made into the 1988 Academy Award-winning movie, *Dangerous Liaisons*, starring Glenn Close and John Malkovich). Having filmed *Cruel Intentions* during a break from her rigorous television schedule, Gellar maintains a fast-paced career. "I like having the family atmosphere on my show," she told *US* magazine, "and it's fun to travel for three months a year [for a movie] and meet different people and do a different character. Now if I could just find a way to fit in a Broadway show, I would be doing great."

Sources

Abele, Robert. "1998 Breakthroughs." *US*, April 1998. [Online] Available http://rc.simplenet.com/smg_page/ (February 4, 1999).

Baldwin, Kristen. "Heavy Necking." *Entertainment Weekly*, September 12, 1997.

Bellafante, Ginia. "Bewitching Teen Heroines." *Time*, May 5, 1997.

Decker, Sean. "Interview with a Vampire Slayer." *Dungeon of Darkness*, October, 1997. [Online] Available http://rc.simplenet.com/smg_page/ (February 4, 1999).

"The Fabulous 50: Sarah Michelle Gellar." People Online. [Online] Available http://rc.simplenet.com/smg_page/ (February 4, 1999).

"Girl Power!" *Fortune*, December 8, 1997.

Graham, Jennifer and Jeanne Wolf. "slay anything." *YM*, January, 1998.

Hine, Thomas. "TV's teen-agers." *The New York Times*, November 10, 1997.

Hobson, Louis. "To Die For." *Calgary Sun*, December 1, 1997.

Mendelsohn, Jennifer. "The sexiest vampire slayer alive." *The Detroit News and Free Press, USA Weekend*, October 23-25, 1998, p.10.

Rochlin, Margy. "Cruel, Cruel World." *Premiere*, April 1999, pp. 90-95.

"Sarah Michelle Gellar's Biography." [Online] Available http://rc.simplenet.com/smg_page/ (February 4, 1999).

Solin, Sabrina. "Girl Meets Boy." *Seventeen*, August 1994.

Villanueva, Annabelle. "Slay ride." *Cinescape*, January/February 1999, pp. 36-41.

Martha Graham

Born May 11, 1894
Allegheny, Pennsylvania

Died April 1, 1991

Dancer, choreographer

In a life that spanned almost a century, Martha Graham got a relatively late start as a dancer. Soon, however, she established herself as one of the world's leading performers. "Much of what makes Graham such a magnificent, mysterious figure is that she invented a completely new way of moving: She supplanted [replaced] spectacle with intensity," Ann Daly wrote in the *Journal of American History*. One of the art's first women choreographers, she went on to become one of the world's most successful choreographers—male or female. Graham left behind a rich and varied body of choreographic work, having created more than 170 dances, and ran one of the country's most enduring dance companies. Awarded the Legion d'Honneur by the French government, Graham has been credited with revolutionizing ballet and bringing to it a new respectability. *Time* magazine's Terry Teachout summarized Graham's impact on the art of dance: "Did she invent modern dance? No, but she came to embody it, arrogantly and spectacularly—and, it appears, permanently."

> "People have asked me why I chose to be a dancer. I did not choose. I was chosen to be a dancer, and with that, you live all your life. "

(Library of Congress)

Raised to be a proper young lady

Born in Allegheny, Pennsylvania, on May 11, 1894, Martha Graham was the first of three daughters born to Dr. George Greenfield Graham, a doctor of nervous disorders, and Jane ("Jenny") Beers Graham. In May 1896, a second girl, Mary, was born, followed in March 1900 by a third child, Georgia (known as "Geordie" by the family). The couple's youngest child, William Henry Graham, died when he was just eighteen months old. The Grahams' relationship was one of mutual respect and adoration—which is not to say that it was based on the notion of sexual equality. Graham explained her parents' relationship in her autobiography: "Mother's relationship to our father was almost like a child's. She was treasured because she was so little, so young and beautiful. Theirs was a warm, strong relationship and it had nothing to do with women's liberation, which she didn't understand. She wanted to be her husband's wife."

Raised to be prim and proper, the Graham girls wore spotless white gloves when they went out in public. Martha, however, was a rebellious girl who cared nothing about what was required of a "proper young lady." She wrote in her autobiography, "My great-grandmother tried to make proper young ladies out of all of us, which really never interested me." She continued, "We were brought up to be ladies, with the plan that one day we would be wives. What else was there except a wife?"

In 1908 the Graham family took a nine-day train trip from Pittsburgh to relocate in Santa Barbara, California. Graham was ecstatic about the move. Allegheny had been a bleak place that was dominated by the coal-mining industry. To avoid breathing soot (released into the air by burning coal), the girls wore veils that covered their faces. In contrast with the sooty coal town, Santa Barbara looked like paradise. Graham recalled in her autobiography, "California was a world of flowers, Oriental [Asian] people, people with Spanish blood, a life completely different from our life in Pittsburgh. It became a time of light and freedom and curiosity. I was thrilled with it."

First steps

When Graham was seventeen, she saw a poster advertising a dance performance to be given by Ruth St. Denis. She begged her parents to take her to Los Angeles, where St. Denis was appearing. Graham's experience at the Mason Opera House in Los

Angeles would alter the course of her life. "I became so enamored [in love] of Ruth St. Denis as a performer," she recalled in her autobiography; "She was more than exotic—I realize now she was a goddess figure. I knew at that moment I was going to be a dancer."

Graham enrolled in the Cumnock School of Expression in Los Angeles, where she studied acting, speech, and dance. But it was not until she was nineteen—exceptionally late for an aspiring dancer—that she enrolled in the Denishawn school (run by St. Denis and her husband, Ted Shawn) to begin her first serious dance training. Graham recalled her first session at Denishawn in her autobiography: ". . . . suddenly Ruth St. Denis appeared. She said, 'Dance for me.' I said, 'Miss St. Denis, I have never danced before and don't know anything about it.' 'You must know how to do something,' she said. 'No I don't.'" St. Denis was not impressed by Graham's interpretation of the music. Jane Sherman, an authority on the Denishawn company, told *Dance Magazine* that St. Denis said to her husband, "Darling, why does a girl like that come to us? Can't she look in the mirror and see that she is hopeless?"

Although Shawn found Graham to be a slow learner, he recognized in her a burning desire to dance. Helping her through her formative years as a dancer, he eventually created at least five solos for her and danced with her as his partner in several duets. Appointed as a teacher after just two years in the school, Graham danced with the company from 1919 to 1923. Appearing in such title roles as Xochitl, she was hailed as an electrifying performer. Graham, however, did not yet see herself as an artist. Shortly after *Xochitl* premiered in California in June 1920, she told the *Santa Barbara News* (cited in her autobiography): "So far the only value of my work—if it has art value—is absolute sincerity. I would not do anything that I could not feel. A dance must dominate me completely, until I lose sense of anything else. Later what I may do may be called art, but not yet."

A new way of moving

While Graham's years at Denishawn were formative, she eventually struck out to find her own mode of self-expression.

Shooting Hoops

"In high school I also played on the school's basketball team. All the women on the team wore the same brown uniform. I wore my long hair in a single braid that swung across my back as I ran across the gymnasium floor in an attempt to make a hoop [basket]. I believe I took quite naturally to this sport because I wanted to move. Many of my girlfriends at this time knew how to dance, but not me. I think this is one of the reasons I took up basketball in the first place."

—Martha Graham in her autobiography, *Blood Memory*

After performing for two years in the Greenwich Village Follies, she took on the difficult life of an independent artist—in a career that would last a lifetime and rock the foundations of the dance world. One of the first women choreographers (one who arranges or maps out a dance), she developed her own style, avoiding traditional aesthetics (ideas of beauty or art)—such as those she had learned at Denishawn—as well as the sentimental aspects of ballet. Interested in expressing pure emotion, she developed a style of movement that was both raw and revolutionary. Her pared-down approach to dance removed the arms, hands and face in order to focus on the torso and spine as expressive instruments. De Mille recalled: " . . . she concentrated on the torso as the source of life, the motor, the workroom, the kitchen. The arms and legs might be useful for servicing or locomotion [movement], and the head for judging and deciding, but everything, every emotion, she believed, starts or is visible in the torso first."

Central to Graham's technique was the rhythm of breathing. "I have based everything that I have done on the pulsation of life, which is, to me, the pulsation of breath," she explained in her autobiography. "Every time you breathe life in or expel it, it is a release or a contraction. It is that basic to the body. You are born with these two movements and you keep both until you die. But you begin to use them consciously so that they are beneficial to the dance dramatically. You must animate the energy within yourself." Mirroring the process of breathing, Graham's technique employed a contraction and release of the body's center to spark gesture.

Graham also experimented with the dancer's relationship to the floor, creating new types of floorwork and unusual falls. Many of the elements of her dance style—such as inwardly rotated leg positions, pelvic tension, and body opposition—have so thoroughly become a part of the vocabulary of modern dance that it is impossible to measure her impact on the discipline. De Mille—a respected dancer and choreographer—summarized Graham's achievement: "She had discovered a new way of moving that was beautiful and significant, and her discoveries and inventions amounted to a new speech: she had enlarged our language." Further, Graham brought a new respectability to the art of dancing and, in so doing, to the dancers themselves. What's more, Graham helped to establish dance as a major art form worthy of government support. Her one-act ballet, *Appalachian Spring,* which premiered in Washington, D.C. in October 1944, was the first government-commissioned dance work; it would not be the last.

Dancing for decades

Having opened the Martha Graham School of Contemporary Dance in 1927, Graham first created pieces—such as *Immigrant, Vision of the Apocalypse,* and *Lamentation*—that dealt with social problems. During the 1930s she created *Chronicle* (a statement against imperialism), *Deep Song* (about the civil war in Spain), *Primitive Mysteries* and *Frenetic Rhythms* (about Native American and Mexican traditions). By the end of the decade, Graham had turned to themes that were often American—such as *Frontier,* which became her signature piece for the 1930s. In 1938 she created *American Document* (based on the theme of American independence) to perform at the White House, on the invitation of Eleanor Roosevelt (1884–1962) and President Franklin D. Roosevelt (1882–1945). It was the first such invitation extended to a dancer. It was not, however, the last: Graham would be invited to dance at the White House by seven other presidents. Also in 1938, Erick Hawkins—who would eventually marry Graham—became the first man to join the dancer's company.

By the 1940s, Graham's work began to explore the realm of human emotion. She created dances that explored the inner lives of her characters, many of whom were women. Feminists (those who believe in equal rights for men and women) have noted that Graham created a collection of works that spoke from a woman's perspective.

In the 1950s, the financial support of Batsheva de Rothschild allowed Graham to commission sets and musical scores, and to send her company on tours as far away as Burma (now called Myanmar) and Thailand. She continued to dance well into the 1960s, stubbornly refusing to leave the stage, even though age and arthritis had weakened her ability to dance. Having taken her final bow as a dancer in *Cortege of Eagles*—at the age of seventy-six—Graham became depressed. "A dancer, more than any other human being, dies two deaths," she wrote in her autobiography, "the first, the physical when the powerfully trained body will no longer respond as you

"When any young student asks me, 'Do you think I should be a dancer?' I always say, 'If you have to ask, then the answer is no.'"

would wish. . . . I only wanted to dance. Without dancing, I wished to die."

Graham turned much of her focus to preserving her life's work. During her later career, she revived a number of her classics, including a spectacular 1987 presentation of *Appalachian Spring* (first composed in 1944, with music by American composer Aaron Copland) with dancers Rudolph Nureyev (1938–93) and Mikhail Baryshnikov (1948–) in leading roles. Graham continued to choreograph up until the time of her death, in 1991, at the age of 96. At the time of her death, she was working on *The Eye of the Goddess,* a ballet for the Spanish government to celebrate the 1992 Olympic Games in Barcelona, Spain. She wrote in her autobiography, "I am sure it will be a terror and a joy, and I will regret starting it a thousand times, and think it will be my swan song, and my career will end like this, and I will feel that I have failed a hundred times, and try to dodge those inevitable footsteps behind me. But what is there for me but to go on? That is the life for me. My life."

Sources

De Mille, Agnes. *Martha: The Life and Works of Martha Graham.* New York: Random House, 1991.

"Equity Online Woman of the Week: Martha Graham." [Online] Available http://www.edc.org/WomensEquity/WOW/graham.html (January 17, 1999).

Graham, Martha. *Blood Memory.* New York: Doubleday, 1991.

"Martha Graham Centennial Celebration." *The Nation,* December 12, 1994, pp. 736 ff.

"Martha Graham: Her biography." [Online] Available http://www.ens-lyon.fr/~esouche/danse/Graham2.html (January 17, 1999).

Philip, Richard. "Moments." *Dance Magazine,* August 1998, p. 7.

Sherman, Jane, and Owen Norton. "Martha Graham & Ted Shawn." *Dance Magazine,* July 1995, pp. 42 ff.

Teachout, Terry. "The dancer: Martha Graham." *Time,* June 8, 1998, pp. 200-202.

Tom Hanks

Born July 9, 1956
Concord, California

Actor, director, producer

UPDATE

Painfully shy as a child, Tom Hanks immersed himself in acting as a student in junior college in California. First acting in festival theaters, he attracted positive reviews as a Shakespearean player before moving to New York, where he landed a role in the popular ABC sitcom, *Bosom Buddies*. Although short-lived, the series did much to further Hanks' career. Impressed with the young actor's portrayal of Kip Wilson in that series, director Ron Howard cast him in *Splash* (1984), as a man who falls in love with a beautiful mermaid (played by Daryl Hannah). A box office success, the film earned more than $100 million. Following a string of mediocre films, Hanks' supporting role in the successful 1992 baseball drama *A League of Their Own* (1992) marked a turning point in his career. In an interview with *Vanity Fair*, the actor called the work he has done since then as his "modern era of moviemaking." Hanks' "modern era of moviemaking" produced a series of critical and box-office hits, including *Sleepless In Seattle* (1993), a romantic comedy directed by Nora Ephron, *Philadelphia* (1993), for which Hanks garnered an Oscar for his portrayal of a gay

"[H]e's the real deal. All the clichés are true. Ask him to work Saturdays, ask him to reshoot a scene—his answer is always 'Whatever you need.' What a pleasure!"
—Lauren Shuler Donner, producer of *You've Got Mail*.

(AP/Wide World)

lawyer with AIDS, and *Forrest Gump* (1994), which landed the actor a second Academy Award. **(See original entry on Hanks in** ***Performing Artists,*** **Volume 2.)**

Out of this world

"Everyman" is a word often used to describe Hanks. About the actor's performance in *Apollo 13* (1995), *New York Times* critic Janet Maslin wrote that he was "wonderful again, as the Everyman in the driver's seat." A fact-based account of the 1970 Apollo lunar mission, *Apollo 13* features Hanks as astronaut Jim Lovell. "Playing the tough, commanding Jim Lovell is a substantial stretch for Hanks, but as usual his seeming ingenuousness [sincerity] overshadows all else about the role. There's not a false move to anything he does on screen. Once again, he gives a performance that looks utterly natural and is, in fact, subtly new." Hanks collected numerous awards for his role in the film, including a 1995 Screen Actors Guild Award for Outstanding Ensemble Performance in a Motion Picture and a 1996 People's Choice Award for Favorite Actor in a Movie. A tremendous popular success, *Apollo 13* pulled in $500 million at the box office—becoming the *second* Hanks blockbuster to do so. (*Forrest Gump,* directed by Robert Zemeckis, raked in $500 million in 1994.)

Although Hanks' next project involved some on-camera work, his primary responsibility took place behind the scenes. Written during the filming of *Forrest Gump, That Thing You Do* marks Hanks' first effort as a screenwriter. "I was in a lot of hotel rooms and planes, and talking about myself in a very unhealthy way," he later told a news conference. "I needed an artistic and creative outlet that had absolutely nothing to do with some movie I'd already made." That "creative outlet" produced a story about a rock-and-roll band from a small town in Pennsylvania whose hit, "That Thing You Do," launches them to sudden stardom.

Released in 1996, *That Thing You Do* also marked Hanks' debut as director—a responsibility he took on with the encouragement of *Philadelphia* director, Jonathan Demme, who vowed to help produce the film. Hanks later described his experience as actor-turned director to *New York Times* reporter Betsy Sharkey: "As an actor you're able to be moody and mysterious, to have

Tom Hanks as Captain John Miller in the World War II drama *Saving Private Ryan. (The Kobal Collection)*

your own way of working that everyone sort of respects because you're the actor and you don't have to explain anything to anybody. As a director, however, you have to be constantly telling people what you want. You have to be able to imagine it first of all, then you have to be able to verbalize it secondly. That's the antithesis [opposite] of being mysterious and moody."

While Hanks' freshman effort as director received mixed reviews from critics, the light-hearted film was well-received by movie-goers (and the catchy title tune, "That Thing You Do," was nominated for an Oscar for Best Song).

War and romance

Next Hanks took part in Steven Spielberg's violent and harrowing war drama, *Saving Private Ryan*, released in the summer of

Spacing Out

Hanks' fascination with space travel began when he was a child. Recalling the night of July 20, 1969, when Apollo 11 landed on the moon's surface, Hanks told an HBO interviewer, "I was sitting on my mom's floor, in the living room watching, waiting, for [astronauts] Neil [Armstrong] and Buzz [Aldron]. I had the model kits [of the Apollo 11 ship]. . . . In my own head, I probably made about 6,000 landings that day."

When Hanks landed a role in the fact-based account of the 1970 Apollo 13 lunar mission that ran into a "problem" 205,000 miles from home, it was a dream come true. Hanks plays the part of astronaut Jim Lovell, on whose 1994 book, *Lost Moon*, the script is based. (Lovell has a small role in the movie, as the Navy captain who welcomes the astronauts aboard the recovery ship). Jim Lovell is also responsible for uttering what has become one of the most famous lines in the history of lunar exploration: referring to an explosion that short-circuited the ship's electrical system and compromised the team's oxygen supply, Lovell told space mission personnel in Houston, Texas, "Houston, we've had a problem." (In the movie, Lovell's statement is changed to, "Houston, we have a problem.")

Hanks' involvement with space-related projects did not end there. In 1998, he produced a highly acclaimed 12-part dramatization of the Apollo era for HBO. *From Earth to the Moon* was a project Hanks took seriously. "For good or bad," he told *The Journal of American History*, "we are going to be something of a definitive history. I feel a responsibility to be as authentic as possible." Both educational and entertaining, the series received an Emmy Award.

1998. Set during World War II (1939–45), it is a fictional account of an American army unit's attempts to find a private (a person of low rank in the army) whose three brothers have been killed in action. Widely acclaimed for its graphic—yet realistic— depiction of war, the movie is considered by many to be the definitive war drama. Hanks was credited with a tour de force (highly skilled) performance as Captain John Miller, the experienced commander who leads his young troop on the quest to find Ryan. His powerful and moving performance as Miller earned Hanks another Academy Award nomination for Best Actor. (While the film did go on to win five Academy Awards—including Spielberg for Best Director—Hanks did not win for Best Actor.)

Star of the decade

Returning to lighter material, Hanks reunited with *Sleepless in Seattle* co-star Meg Ryan in the 1998 romantic comedy, *You've Got Mail*. Written by *Seattle* screenwriter Nora Ephron (with her sister, Delia Ephron), the story is a late 1990s version of the 1940 Ernest Lubitsch comedy, *The Shop Around the Corner*. As Joe Fox, a corporate tycoon who falls for a small bookstore owner over the Internet, Hanks again won critical raves. "The movie is unimaginable without Hanks," wrote *Newsweek*'s David Ansen. Janet Maslin found comparisons to Hanks' popular predecessor inevitable. "[Hanks] continues to amaze. Once again, he fully inhabits a new role without any obvious actorly behavior, to the point where comparison to James Stewart (who starred with Margaret Sullavan in the Lubitsch film) really cannot be avoided."

Named the Box Office Star of the Decade by theater owners in 1999, Hanks is, by all accounts, very much the pleasant Everyman he portrays on screen. Even Hanks himself says so. "I think I'm a very pleasant person," he told *Time*. "I'm a sunny individual. I think I can work with just about everybody. But this is a pretty protective atmosphere we're [actors] in here. It's very easy. In all honesty, why not be pleasant? I've never been a fan of people who operate from the school of 'the squeaky wheel gets the grease.' In my mind, the squeaky wheel gets replaced."

Sources

Corliss, Richard, and Cathy Booth. "Tom Terrific." *Time,* December 21, 1998, pp. 152 ff.

Crouch, Tom D. "From Earth to the Moon." *The Journal of American History,* December 1998, pp. 1197-1199.

"Rock n'roll heyday revisited in Hanks' directing debut." Jam! Movies Archive, September 14, 1996. [Online] Available http://www.acmi.canoe.ca/. (March 8, 1999)

Schneider, Karen S., et al. "Tom on top." *People,* August 3, 1998, pp. 3 ff.

Sharkey, Betsy. "In the Director's Chair, It Was the Year of the Actor." *The New York Times,* January 12, 1997.

"Tom Hanks." Lycos Celebrity Guide. [Online] Available http://www-spry.lycos.com/entertainment/ (March 8, 1999).

"Tom Hanks Biography." Mr. Showbiz. [Online] Available http://mrshowbiz.go.com/ (March 8, 1999).

Melissa Joan Hart

Born April 18, 1976
Sayville, New York

Actress

> "Teens are drawn to Sabrina [Hart's character] because she deals with fitting in—and teen angst. I know all about teen angst. In fact, I think I'm still going through it."

Born into a show business family (her siblings are actors, and her mother and stepfather are producers), Melissa Joan Hart broke in show business at age four and has worked steadily since then. A longtime fan of Shirley Temple (1928– ; a child star in the 1930's), she landed the title role in the Nickelodeon series, *Clarissa Explains It All* when barely into her teens. It soon became apparent that her fresh-faced girl-next-door quality appealed to audiences. Cast in the lead role in ABC's *Sabrina, the Teenage Witch,* she gained legions of young fans. Said ABC programming vice president Jeff Bader, "To say Melissa has a huge following is putting it mildly."

Off to a running start

Born in Sayville, New York, on April 18, 1976, Melissa Joan Hart was the oldest of five children. Her father, William (Billy) Hart, a shellfish supplier, and mother, Paula, a show-business manager for children, divorced when she was young. Paula later married television executive Leslie Gilliams. In addition to Hart's four siblings—Trisha, Elizabeth, Brian, and Emily—she has two half-sisters, Alexandra and Samantha. Named "Joan" after her maternal grandmother, Hart was given the name "Melissa" after the Allman Brothers song of that title.

At the age of four, Hart shot her first national television commercial—a spot for a bathtub doll called "Splashy." In a *People* interview, the actress recalled that as a four-year-old aspiring actress, she was "really embarrassed about being naked" in the bathtub scene. Hundreds of commercial appearances followed, marking the beginning of what would become a non-stop series of roles in show business.

When Hart was in junior high school, she added live theater to her growing resumé. She appeared in a Broadway production of *The Crucible,* opposite veteran actor Martin Sheen. (Hart's theater credits also include a starring role opposite William Hurt in the Circle Repertory off-Broadway production of *Beside Herself,* and as Valerie in the same company's production of *Imagining Brad.)*

Sweet Melissa

Born in 1976, Hart was named "Melissa" after the popular Allman Brothers song of the same name. "Melissa" appeared on the 1972 album, *Eat a Peach.* The song begins:

> Crossroads, seems to come and go
> The gypsy flies from coast to coast
> Knowing many loving none
> Bearin' sorrow havin' fun
> For sweet Melissa
> Freight train, each car looks the same
> No one knows the gypsy's name
> No one hears his lonely sighs
> There are no blankets where he lies
> Though in his deepest dreams he flies
> To sweet Melissa

Clarissa explains all

During her stint on Broadway in *The Crucible,* Hart began to attract the notice of television and film producers. Soon followed a host of brief appearances in movies and television series, including a role as Florentyna in the 1985 NBC miniseries *Kane and Abel* and regular spots on the CBS series *The Lucie Arnaz Show* and the NBC soap opera *Another World.* She also had parts in five episodes of *Saturday Night Live* during the 1984–85 season, appearing in skits with some of the regular cast members. Hart's first major breakthrough came in 1990 when she landed the title role in the Nickelodeon series, *Clarissa Explains It All.* Nickelodeon's vice president of talent relations, Rich Ross, told *People* that Hart was cast as Clarissa because "she's a little quirky [offbeat], but not put-offish. There's not a jaded [dulled] quality about her." The long-running sitcom earned Hart a loyal following. Cool, wise, and outspoken, Clarissa appealed to teens as a role model. "[S]he shows kids not to give in to peer pressure," Hart explained to *People.* "I like her." Hart's straightforward manner and natural rapport with the camera helped viewers to see her as a real person. "Because I used to talk to the camera on *Clarissa*," she explained to *People*, "people would really feel like they knew me. They'd come up and hug me on the street and I'd be like, 'Who are you?'"

For her portrayal of Clarissa, Hart was nominated for a Cable ACE Award for Best Actress in a Comedy Series. The sitcom, which ran for sixty-five episodes in four years (finishing production in December 1993), was nominated for a 1994 Primetime Emmy Award, and has bred a wide assortment of books—such as *Clarissa's All-In-One Perfect Book of Everything Important (Until I Change My Mind)*—CDs, a board game, and Clarissa "home" videos. Although CBS aired a pilot of Clarissa—also starring Hart—the network never picked up the series.

Hart's experience in the long-running cable series was not without pitfalls. ET Spotlight reported that "from the time she was 13 until she reached adulthood at age 18, she practically lived in a windowless studio in Orlando, Florida, where *Clarissa* was filmed." Having attended the Professional Children's School, Hart worked with a tutor to earn a degree from Dr. Phillips High School in Orlando. Removed from the regular school routine, she grew up surrounded by adults, with few friends her own age. "Sometimes I feel like I kind of missed out on high school," she confided to a *Star* (UK) reporter. "I missed out on learning to relate to people my age, and I missed out on a social life, going to dances and things like that." After her stint on *Clarissa* ended, Hart put her career on hold, for two years, to attend New York University.

Magic tricks

"When you play a character [such as Clarissa] for so long," Hart explained to *People*, "you really begin to wonder if you can do anything else." Assuming the lead role in ABC's *Sabrina, the Teenage Witch* in fall 1996, she proved her ability to create a new and convincing character. A good witch with magical powers, Sabrina sometimes lands in trouble when her magic backfires. Asked to compare herself to the character she portrays, Hart told *Nickelodeon* magazine, "I think I'm more secure than Sabrina is. She's more confused. When Sabrina finds out she's a witch, she really doesn't know what to do with herself. I'm more like Clarissa, because I'm very good at working through my problems." Hart saw her role in the popular series as an opportunity to work on her acting skills. "With Clarissa, I just kind of went in and did it. I was just saying the lines," she told the *Los Angeles Times*. "Now I concentrate more on the jokes, timing and acting."

Sabrina the Teenage Witch has become somewhat of a family affair for Hart, whose mother is the show's executive producer. Paula Hart—who shares the helm of a production company called Hartbreak with the actress— told *People* that working with her daughter is "fantastic, even though sometimes I have to switch off the mom hat and put on the producer one if Melissa wants to, say, go to a party and we need to finish working." Brother Brian and sisters Elizabeth and Emily have also appeared on the show.

Impressed with the success of the popular sitcom, UPN created an animated prequel, which takes the lead character back in time, to the age of 12. [A *prequel* depicts the events leading up to a particular event; a *sequel* depicts events that come after a particular event. These devices are used in movies, books, and TV shows.] *Sabrina the Animated Series,* scheduled to debut in the fall of 1999, features Hart in the voice parts of Sabrina's aunts Hilda and Zelda. Adults in the original series, Hilda and Zelda are teenagers in the animated prequel. Hart's younger sister, Emily, will provide the voice for the young Sabrina.

Beyond *Sabrina*

Hart's long list of film credits includes lead roles in the 1994 Disney movie, *Family Reunion: A Relative Nightmare* and NBC's *Christmas Snow;* guest appearances in the CBS series *Touched By An Angel,* and *Nickelodeon's Are You Afraid of the Dark*; as well as a guest-host appearance on NBC's *America's Funniest People.* In the spring of 1996, during her first season on *Sabrina,* Hart took on her first "bad girl" role in the NBC Movie of the Week, *Twisted Desire.* Also that year, she appeared in a feature film version of *Sabrina the Teenage Witch.* After appearing in *The Right Connections* and *Two Came Back* in 1997, she appeared in *Silencing Mary* and resumed the role of the teenaged sorcerer in the 1998 feature, *Sabrina Goes to Rome.* She also co-starred with Ethan Embry and Jennifer Love Hewitt in that year's *Can't Hardly Wait,* a film that has been praised for reviving the teen comedy genre. Future projects include a deal to star in NewStar Television's made-for-TV version of *Jacob's Hands,* the story of a simple healer who eventually learns that he can heal the bodies—but not the souls—of his followers. Hart is also slated to produce the film, which is based on a newly discovered screenplay by Aldous Huxley (1894–1963) and Christopher Isherwood (1904–86).

Hart's recording ventures have extended beyond the Clarissa-related albums she has recorded for SONY Wonder, including a role in the Boston Symphony Orchestra's SONY production of *Peter and the Wolf,* Young People's Guide to the Orchestra. Active in charitable causes, Hart was the 1995–96 spokesperson for the Center for Disease Control Hepatitis B Immunization Program. She also appeared as spokesperson for Starlight Foundation, Audrey Hepburn's Hollywood for Children Fund, Pediatric AIDS/Kids for Kids and other charities. Hart—who takes seriously her former role as the teenage know-it-all—also writes a monthly advice column in *Teenbeat* magazine.

Sources

"ET Spotlight: Melissa Joan Hart." ET Online. [Online] Available http://www. etonline.com/html/NewsItems/4521.2html (January 28, 1999).

"Fact sheet: Melissa Joan Hart." E! Online. [Online] Available http://www. eonline.com/Facts/People/0,12,38342,00.html (January 28, 1999).

"Interview with Melissa Joan Hart." [Online] Available http://obkb.com/ info/mjhpages/paula.html (January 28, 1999).

Jedeikin, Jenny. "A Home with Hart." *InStyle.* March 1999, pp. 309–13.

Lang, Steven. "Witchy Woman: Melissa Joan Hart casts her spell as Sabrina." *People.* [Online] Available http://www.pathfinder.com/people/ 961209/features/hart.html (January 28, 1999).

"Meet Melissa Joan Hart." [Online] Available http://www.lls-online.com/ rdrnyouth/youthpages/3hrtintvw.htm (January 28, 1999).

"Melissa Joan Hart: Scans of People on the Move." People Online. [Online] Available http://www.casenet.com/people/melissajoanhart.htm (January 28, 1999).

Nickelodeon Magazine, October 1996. [Online] Available http://www.ezz. u-net.com/clar.html (January 28, 1999).

"Quick Hits: News on Ivana Trump, Bill Murray and More . . . " Mr. Showbiz. [Online] Available http://mrshowbiz.go.com/archive/news/Todays_ Stories/98029/quickhits092998.html (January 28, 1999).

Review of *Can't Hardly Wait. Entertainment Weekly* Online, May 15, 1998 [Online] Available http://cgi.pathfinder.com/ew/features/980515/ smp/june/cant_hardly.html (January 28, 1999).

"*Star* Newspaper Article." [Online] Available http://www.ezz.u-net.com/clar. html (January 28, 1999).

"Voice of Experience." *People,* June 10, 1991. [Online] Available http://www. ezz.u-net.com/voicexp.html (January 28, 1999).

Amy Heckerling

Born May 7, 1954
New York, New York

Director, writer, producer

A lmost overnight, film director Amy Heckerling broke into the Hollywood mainstream—to stake her claim in a profession that had long been dominated by men. From her first feature, *Fast Times at Ridgemont High*, to later films, such as *Clueless*, her movies feature fast-paced dialogue and witty humor that pokes fun at the sexism and shallowness of America's consumer culture.

Fast times in Hollywood

The daughter of a certified public accountant and a bookkeeper, Amy Heckerling was born on May 7, 1954, in the Bronx, one of the five boroughs of New York City. After graduating from the High School of Art and Design in New York, she attended the Institute of Film and TV at New York University. In 1974 she graduated from the American Film Institute in Los Angeles, California, with a master's degree in directing.

Heckerling made a dazzling Hollywood debut with the feature film *Fast Times at Ridgemont High*. An amusing and insightful look at California teens in the early 1980s, the film is

"I love losers. I mean, it's not unusual. I feel like everybody feels this way. That somewhere out there is something really wonderful, but they're not going to let you in. Whether it's a club or show business . . . or whatever."

(The Kobal Collection)

109

based on a book by Cameron Crowe, who, at age 22, returned to high school to get a sneak peek at contemporary adolescents. Heckerling turned the screenplay, adapted by Crowe, into a box-office smash that earned the studio millions of dollars. Released in 1982, the film featured a strong cast, including Sean Penn as a dazed and confused surfer, Judge Reinhold as a well-meaning senior, Jennifer Jason Leigh as his mixed-up younger sister, and Ray Walston as a frustrated high school teacher. The film also marked the Hollywood debuts of Anthony Edwards (from TV's *ER*), Eric Stoltz, Forest Whitaker, and Nicolas Cage (then using the last name Coppola) all of whom moved on to successful careers in film or television. A light-hearted parody (imitation) of formulaic teen-age comedies, Heckerling's film was widely praised as a fresh and clever treatment of familiar material, and has become somewhat of a cult classic. (Heckerling later directed several episodes of the short-lived CBS television series, *Fast Times*, which aired in March and April of 1986.)

Hits and misses

Heckerling's next feature, *Johnny Dangerously* (1984), was less successful. A clever take-off of gangster movies of the 1930s, the film portrays an honest man (played by Michael Keaton) who turns to crime to pay for the hospital bills of his ailing mother. His brother, meanwhile, a district attorney, knows nothing about his sibling's illegal activities. A box-office failure, *Johnny Dangerously* received a lukewarm reception from film critics, many of whom found the parody to be strained and exaggerated. Roger Ebert later wrote, "The opening scenes of *Johnny Dangerously* are so funny you just don't see how they can keep it up. And you're right: They can't . . . the movie keeps trying, but it runs out of steam."

National Lampoon's European Vacation, released in 1985, fared no better with critics—or at the box office. A comic send-up of the stereotypical American family, the film features Chevy Chase and Beverly D'Angelo as Clark and Ellen Griswold, a couple who win a cut-rate trip to France on a game show. The second, and possibly weakest, entry in the "Vacation" series, the film is marred by a weak screenplay and strained comedy.

Hoping to produce her screenplay, *My Kind of Guy*, Heckerling approached numerous studios—including MGM, Universal, and Warner's Bros.—all of whom turned her down. Undaunted by rejection, she started working on another screenplay, *Look Who's Talking* (1989). Inspired by her pregnancy, (Heckerling had daughter Mollie Sara Israel, born in 1986, by husband Neal Israel, whom she divorced in 1991) the story revolves around a single mother-to-be (Kirstie Alley) who is looking for the perfect father for her baby—whom she finds, unexpectedly, in a helpful cab driver (John Travolta). The film's comedy revolves around baby Mikey (the voice of Bruce Willis), who expresses his amusing (and surprisingly adult) opinions and observations. A surprise hit, the film marked Heckerling's Hollywood "comeback" and spawned two sequels, the first of which (*Look Who's Talking, Too*, 1990) she directed.

Clued into what movie-goers like

A contemporary adaptation of Jane Austen's 1816 novel, *Emma*, *Clueless* (1995) became a huge commercial and critical hit. Another clever parody of teen-age movies, the film is filled with bright colors and witty dialogue. Alicia Silverstone, in the career-making lead role of Cher Horowitz, plays a popular Beverly Hills teenager who acts as her classmates' matchmaker, her best friend's makeover advisor, and her father's confidant. Although spoiled and self-involved, Heckerling's appealing teenage heroine expresses surprising self-awareness—concerning matters such as sexism and the shallow values of her suburban upbringing. Popular with both adult and adolescent audiences, the film makes lighthearted fun of both teenage preoccupations and the materialistic concerns of a consumer-driven society. As Richard Corliss noted in *Time*, "The movie is about conspicuous consumption: wanting, having and wearing, in style. And in L.A." Heckerling received the top writing award from the National Society of Film Critics for the screenplay.

Hoping to trade on the success of the feature film, ABC launched a sitcom, also called *Clueless*, with Heckerling as executive producer. Many television critics complained that the television series, which featured Rachel Blanchard in the lead role, paled in comparison to the original film. Fans of the show, however, made it a hit.

Amy Heckerling blocks a scene from Clueless with Stacey Dash and Alicia Silverstone. (The Kobal Collection)

A Night at the Roxbury

Heckerling arrived at the idea for her next film project after seeing an episode of the television show, *Saturday Night Live*. The idea grew from a skit—featuring regular cast members Will Ferrell and Chris Kattan—that revolved around the dance club-hopping Butabi brothers. *New York Times* critic Anita Gates described the brothers, who constantly bob their heads in time with music: "Week after week, they drive to the trendy clubs, appall the women they try to dance with and deal with rejection by trying even harder to look cool." Heckerling found the brothers hilarious—and believable. "I just loved those characters and they're so much like guys I know, [who I] grew up with," she told TNT interviewer Andy Jones. A champion of losers in her movies, Heckerling described the Butabi brothers' appeal: "They're just so identifiable. Nobody wants them. They just keep plugging along. They're very optimistic. Nobody wants them to come into their clubs and yet they keep trying and trying. They hit on women. Everybody rejects them, but they just never lose their nerve."

An amusing skit, however, does not necessarily guarantee laughs in a feature-length film. Based on characters who were never meant to speak, *A Night at the Roxbury* (1998)—which Heckerling co-produced with *Saturday Night Live* producer Lorne Michaels—was a critical failure. As *New York Times* critic Anita Gates noted, "The Butabi brothers movie, *A Night at the Roxbury,* is a lot like the brothers themselves: undeniably pathetic but strangely lovable. Still, do you really want to spend an hour and a half with them in a dark room?" Also in 1998, Heckerling produced *Rescue Me* (1998).

Heckerling cites Martin Scorsese, Sydney Lumet, Sydney Pollack, Lina Wertmuller, and Federico Fellini as some of her favorite directors. A graduate of the American Film Institute, she was presented with that institution's Franklin Schaffner Alumni Award in 1998. Best remembered for her insightful and comic screenplays, she once described her writing routine in a masters seminar at her former school: "I sort of do it in my sleep, kind of. It's like the middle of the night, I'm watching David Letterman, I'm scribbling a little, I'm watching some videos, I guess I have to work on this scene, I do a few pages, I decide to re-read other stuff and then I go to sleep. And then it seems like there's a pile of yellow pages suddenly. I go, 'There must have been elves here or something.'"

Répondez, s'il vous plait

Although self-absorbed and spoiled, Cher Horowitz, the lead character in *Clueless,* has a social conscience. Here's her take on whether Haitian immigrants should be allowed into the United States:

"The Haitians need to come to America. But some people are all, 'What about the strain on our resources?' Well, it's like when I had this garden party for my father's birthday. I put RSVP [French for "please respond"] 'cause it was a sit-down dinner. But some people came that, like, did not RSVP. I was totally buggin'. I had to haul ass to the kitchen, redistribute the food, and squish in extra place settings. But by the end of the day it was, like, the more the merrier. And so if the government could just get to the kitchen and rearrange some things we could certainly party with the Haitians. And in conclusion may I please remind you it does not say RSVP on the Statue of Liberty! Thank you very much."

Sources

"*Clueless* lacks color, except maybe, like, in clothing." *The Detroit News,* September 20, 1996. [Online] Available http://detnews.com/1996/menu/stories/65898.htm (February 2, 1999).

Corliss, Richard. "To Live and Buy in L.A." *Time,* July 31, 1995. [Online] Available www.time.com. (February 2, 1999).

Ebert, Roger. *Roger Ebert's Movie Home Companion.* Kansas City: Andrews and McMeel, 1992, p. 308.

"Fact Sheet—Amy Heckerling." E! Online. [Online] Available http://www.eonline.com/Facts/People/Bio/0,128,40459,00.html (February 2, 1999).

Gates, Anita. "*A Night at the Roxbury*: A Lucky Break for the Terminally Uncool." *The New York Times,* October 2, 1998.

"Harold Lloyd Master Seminar: Amy Heckerling." [Online] Available http://www.afionline.org/haroldlloyd/heckerling/script.5.html (February 2, 1999).

Jones, Andy. "Baby Don't Hurt Me." TNT's Rough Cut, September 28, 1998. [Online] Available http://www.roughcut.com/ (February 2, 1999).

"Memorable Quotes from Clueless." Internet Movie Database. [Online] Available http://us.imdb.com/Name?Heckerling,+Amy (February 2, 1999).

Ross, Bob. "Actor: Amy Heckerling." *The Tampa Tribune,* October 9, 1996. [Online] Available http://www.tampatrib.com/baylife/rent208u.html (February 2, 1999).

Seymour, Gene. "It's a Slow *Night at the Roxbury.*" *The Los Angeles Times,* October 2, 1998, [Online] Available http://www.newstimes.com/archive/ (February 2, 1999).

Jennifer Love Hewitt

Born February 21, 1979
Waco, Texas

Actress, singer

Having started to perform shortly after she learned to walk, Jennifer Love Hewitt convinced her mother to let her try her hand at acting in Hollywood at the age of ten. Moving quickly from commercials to TV roles she soon landed a career-altering part in the popular *Party of Five* series. Next came substantial movie roles, including *I Know What You Did Last Summer* and its sequel. Concerning her rapid rise to celebrity, Hewitt told TNT Rough Cut interviewer David Poland, "[A]ll this is like, 'Whoa.' It almost feels like a big wind machine, but instead of blowing wind, it's like blowing my career."

From Texas to Hollywood

Jennifer Love Hewitt was born in Waco, Texas, on February 21, 1979. Her mother, Pat, a speech pathologist, and father, Danny, a medical technician, split up when she was six months old. Pat remarried in the early 1980s, but divorced when Hewitt was eleven years old. Hewitt—who was named "Love" by her mother, after a college roommate—had the urge to entertain from a very young age. When she was just three

"I have this fear of [fame] hitting me and going to my head and I never want that to happen. I just keep reminding myself that I'm a working actor. I go to work every single day."

(The Kobal Collection)

years old, she stole away from her parents in a club so that she could sing "Help Me Make It Through the Night" on stage. At the age of five she enrolled in dance lessons, and soon garnered the title of "living doll" in a Texas beauty pageant. When she was just nine years old, she joined the Texas Show Team, a dance troupe, and traveled abroad with them—including a special performance tour of Russia as goodwill ambassadors. The following year she convinced her mother to leave Texas so that she could pursue her dream of breaking into Hollywood. On her tenth birthday, Hewitt moved with her mother and brother, Todd, who was eighteen at that time, to Los Angeles—with the idea of staying one month.

Hewitt found work almost immediately. She appeared in numerous commercials, including ads for Circuit City and Chex cereal, in addition to approximately twenty spots on national commercials for Mattel's Barbie Dolls. As a ten-year-old spokesperson for the sportswear line L.A. Gear, she went on an international tour. While touring with L.A. Gear, Hewitt released her first album, *Love Songs*. Released in Japan in 1992, the album included a dance single, "Dancing Queen," which enjoyed the top spot on Japanese pop charts for three weeks.

Hewitt landed her first television role in 1989, playing Robin on *Kids Incorporated,* a Disney variety show. One episode featured Hewitt's performance of "Please Save Us the World," which later became the show's theme song. Ending her stint with Kids Incorporated in 1991, she later appeared on television shows such as *Shaky Ground* (1992), and the short-lived prime-time series *Byrds of Paradise* (1994) and *McKenna* (1994). In addition to television work, Hewitt earned screen time in a handful of films, including *Munchie* (1992) and *Sister Act 2* (1993). She also starred in *Little Miss Millions* (1993), the story of a runaway twelve-year-old whose wicked stepmother hires a bounty hunter to bring her back.

A *Party* girl

Hewitt's big break came in 1995 when she was cast as Sarah Reeves in *Party of Five*—the popular Fox drama that helped to launch the careers of other cast members, including Neve Campbell and Scott Wolf. "Most of my association is because of the great character that I get to play on *Party of Five,*" she

Hewitt and Scott Wolf share a scene from Party of Five. *(The Kobal Collection)*

told Jose Martinez of MSNBC. "I feel incredibly honored by that. I don't think there's a better role model around than Sarah. She's my role model." Joining the cast during the show's second season, as Scott Wolf's girlfriend, Hewitt won a solid following of fans. In fact, she was so popular with audiences that Fox created a spinoff series called *Time of Your Life*, to be launched in 1999, in which Hewitt's girl-next-door character travels to New York to find her birth father.

One year after joining *Party of Five,* Hewitt appeared in the 1996 comedy, *House Arrest.* As Brook Figler, she joins her siblings in a plan to lock their parents (played by Jamie Lee Curtis and Kevin Pollak) in the basement until they decide not to divorce. Hewitt (who for a while played the leader of a rock band on *Party of Five*) provided the music for the film's final credits. "It's Good to Know I'm Alive," was taken from Hewitt's third album, *Jennifer Love,* released in September of 1996. Her most successful release, the CD also included the tracks, "No Ordinary Love" and "I Believe In..." Her second album, *Let's Go Bang—* her first to be released in the United States—debuted in 1995 and included the single, "Couldn't Find Another Man."

On the silver screen

Hewitt's first starring role in a feature film came in 1997, when she headlined the cast of *I Know What You Did Last Summer.* Directed by Kevin Williamson, whose previous credits include the popular horror film, *Scream,* the horror-thriller follows the chilling consequences of four teenagers' attempts to cover up a (supposedly) fatal hit-and-run accident. Hewitt attracted positive reviews for her performance as the guilt-ridden teenager, Julie James. *New York Times* film critic Stephen Holden wrote: "Jennifer Love Hewitt as Julie James, the most conscience-stricken of the four, made quivering, teary-eyed guilt seem most attractive." A smash hit with audiences, the film grossed $72 million—on a $17 million budget.

Next Hewitt co-starred with Will Friedle in an off-beat comedy entitled *Trojan War,* a 1997 straight-to-video release. Hewitt plays Leah, a high school girl who falls in love with her best friend, Brad, who happens to be infatuated with another girl. The tables were turned in *Can't Hardly Wait,* released in June 1998. As Amanda Beckett, Hewitt plays the love interest of aspiring writer Preston Meyers (played by Ethan Embry), who is too shy to admit his feelings. "[M]y character is some-

"The one thing I've been really happy with is that right now, there's a lot of really good roles for people my age. The people in the [movie] industry are now seeing that somebody eighteen or nineteen years old can carry a film without having to fall back on teenage stereotypes."
–Hewitt, *Love Story*

body that I've never played before," Hewitt explained to Poland. "She's such a dream girl: perfect hair, perfect make-up, perfect outfit, perfect everything. I've never gotten to do that. I always play the all-American girl next door, super-natural kind of thing." Critics, however, were not convinced by Hewitt's portrayal of dream-girl Beckett. Janet Maslin, for instance, wrote in *The New York Times* that Hewitt "has been more believably cast than she is as the glamour queen of fictitious Huntington Hills High School."

Playing a high school student was not a part for which Hewitt could draw from her own experience. Her professional schedule required demanding hours, which made it impossible to attend classes. "I was the freak that wanted to act and not play Nintendo," she told Martinez. "I was looked at as off-the-wall even by my teachers. They thought I was ruining my education by going to auditions." Although she was tutored through most of high school, she did manage to participate in one high school ritual— attending her school's homecoming dance.

Beyond *Last Summer*

Hewitt returned to the horror genre with *I Still Know What You Did Last Summer,* released in 1998. "I'm still not a fan of horror movies," she confessed in an ET Spotlight interview. "I like making them, but I don't like watching them." Resuming the role of Julie James, Hewitt found the sequel to be more fun than the original. "This latest film . . . takes place in Julie's head, which no longer has any source of reality in it at all. This one was allowed to be a little crazier, a little more violent, and a lot bloodier. It was more psychotic and strange and off, because it all started in her head—and her head was not okay."

Still involved in recording, Hewitt released a single on the soundtrack to *I Still Know What You Did Last Summer.* "How Do I Deal" drew little praise from music critics, although the accompanying video enjoyed frequent play on MTV.

Since appearing in the popular horror sequel, Hewitt has lined up a number of film projects, including an updated remake of the 1970 Erich Segal tearjerker, *Love Story,* and an ABC

No Time for Music

Although Hewitt first ventured onto stage as a three-year-old to belt out her interpretation of "Help Me Make It Through the Night," she finds it hard to make time to record music. "Singing is something that I love so much," she told David Poland of TNT's Rough Cut, "and all the other albums that I've done I put 100 percent into it. I put 100 percent of my soul but not 100 percent of my time, and there has to be both for it to turn out the right way. . . . so I want to wait until there's a clear path that I can give to it."

television biography about the Academy-Award winning actress Audrey Hepburn (1929–93), whom, Hewitt confessed to *Entertainment Weekly,* she has idolized for a long time. "When I was growing up," she said, "my mom showed me *Breakfast at Tiffany's* [1961], and I've never been the same." About *Rescue Me,* a teen romance, she told E! Online, "I play the sort of girl you would picture [pop singer] Alanis Morrisette to have been in high school." Slated to star in *Cupid's Love,* a romantic comedy by New Line, she was credited as the film's executive producer—for having provided a ten-page summary of the plot. "I woke up from a romantic dream and said . . . I want to share this dream with people," she told Martinez.

Almost constantly employed in show business since she moved to Hollywood at the age of ten, Hewitt remains philosophical about her success. "I think life is made of moments," she told *US* reporter, Johanna Schneller. "And moments don't last forever. And moments don't happen when you want them to happen, they happen when life wants them to happen. Right now I'm having really great moments."

Sources

Corliss, Richard. "The class of '98." *Time* Online. [Online] Available http://cgi.pathfinder.com/time/magazine (January 27, 1999).

Errico, Marcus. "Jennifer Love Hewitt Updates *Love Story.*" E! Online, September 18, 1998. [Online] Available http://www.eonline.com. (January 27, 1999).

"ET Spotlight Interviews Jennifer Love Hewitt." [Online] Available http://etonline.com (January 27, 1999).

Friedman, Linda. "Summer Time." *Teen People,* December 1998/January 1999, pp. 64-70.

Hayden, Chaunce. "Jennifer Love Hewitt." *Teen Celebrity,* February 1999, pp. 44 ff.

Holden, Stephen, *"I Still Know What You Did Last Summer:* An Empty, Farcical Bloodbath." *The New York Times,* November 13, 1998.

"The It List." *Entertainment Weekly,* June 19, 1998 [Online] Available http://cgi.pathfinder.com/ew/. (January 27, 1999).

"Jennifer Love Hewitt Profile." Mr. Showbiz. [Online] Available http://mrshowbiz.com (January 27, 1999).

"Jennifer Love Hewitt Source Biography Page." [Online] Available http://www.geocities.com/ (January 27, 1999).

"Love Hewitt's New 'Deal.'" Mr. Showbiz. [Online] Available http://www.mrshowbiz.com (January 27, 1999).

Martinez, Jose. "Jennifer Love Hewitt finds stardom worth the wait." MSNBC Celebrity Bar. [Online] Available http://www.msnbc.com/ (January 27, 1999).

Maslin, Janet. *"Can't Hardly Wait:* Pat but Entertaining Teen-Age Comedy." *The New York Times,* June 12, 1998.

"People." *Time* Online, November 23, 1998. [Online] Available http://cgi. pathfinder.com/time/. (January 27, 1999).

Poland, David. "Party Girl." TNT's Rough Cut. [Online] Available http://www. roughcut.com/ (January 27, 1999).

Shapiro, Marc. *Love Story: The Unauthorized Biography of Jennifer Love Hewitt.* New York: Berkeley Boulevard Books, 1998.

"Sizzlin' Sixteen: Jennifer Love Hewitt." E! Online. [Online] Available http://www.eonline.com (January 27, 1999).

"The Star Boards: Jennifer Love Hewitt." E! Online. [Online] Available http://www.eonline.com (January 27, 1999).

"Star Talk with Jennifer Love Hewitt." [Online] Available http://www.tvgen. com (January 27, 1999).

"The True Love Site." [Online] Available http://members.xoom.com/true lovesite/ (January 27, 1999).

Wolf, Jeanne. "The *Party* girl confronts crazed fishermen, Jay Leno and cleavage." E! Online. [Online] Available http://www.eonline.com/ (January 27, 1999).

Whitney Houston

Born August 9, 1963
Newark, New Jersey

Singer, actress

UPDATE

> "My mother always said, if you can sing, you can sing."

Since her debut on the music scene in the mid-1980s, Whitney Houston has established herself as an American pop institution. Born into a musical family, she released her first album at the age of twenty-one. That recording, titled *Whitney Houston,* sold millions of copies and remained at the top of the charts for forty-six weeks. Her second album, *Whitney,* was equally successful. In 1992, having turned out a third album, which sold six million copies worldwide, Houston married singer Bobby Brown and made her feature film debut beside Kevin Costner in *The Bodyguard.* The success of that film was astonishing. *The Bodyguard* grossed $411 million worldwide, while the movie's soundtrack, which sold more than 33 million units, became the most successful soundtrack ever released. Houston's transition from pop singer to screen star was only just beginning. **(See original entry on Houston in *Performing Artists,* Volume 2.)**

Movie magic and marital woes

Houston's second film project, *Waiting to Exhale* (1995), proved to be equally successful. Based on the best-selling Terry McMillan novel and set in Phoenix, Arizona, the film revolves around the lives of four successful contemporary African American women. As Savannah, whose married boyfriend refuses to leave his wife, Houston played opposite Angela Bassett, Lela Rochon, and Loretta Devine. Although the film and soundtrack were phenomenally successful with audiences, Houston failed to garner rave reviews for her acting ability. Author (and co-scriptwriter) McMillan told *Time,* that "[Houston is] going to be a really better actress when she starts seeing herself as an actress and not a singer who acts." The film's soundtrack, compiled by Houston with producer-composer Kenneth "Babyface" Edmonds, has been dubbed a "Who's Who of divadom." Featuring women singers exclusively, the album includes songs by a number of respected rhythm-and-blues performers, including Mary J. Blige, Toni Braxton, and Aretha Franklin.

Houston next took a role in Penny Marshall's *The Preacher's Wife,* an adaptation of a 1947 romantic comedy starring Cary Grant and Loretta Young. She explained to *The Seattle Times* that co-star Denzel Washington was instrumental in convincing her to do the film. "In his convincing voice, he said to me, 'We have to do this movie. It must be done. It is essential that African American actors play these roles of people who have a life, who care, believe and have faith in the community and stick with that,'" she said. Again, Houston's singing overshadowed her talent for acting. A TNT Rough Cut reviewer wrote, "while not the greatest actress, Houston does a good job as the gospel-singing, choir-directing wife of a preacher, who, of course, has an amazing singing voice." While *The Preacher's Wife* did not perform exceptionally at the box office, the soundtrack, which allowed Houston to return to her gospel beginnings, was a commercial success.

Also in 1996, Houston co-starred with pop singer Brandy in a $12 million Walt Disney Television production of *Cinderella*. The updated fairy tale, in which Houston played the Fairy Godmother to Brandy's Cinderella, was a critical and popular

Waiting to Exhale—The Phenomenon

Waiting to Exhale, a 1995 film that follows the lives of four professional African American women, was so popular that some critics referred to it as a phenomenon. The directing debut of actor Forest Whitaker, the film was based on a novel by Terry McMillan. Like the novel, which enjoyed a third-place position on *The New York Times'* 1992 hardcover bestseller list, the movie struck a chord with audiences nationwide. During its opening weekend, the film grossed in excess of $14.1 million. Especially popular with women, the film was noted for its broad appeal in terms of age and ethnicity. Tom Sherak, executive vice president for 20th Century Fox distribution, told *The New York Times,* "It's attracting women 18 to 65, crossing over, up and down, with 65 percent African American and 35 percent Caucasian audiences." Adding to the film's popularity was the soundtrack, which contained three numbers by Whitney Houston (who also co-starred in the ensemble cast).

Whitney Houston and Denzel Washington light up the screen in 1996's The Preacher's Wife. *(Archive Photos)*

success. The television movie garnered one Emmy Award and received seven other nominations.

Houston's marriage to controversial hip-hop artist Bobby Brown, meanwhile, attracted a great deal of unwanted media attention. The singer-turned-actress separated from her husband — who has a reputation for drinking, womanizing, and trouble with the law—for one month in 1997. After their brief separation, the couple decided to reconcile. "We go through our ups and downs," Houston later reported to *Ebony*. "But we vowed to do it [stay married] forever, so that means a lot to us — to fight hard and to love hard, and to fight hard for the love."

Returns to the recording studio

Returning, after a long absence, to the recording studio, Houston produced *My Love Is Your Love*. Released in 1998, the recording was her first studio album in eight years. (Her preceding albums had been movie soundtracks.) The album brought together rhythm-and-blues and hip-hop artists as producers, writers, and singers—including Lauryn Hill, Wyclef Jean, Faith Evans, and Kelly Price. The song, "When You Believe," a duet between Houston and pop singer Mariah Carey, was also featured on the soundtrack for the successful animated film, *The Prince of Egypt*.

Houston next accepted a role to appear with singer-actor Will Smith in *Anything for Love,* the story of a couple who divorce and soon discover that they can't live without one another. "It's very cute," she told *Ebony*, "lots of comedy." While she continues to mature as an actress, Houston, who supervises her own movie production company and record label, remains committed to her career as a singer. "Music is a part of my life I can't forget," she told *Ebony*. "I want to make good music. This is what I do."

Sources

DeWitt, Karen. Review of *Waiting to Exhale. The New York Times,* December 31, 1995.

Farley, Christopher John. "No Miss Prissy." *Time,* December 4, 1995.

Holden, Stephen. Review of *The Preacher's Wife. The New York Times,* December 13, 1996.

Lee, Luaine. "'Preacher's Wife' Houston still learning about marriage." *The Seattle Times,* December 24, 1996.

Norment, Lynn. "Whitney at 35!" *Ebony,* December 1998, pp. 156-162.

Norment, Lynn. "Sounding off: The best in recorded music." *Ebony,* February 1999, p. 28.

Review of *The Preacher's Wife*. TNT Rough Cut. [Online] Available http://www.roughcut.com (March 8, 1999).

Samuels, Allison. "Whitney on the record." *Newsweek,* November 23, 1998, pp. 76-77.

"Whitney Houston Biography." Mr. Showbiz. [Online] Available http://www.mrshowbiz.go.com (March 8, 1999).

Judith Jamison

Born May 10, 1944
Philadelphia, Pennsylvania

Dancer, choreographer,
artistic director

"Dance is a totally committed art that is so hard to do. It requires many hours and much sweat. If you don't love what you're doing and if your goal is to make money, you can forget it."

Devoted to dancing since childhood, Judith Jamison began dancing with the prestigious Alvin Ailey American Dance Theatre in 1965. During her fifteen-year tenure with that company, she emerged as an international dance star—a designation she refused to embrace. "Don't call me a star," she often said, "call me a dancer." In a career that has included ballet, modern dance, musical theater, and choreography, she has been showered with honors and awards. As the founder of the Jamison Project and artistic director of the Ailey troupe, she demonstrated a firm commitment to her art. A presidential appointee to the National Endowment for the Arts, she has received honorary doctorate degrees from numerous universities, including Harvard and Yale.

Growing up in Phillie

Both of Judith Jamison's parents were southerners. Her father, John Henry Jamison, was raised in the segregated (racially separated) community of Orangeburg, South Carolina. When John Henry was six years old, his father died, leaving his mother and four siblings impoverished (poor) and devastated. Jamison's mother, Tessie Belle Brown, was raised in Bartow, Florida. Eventually, both of Jamison's parents left the South, moving to Pennsylvania. There, both attended Mother Bethel African Methodist Episcopal Church, the oldest African American church in the country (established in 1787). After meeting in the church choir, John Henry and Tessie were married on May 3, 1938. They settled in West Philadelphia and had two children. Three years after the birth of John Henry Jamison, Jr., Judith Jamison was born in Philadelphia, Pennsylvania, on May 10, 1944.

A Tall Tale

"When I was six years old I was tall, lean, and long-legged. At ten I could walk down the street and see over everybody's head. I loved being last in line in elementary school and peeking at what was happening up front. I don't remember being little or having to look up at people. I think I was born five feet ten. It's not that I felt especially tall. I was wondering when everybody else was going to catch up."

—Judith Jamison, in *Dancing Spirit, An Autobiography*

The Philadelphia in which Jamison grew up was a vibrant center of African American culture. "I had a great time growing up in Philadelphia," Jamison wrote in her autobiography. "My parents, who loved classical music and opera, tried to expose my brother and me to all the cultural institutions of the city. Philadelphia was full of wonderment for me as a child, full of people interested in artistic expression." Thanks to the pioneering efforts of Essie Marie Dorsey, Philadelphia's African American community enjoyed a thriving dance environment. Encouraged by her parents, Jamison began to study dance at the age six, under the teachings of one of Dorsey's former students, Marion Cuyjet.

The Jamisons' decision to send their young daughter to ballet school was not entirely driven by their interest in the arts. Exceptionally tall and hyperactive, Jamison had trouble sitting still. "My parents had the good sense to channel my energy and put me in dancing school, because I was driving them *crazy*," she reported in her autobiography.

Miss Marion's school of dance

Marion Cuyjet immediately recognized the promise of the gangly six-year-old. "I remember the day Judi's mother came to register her at my first studio on 1310 Walnut Street," Cuyjet recalled in Jamison's autobiography. "Judi was tall. She looked like she was nine years old. She was six. We were rehearsing the *Swan Lake* overture for our recital, and Judi and her mother stood to the side of the studio, watching and admiring the dancers. Judi's mother said to her, 'You'll be doing that one day, Judith.' I was so excited by her that all my husband and I talked about on Saturday nights, the only night I had dinner home, was Judi. Did you see that? Did you see her extension? Judi. Judi. Judi."

In spite of her new student's height and obvious talent, Cuyjet insisted that she begin at the beginning. Jamison started by studying classical ballet, learning the proper ballet terms for the technical skills she acquired. Not least among the things she learned at Cuyjet's school was to treat her art with respect. "In Marion's classes you behaved and you acknowledged the fact that you were in a 'holy' place," she explained in her autobiography. "When you came into her studio you knew you were there to work and you came in there wanting to be a sponge. You did not 'mess around'; you did not drape your belongings across the [dance] barre. You entered ready to dance and you danced every class as if it were a performance."

By the time she was eight, she began studying other disciplines, including tap dance, under the teachings of Ann Bernardino, and acrobatics, a discipline she disliked. As a young student she also studied Afro-Caribbean, jazz, and modern dance. Convinced that broad exposure was beneficial to her students, Cuyjet sent many of her students outside of her school. When Jamison was ten, she began studying with British choreographer (dance arranger) Antony Tudor and Madame Maria Swoboda, whose school became the company school of the Ballet Russe de Monte Carlo.

Soon, Jamison developed a desire to teach others. When she was just fourteen, she began teaching dance to nine-year-olds. "I was a very strict teacher," she recalled in her autobiography. "I wouldn't put up with any nonsense. I treated them as adults. If they didn't respond, I didn't have the experience to know how to keep their attention. I was expecting too much from a nine-year-old because I was such a focused child. When it came to dance, nothing else mattered. It's taken me until the middle of my life to realize that everybody doesn't have the same kind of concentration."

In 1959, at the age of fifteen, Jamison made her formal debut as Myrtha, Queen of the Wilis, in *Giselle*. Young girls who died before they were wed, Wilis rose from the grave to lure their beaus (boyfriends) into a beautiful but deadly dance. Jamison, who was a gifted jumper, was well suited to the part, which required many *grand jetés* (broad leaps).

Dancing with de Mille

After graduating from high school, Jamison enrolled in Fisk University in Nashville, Tennessee, as a psychology major. After three semesters, however, she transferred to the Philadelphia Dance Academy (now the University of the Arts). There, she enrolled in a master class given by Agnes de Mille, the New York-born dancer who is perhaps best known for her choreography of the musicals *Oklahoma* and *Carousel*. De Mille recalled her first encounter with Jamison in *Dancing Spirit*: " . . . I taught a class and there were just the ordinary students, some good, some bad, with this one astonishing girl. After a while I began talking only to her and all the other students just sat down and listened. And it was all right. They saw me talking, I don't know how much they benefited, but they saw me talking to a really responsive body and a really responsive mind and we talked quite seriously." Later, when she was assembling dancers to perform in American Ballet Theatre's production of *The Four Marys,* de Mille remembered her striking former student. Aware that she would not earn much, Jamison traveled to New York to perform with the prestigious ABT, which was then celebrating its twenty-fifth season.

Discriminating Times

Growing up in Philadelphia, Pennsylvania, during the 1940s and 1950s, Jamison profited from the city's thriving African American cultural community. Even so, her childhood was not free from ugly reminders of racial discrimination. Because of her fair skin, Marion Cuyjet, Jamison's first ballet teacher, was able to lease space for her dance school where other African Americans had been refused because of the color of their skin. Cuyjet was forced to move her school seven times, after racist landlords evicted her because black children were discovered on her premises.

After its debut in New York, the ballet traveled to Chicago, Illinois. When *The Four Marys* concluded its engagement at the Chicago Opera House, Jamison returned home without a job. To support herself, Jamison took a job at the World's Fair—selling tickets and helping customers into boats in an amusement ride. Next she auditioned for choreographer Donald McKayle for a Harry Belafonte television special. "I went to the audition but I wasn't very good," she recalled in her autobiography. "In fact, I was dreadful. I hadn't danced the entire summer and I was in very bad shape. . . . If I had been auditioning myself, I would have eliminated myself immediately; I was that bad." Jamison made it to the fourth cut, but was not offered a part.

Nevertheless, the experience marked a turning point in the dancer's career. One of the people who had been present at the audition was Alvin Ailey (1931–89), famed dancer and choreographer who was a friend and colleague of McKayle's. In

spite of Jamison's poor performance, he recognized her obvious ability. Three days after the failed audition, Ailey contacted Jamison to ask her to join his dance company. "Without hesitation," Jamison recounted in her autobiography, "I said yes and danced with his company for the next fifteen years."

Fifteen years with Alvin Ailey

Dancing with the Alvin Ailey American Dance Theater from 1965 to 1980, Jamison came into prominence as a principal dancer during the dance boom of the 1970s. She toured the United States, Europe, Asia, South America, and Africa, and danced with many of the world's most respected male dancers, including Mikhail Baryshnikov, Kevin Haigen, James Truitte, and Dudley Williams. In addition to pieces written by Ailey, she performed works from a diverse repertory (theatre company) that included choreography by Talley Beatty, John Butler, Janet Collins, Ulysses Dove, Louis Falco, Donald McKayle, and Anna Sokolow.

Noted for subtle but expressive style, Jamison evoked a powerful stage presence. An innovative choreographer, Ailey created some of his most remarkable roles for her—including the fifteen-minute solo tour de force (an act requiring great skill or strength), *Cry.* Critic Clive Barnes wrote, "For years it has been obvious that Judith Jamison is no ordinary dancer. She looks like an African goddess and her long body has an unexpected gracefulness to it, but it moves in a manner almost more elemental than human. . . . Now Alvin Ailey has given his African queen a solo that wonderfully demonstrates what she is and where she is. . . . Rarely have a choreographer and dancer been in such accord. The solo, which lasts some 15 minutes and must be one of the longest solos ever choreographed, is called "Cry." Ailey has dedicated it: 'For all black women everywhere—especially our mothers.' You can see why, for here crystallized is the story of the black woman in America. . . ." One of the landmark modern dance works of the twentieth century, *Cry* established Jamison as an international diva.

Whatever it takes

After leaving the AAADT in 1980, Jamison took on a starring role in the Broadway musical, *Sophisticated Ladies.* She ap-

---

Judith Jamison dances in John Butler's "Blood Memories." (Johan Elbers)

peared as a guest artist with companies all over the world, including the Harkness Ballet, Maurice Bejart's Ballet of the Twentieth Century, and the Vienna, Munich, and Hamburg state opera ballets. By the mid-1980s, she had begun to spread her wings as a teacher and choreographer. In 1984, she choreographed her first work, *Divining*, which received its premiere at the Ailey company. Four years later, she formed her own company, the Jamison Project. The company debuted in Detroit, New York, and Philadelphia, and embarked on a critically acclaimed U.S. tour in its second year. Like Ailey, Jamison drew on African American culture as inspiration for her company's choreography.

> "That life force that's within every dancer is worth its weight in gold. It's infectious when you're around that energy. If you are a real dancer, you never lose that. You are always connected to that original heartbeat."

A short time before he died in 1989, Ailey asked Jamison to take over as artistic director of AAADT. Accepting artistic control of the troupe, Jamison upheld Ailey's mission of a repertory featuring works by African American choreographers. "What I tend to do is make programs that take you on a journey, that you don't know necessarily what is around the bend," she told *The Seattle Times*. " . . . you come to Ailey and you see works by a variety of choreographers. The objective is that even if you haven't seen dance, that the program will be such that it will entice you even if you'd rather be at a hockey game."

Although she inherited a company with serious financial debt, Jamison managed to invigorate the organization, both artistically and financially. As her biography in the Alvin Ailey web site explains, Jamison managed to "propel the organization in new directions." She played a role in the development of the Women's Choreography Initiative and has helped to establish a multicultural curriculum that includes the dance of West Africa. In 1997 she realized her dream of taking the company to South Africa. Jamison has also been a key figure in implementing a joint effort between the Alvin Ailey American Dance Center and Fordham University to establish a Bachelor of Fine Arts (B.F.A.) program that combines dance training and liberal arts education. Not least of all, she has implemented a national outreach dance camp program for "at risk" children ages 11 to 14. "I'm not a business person," Jamison explained to *Black Enterprise*, "but I do have my grandmother's common sense. Whatever it takes to make this company grow and thrive, I'm going to do it."

In 1998, the Alvin Ailey American Dance Theater celebrated its fortieth anniversary. For the occasion, Jamison offered a number of premieres, including her own *Echo: Far from Home.* Also that year, she debuted as a conductor, in *Revelations,* a rousing 38-year old Ailey masterpiece inspired by the choreographer's childhood experiences at Sunday school.

Jamison refuses to see her profound commitment to her art as a sacrifice. "I'm doing what I wanted and still want to do," she explained to *Time Out* reporter Gia Kourlas. "Anybody my age should be around young people. That's why the dancers are so important to me—everyone, from the youngest to the oldest. That life force that's within every dancer is worth its weight in gold. It's infectious when you're around that energy. If you are a real dancer, you never lose that. You are always connected to that original heartbeat."

Sources

Davila, Florangela. "Tempo: Ailey: staying a step ahead." *The Seattle Times,* January 23, 1997. [Online] Available http://www.seattletimes.com/extra/browse/html97/altalvi_012397.html (January 11, 1999).

Gardner, Paul. "Is art good for you?" *ARTnews,* March 1994, p. 118.

Gladstone, Valerie, "Judith Jamison Leaps Forward," *Ms. Magazine,* November/December 1991.

Jamison, Judith. *Dancing Spirit, An Autobiography.* New York: Doubleday, 1993.

"Judith Jamison, Artistic Director." [Online] Available http://www.alvinailey.org/jjbio.html (January 11, 1999).

Kourlas, Gia. "A shot of Jamison." *Time Out* New York. [Online] Available http://citysearch-nyc.iconnet.net/timeoutny2/to/picks/167jamison.html (January 11, 1999).

Reiter, Susan, "Ailey Women!!," *Dance Magazine,* November 1993.

Ross, Barbara. "Choreographing the money dance." *Black Enterprise,* December 1991, pp. 82 ff.

Teachout, Terry. "More tricks than treats in new Ailey works." *New York Daily News,* December 8, 1998. [Online] Available http://mostnewyork.com/1998-12-08/New_York_Now/Culture/a-13043.asp (January 11, 1999).

Lucy Lawless

*Born March 29, 1968
Mount Albert, Auckland,
New Zealand*

Actress

"[Celebrity status is] not real to me. . . . It has nothing really to do with my daily life. You get up and put your pants on one foot at a time like everybody else. Then you go out and water the garden or clean up the dishes from the night before."

(Corbis Corporation)

When the actress who had been hired to play a female action hero for a new television series fell ill, Lucy Lawless was not at the top of the studio's list of possible replacement actresses. After changing her appearance, however, she won the part, and soon made the role of Xena, Warrior Princess hers—and hers alone. An actress with a past that includes a stint working in the Australian outback as a gold-miner, Lawless, whose role as Xena has earned her an estimated $10 million, is a prime example of being in the right place at the right time—and making the most of it. The actress once told a Mr. Showbiz interviewer that "as long as you live your life consciously, you're going to pick up on the opportunities and hopefully make the most of them."

Kiwi beginnings

The fifth of seven children and the oldest girl in her family, Lucille Frances Ryan (later known as Lucy Lawless), born on March 29, 1968, was raised in the middle-class suburb of Mount Albert, Auckland, New Zealand. Her father, Frank Ryan, was mayor of Mount Albert for twenty-two years. Her mother, Julie Ryan, a homemaker, was known as a feminist before feminism became a mainstream concern (feminism is the belief in equal rights for men and women). As the mayor's wife, she organized the construction of a bronze statue in a local park honoring the women in Mount Albert who fought for the right to vote.

As a child, Lawless was a tomboy who learned to fend for herself against her four older brothers. "I just knew I wanted to be respected," she told *The Sydney Morning Herald* reporter David Leser. "I wanted to be good at sport. I wanted to be pretty. I wanted to be head librarian. I wanted to be good academically. But I didn't think of myself as pretty or clever and I was never good at sport." In fact, unlike her on-camera character, Lawless had a reputation for being clumsy. "Action-adventure scared me," she said in the *Los Angeles Times*. "I'd never been physically inclined. My nickname [as a child] was Unco [for uncoordinated]."

Coming from a Catholic family, Lawless was educated primarily in convent (religious) schools. A natural performer, she became interested in acting and singing as a child. "She used to get up on the coffee table with a seashell for a microphone and sing away," her mother told *People* reporters Karen Schneider and Kirsten Warner. When Lawless graduated from high school at the age of seventeen, she dreamed of becoming an actress—having appeared in numerous musical and theatrical productions as a student. She enrolled briefly in Auckland University, where she studied opera singing and languages (a gifted linguist, one who speaks fluently many languages, she speaks German, French, and some Italian—and can accurately imitate a middle-American accent).

Gold-digging in the outback

Wanderlust (a strong desire to travel) soon struck, however, and she headed for Europe with her boyfriend, Garth Lawless. (The two met while she was a part-time waitress at Club Mirage, Auckland's hottest night-spot, where Garth Lawless bartended.) Traveling through Germany (where Lawless picked grapes along the Rhine River), Italy (where she studied opera), and Switzerland, the pair started to run low on money. "We were in Europe and wanted to go on a trip through Russia and I thought, 'I've got a brilliant idea,'" she told Leser. "'Let's go to Kalgoorlie [a small town in the remote Australian outback, about 500 miles from Perth] to earn the money to get there.' That's how dull-witted we were."

Both took jobs at a remote gold-mining company two hours further from civilization. One of very few female miners, Lawless took on the same grueling duties as the male miners, digging and pushing large amounts of dirt through a diamond saw. "I started working for a gold-mining company sawing core — this poor, stinking Kiwi [a nickname for New Zealanders] in need of work," she told Leser. "I was there at 7 A.M. in the freezing desert sitting at this diamond saw with water spraying all over me and I'm freezing and wearing garbage bags. I felt like the girl from Rumpelstiltskin who used to spin mountains of straw." After taking another job—driving trucks through the outback, measuring earth, and mapping with a compass—Lawless became pregnant. After marrying, Lucy and Garth Lawless moved back to Auckland, where daughter, Daisy, was born. (The couple divorced in 1995.)

A slow start

Back in her native New Zealand, Lawless renewed her interest in acting. She began doing television commercials—the first of which she described as a "really bad, cheesy commercial for travel." At the age of 20 she landed her first real acting role, with a television comedy troupe on a show called *Funny Business*. Although she landed a number of guest-starring roles in several television series' she was rarely offered choice roles. "I didn't fit the mold of New Zealand drama," she told Leser. "I don't know why. I often thought I was too big [Lawless stands five feet ten inches tall], too in their face. I think that was part of the truth and, possibly, I wasn't very good."

Determined to improve her acting skills, Lawless moved with her family to Vancouver, Canada, to study drama at the William Davis Center for Actors Study. After an eight-month stint at the Davis Center, she returned to New Zealand in 1992. There she accepted a job as co-host of *Air New Zealand Holiday*, a travel magazine program broadcast in New Zealand and throughout Asia. Working two seasons as the show's co-host, she traveled around the world.

From Amazon woman to warrior princess

Lawless's first significant exposure on American television came when she took the role of Lysia, a renegade [outlaw]

Amazon enforcer, in the television movie, *Hercules and the Amazon Women*. Produced by Rob Tapert, the movie helped launch the weekly one-hour series, *Hercules* (starring Kevin Sorbo in the lead role). Soon Lawless was cast in a role in the popular series, as Lyla, the courageous wife of Deric the Centaur. In 1995, the show's American producer—who also produced horror cult films such as *The Evil Dead* and action films such as *Hard Target* and *Time Cop*— was interested in creating the character of a female superhero for television. He was influenced by the action films produced by Hong Kong filmmakers, whose heroines were often "tough, strong women in very dubious [questionable] moral positions," he told Leser.

The character of Xena—a tough, strong woman who finds herself in questionable moral positions—was introduced in a three-episode sequence of *Hercules*. At first, Lawless was not considered as a candidate to play Xena. "Since she had already played two different parts in *Hercules,* the studio wanted another actress," Tapert explained to the *Los Angeles Times*. After several well-known actresses refused the part, American actress Vanessa Angel was cast as the Warrior Princess. But when Angel fell ill en route to Auckland (where the series is filmed), the show's producers needed a last-minute replacement. Lawless, whose natural hair color is light, dyed her hair much darker. Convinced that her new look was sufficiently different from her previous appearance, the show's producers cast Lawless as Xena. Within one week, she began filming as the Warrior Princess. In September 1995, the female superhero debuted in a one-hour spin-off series, *Xena: Warrior Princess*.

"It was like everything I had done in my life came into play in [the first] episode," Lawless told Marc Shapiro, author of *Lucy Lawless Warrior Princess*. "All the rough-and-tumble play with my family and the running and jumping I did at play. It was like just about every physical challenge that came up, I could reach into my bag and pull out an appropriate ability." Having had no special training in martial arts or swordplay, however, Lawless needed a crash-course to make her portrayal of the Warrior Princess more believable. (Xena, after all, is able to do back-flips into her horse's saddle, can leap two stories into the air, and is an expert fighting with knives, crossbows, tridents, swords, and staffs—as well as her signature circular metal ring, called a chakram.) Lawless trained

"I met so many women and young girls who feel . . . empowered, by watching [Xena]. I realized this isn't a burden, this is an honor."

briefly with martial arts expert Douglas Wong (*Dragon: The Bruce Lee Story*) to learn some basic kung fu moves, high kicks, and sword- and staff-fighting techniques. "She was frustrating herself the first couple of days of training," the martial arts instructor told Shapiro. "Lucy was having trouble remembering the movements. By the third day she was very much on it. I could tell right away that Lucy was very strong-minded. She kept telling herself she was going to master these skills and she did."

The Xena phenomenon

A hit with television critics from the start, *Xena* quickly developed a large and varied cult following. A pop-cultural icon, *Xena* spawned scores of fan Web sites, fanzines, trading cards, action figures, and CD-ROMs. In January 1997, Burbank, California hosted the first official Hercules/Xena convention. The highest-rated syndicated drama on American television, *Xena* is seen in more than sixty countries. Known for its campy (silly) humor, the show has often been spoofed by other network television programs.

Xena proved to be especially popular among women. "I tend to think of people generically [as one]," Lawless explained in a Mr. Showbiz interview. "I thought it would be successful with everybody, of every age group. But I'm thrilled that it has struck a chord with women, because it's been brought to my attention that an awful lot of women need that." Feminists enjoy Lawless's portrayal of a powerful, independent woman. "Many feminists have been dreaming of mass-culture moments like this since feminism came into being," a *Ms.* cover story proclaimed. "No woman television character has exhibited the confidence and strength of the male heroes of archetype [myth] and fantasy [as Xena]." Although reluctant at first to be considered a feminist role model, Lawless came to appreciate the position. "I met so many women and young girls who feel . . . empowered, by watching. I realized this isn't a burden, this is an honor."

On Broadway

In September and October of 1997, Lawless made her Broadway debut when she took on the role of tough-talking Betty

Rizzo in the musical, *Grease.* Again, she seemed to have been in the right place at the right time. During a guest appearance on the Rosie O'Donnell Show, she sang "I'm An Old Cowhand." The conversation eventually turned to the character of Rizzo—a part O'Donnell had previously played in the popular musical. The producers of *Grease* saw the New Zealander's performance and soon offered her the part. "Rizzo is a tough, hard woman with a heart," the actress told biographer Shapiro. "It's a great role for me. They could hardly cast me as the good girl." Although trained in opera (she is the voice behind all Xena's songs in *Hercules and Xena—The Animated Movie: The Battle for Mount Olympus,* produced in 1997), Lawless had to face her fear of singing in public. "I had always been terrified to sing in public," she told Shapiro. "I guess that's why I chose to do *Grease.* It really forced me to confront my fears."

Married to the show's executive producer Rob Tapert in March 1998, Lawless sees the role of Xena as "The best [role] for a woman in the past 30 years of television." But she doesn't plan to play the Warrior Princess indefinitely. "Xena isn't going anywhere soon," she told Shapiro, "but Lucy Lawless does have other aspirations [ambitions]. I don't want to be fifty and walking around in a leather skirt, saying, 'Hey! Remember Me?' I would like to go out on a high. So I'll just go until it feels right."

I'm Not A Superhero, But I Play One On TV

While the TV character Xena is a powerful warrior princess, Lucy Lawless proved she's only human. Lawless was injured while taping a skit on horseback for *The Tonight Show with Jay Leno* in October 1996. Suffering multiple fractures in her pelvis, she was hospitalized for two weeks and was unable to work for two months.

Sources

Graham, Jefferson. "The fall and rise of Xena." *USA Today,* January 15, 1997, p. 3D.

Graham, Jefferson. "*Xena* makes Lawless an accidental action star." February 15, 1996, p. 3.

"A Herculean spinoff." *Newsday,* November 8, 1995.

Leser, David. *The Sydney Morning Herald Magazine,* January 30, 1999. [Online] Available http://www.xenamedia.com/ (February 2, 1999).

"Lucy Lawless Biography." [Online] Available http://sword-and-staff.com/biography.htm (February 2, 1999).

"Lucy Lawless down under on top." People Online. [Online] Available http://www.pathfinder.com/people/profiles/lucy/index.html (February 2, 1999).

"Lucy Lawless Interview." Mr. Showbiz. [Online] Available http://mr.showbiz.com (February 2, 1999).

Ryan, Joel. "Xena Plays Blushing Bride." E! Online. [Online] Available http://www.eonline.com/News/Items/0,1,1895,00.html (February 2, 1999).

Shapiro, Marc. *Lucy Lawless Warrior Princess*. New York: Berkley Boulevard Books, 1998.

Sosin, Michelle. "Xena Sings on Broadway." E! Online. [Online] Available http://www.eonline.com/News/Items/0,1,1728,00.html (February 2, 1999).

John Leguizamo

Born July 22, 1965
Bogota, Colombia

Comedian, actor

"When you grow up in the inner city and you're a minority person, you don't see yourself belonging to the fabric of society," Colombian-born comic John Leguizamo once explained. "You never think of the future." Urged to put his mischievous humor to good use, the young actor/comedian started to think of the future—a future in which he envisioned equal opportunity for Latin entertainers. Inspired by the urban humor of comics such as Richard Pryor and Lily Tomlin, he created an ethnic comedic style that has earned critical praise—and more than a little controversy.

An obnoxious goofball

John Leguizamo was born in Bogota, Colombia on July 22, 1965. When he was three years old, he and younger brother, Sergio, were sent to stay with his grandparents while their father, Alberto, and mother, Luz, looked for work in the United States. The next year, the two boys traveled to New York City, where their parents had found jobs. Luz worked in a factory, while Alberto was employed as head waiter in a French restau-

"I want to present everyday characters created from a Latin point of view, Latin interests, Latin cultural-specific things, and then translate them so that there's larger appeal to audiences."

(The Kobal Collection)

141

rant—or so he told his family. Leguizamo later discovered that his father—who had once hoped to be a filmmaker, and had studied at Cinecitta in Rome, Italy—worked as a dishwasher. (Leguizamo's father later became a real estate agent, while his mother became involved in Latin activism.)

Leguizamo grew up in a rough neighborhood in the Jackson Heights section of Queens (one of the five boroughs of New York City)—in an area known as the "Bogota Belt" because of the number of Colombian immigrants who settled there. Struggling to make ends meet, Leguizamo's parents worked long hours, leaving their young sons unsupervised. The couple fought often, and finally divorced when their oldest son was fourteen. Reacting to his parents' divorce—and to his father's abusive behavior—Leguizamo started getting into trouble. He once took over the conductor's booth on a subway train and announced, over the loudspeaker system, "This is our train, people." The young performer's comedy routine was well received by passengers; the New York City police who came to arrest him, however, were less sympathetic. Leguizamo was arrested a second time—for truancy [unexcused absence from school]—when he and a friend skipped school to attend an X-rated movie.

Concerned about their son's future, the Leguizamos shipped their son back to Colombia—hoping that a change of environment would have a positive effect on his behavior. After staying with relatives in Bogota for one year, Leguizamo returned to New York—and to his trouble-stirring ways. "I was an obnoxious goofball in high school," he told *Hispanic.* "I used to do all kinds of crazy things, like locking teachers out of the room, 'snapping' on people. That's where it started." Recognizing the young trouble-maker's comic potential, a guidance counselor suggested that he put his antics to good use—to earn a living as a comic. That suggestion set Leguizamo—who, as *The Village Voice* noted, was "another quality-of-life offender on his way to becoming a hood"—on the road to success.

Beyond Off Center

Although his family encouraged him to pursue a more stable career—like accounting—Leguizamo enrolled in acting school. Working at Kentucky Fried Chicken to pay for classes, he honed his natural talent for performance. A gifted imitator, he already had plenty of experience creating caricatures [exaggerated imitations]—having entertained relatives with comic impersonations at family gatherings. The decision to pursue acting marked a turning point in his life. "If acting hadn't come along, I'd either be a doorman or in jail," he told *Cosmopolitan* reporter Nancy Mills.

After spending one year at New York University, Leguizamo left school to perform with a comedy troupe called Off Center Theater. He also landed a number of insignificant roles in small, off-Broadway theatrical productions. Typically, he was cast as a Latino junkie (drug addict)—a form of stereotyping that reflected the lack of positive roles for Latin actors. In 1984, he broke into television, appearing on the first season of the popular NBC police drama, *Miami Vice* (co-starring Don Johnson and Philip Michael Thomas).

Leguizamo landed his first major film role when director Brian De Palma cast him in the fact-based Vietnam War (1964–75) drama, *Casualties of War.* Co-starring with Sean Penn and Michael J. Fox, he played a soldier who is coaxed into raping a young Vietnamese girl. Released in 1989, the film received positive reviews. It was not long before Leguizamo—who had attracted the attentions of legendary acting coaches Lee Strasberg, Herbert Berhoff, and Wynn Handman—began to command more offers. In 1990, he appeared in *Street Hunter, Revenge, Gentile Alouette,* and *Die Hard 2*. The following year, he shared screen time with Steven Seagal in *Out for Justice,* and with Harrison Ford in *Regarding Henry.* He was also cast in that year's *Hangin' with the Homeboys,* a coming-of-age story about four young men from the South Bronx in New York. Written and directed by the late Joseph Vasquez, the film won the 1991 Sundance Film Festival award for best screenplay.

Also in 1991, Leguizamo launched a one-man off-Broadway show called *Mambo Mouth*. Presented in seven sketches, the show featured characters the comic had created and refined in theater workshops—such as a slow-witted boxer and a fast-talking talk-show host. The comic drew criticism for creating characters that did little to combat negative stereotypes of Latinos. "To some Latin people," he explained to *Time* reporter Guy Garcia, "we're not allowed to mock ourselves." A critical success, *Mambo Mouth* garnered numerous awards, in-

"A stereotype is a negative portrayal based on other negative portrayals. But a prototype is something invented. It's the first of its kind. That's what I try to do." –Leguizamo, *Village Voice.*

cluding an Obie Award from the Village Voice, an Outer Critics Circle Award, and a Vanguard Award. Later presented as part of HBO's Comedy Theater, Leguizamo's act won a Cable Ace Award. (And in 1997, the comic launched his record label, Minimum Wage Records, with the release of the comedy album, "Mambo Mouth.")

Spic-O-Rama

Eager to cash in on Leguizamo's growing popularity, a number of television networks approached the up-and-coming comic about doing a situation comedy. He refused. "I wasn't into sitcoms," he later explained to *Hispanic* reporter Valerie Menard. "I didn't think the first Latin show should be a sitcom where everyone's nice and lovable, PC [politically correct], cute and boring." Sharply aware of the absence of Latin characters on television, he believed it was high time for television to present realistic portrayals of Latin-Americans. "[It's] more than time for us to be out there," he told Menard. " . . . It's taken so long, and it shouldn't have."

Next Leguizamo created *Spic-O-Rama,* a one-man show about the Gigantes, a dysfunctional Latin family planning a wedding. Beating critics to the punch, he informed audiences that the Gigante family is "not representative of all Latin families," adding, "If your family is like this one, please seek professional help." After a successful run in Chicago, the show appeared at the Westside Theater in New York, where it received rave reviews from theater-goers and critics. A *New Republic* critic, for example, dubbed the piece "brilliant." The recipient of numerous awards—including a Drama Desk Award, A Dramatist's Guild Hull-Warriner Award, and the Lucille Orttel Outstanding Achievement Award —*Spic-O-Rama* was broadcast on HBO cable television in 1993.

Briefly buggin'

Encouraged by the success of *Spic-O-Rama,* the HBO production company gave the comic free reign to create a project of his choice. Even before he was first approached about doing a sitcom, he had known what kind of show he wanted to create. "I wanted to do a variety show," he told Menard. "Being the first Latin show, it could be daring, political, social, nasty, wicked— better than a sitcom." After assembling a six-member comedy troupe—including his then-wife, Yelba Osorio—he hit the New

York comedy club circuit so the group could gain experience working together. "Some nights it would be so dead you could hear crickets," he told Menard, "but other nights people would be screaming and going, 'No they didn't! No they didn't! Oh my God, yes they did!'"

After two pilot episodes were shot, Fox network bought the rights to Leguizamo's comedy series. *House of Buggin'*, which debuted in 1995, drew impressive ratings in urban markets across the country—including a number-one ranking in Los Angeles, California. Frequently compared to *In Living Color*—a Fox comedy series that featured mostly African American players—Leguizamo's show pulled no punches with regard to racial stereotypes. Like *In Living Color*, it featured exaggerated caricatures (imitations) that forced stereotypes into the open. The show drew positive reviews. Menard, for example, wrote in *Hispanic*, "Beginning with the Latin hip-hop opening theme to *House of Buggin'* . . . it's clear that Hispanics have finally returned with starring roles to TV, and we can revel in it." In spite of its success, the show was canceled after only ten episodes.

Latinos On Television

When Leguizamo's comedy series, *House of Buggin'*, debuted on the Fox network in 1995, it was the first prime-time series in over twenty years to feature Latin actors as main characters. Although a few Hispanic characters have appeared in leading roles—such as Jimmy Smits in the popular ABC crime drama *NYPD Blue*—none, since Freddie Prinze's *Chico and the Man*, had addressed the characters' ethnicity.

Chico and the Man, which first aired on NBC in September 1974, was the first television series to be set in a Mexican American neighborhood. The show was criticized, however, by many Chicano organizations because there were no Mexican Americans in the cast when the show began. Freddie Prinze, who played the lead role, was of Puerto Rican and Hungarian descent. Prinze, who found it difficult to deal with the pressures of his overnight success, committed suicide in January 1977, when his son—actor Freddie Prinze, Jr.—was ten months old. The series continued until July 1978, with twelve-year-old Gabriel Melgar in the role as a Mexican youngster.

Shakespeare, drag queens, and more

A fan of the late African American comedian Flip Wilson—famous for his portrayal of a female character named "Geraldine"—Leguizamo donned high heels, makeup, and slinky dresses in the 1995 blockbuster comedy *To Wong Foo, Thanks for Everything, Julie Newmar*. Co-starring with actors Wesley Snipes and Patrick Swayze, Leguizamo was nominated for a Golden Globe award for Best Supporting Actor for his portrayal of drag queen (man dressing in women's clothing) Chi-Chi Rodriguez. Also that year, he appeared as narrator Sergio in *A Pyromaniac's Love Story*, an offbeat—and poorly received—romantic drama.

In 1996, Leguizamo did time again with action star Steven Seagal in the unexceptional hijack drama, *Executive Decision*.

"Working with Seagal is just always, always difficult," he later told TNT interviewer David Poland. ". . . .It was the longest shoot of my life." Panned by critics, the film earned Seagal a Golden Raspberry Award as Worst Supporting Actor. Also that year Leguizamo appeared in *The Fan* (co-starring Robert DeNiro and Wesley Snipes) and in *Romeo and Juliet* (co-starring Leonardo DiCaprio and Claire Danes), as Juliet's cousin, Tybalt.

From evil clown to Tony-winning *Freak*

Leguizamo made a number of other film appearances in 1997—including roles in *A Brother's Kiss* and the special-effects laden comic-book adaptation, *Spawn*. As the evil clown, Violator, the actor—who wore forty pounds of costume devices for the part—was unrecognizable. That year's *The Pest,* written and co-produced by Leguizamo, did nothing to further his reputation as a film actor. *Village Voice* reporter Richard Goldstein referred to the movie as one of the comic's "spectacular movie flops" (along with the dismal 1993 flop, *Super Mario Brothers*).

Far more successful was Leguizamo's solo stage act, *Freak.* Having moved to New York after opening in San Francisco, California, *Freak* was the first one-man Broadway show to feature a Latino actor. Based largely on the comic's life, the show was billed as a "demi-semi-quasi-pseudo-autobiographical comedy." Although presented humorously, the show dealt with painful memories of an abusive father and feelings of ethnic isolation. "It's the story of not fitting in, being an outsider, feeling freakish wherever you go," the actor told *Hispanic* reporter Tony Lellela. "Mostly as an adolescent you feel that . . . you have to overcome things, no matter what kind of childhood you had."

Freak—which required the comic to play forty different characters—was a smashing success with theater critics. Extended twice during its run at Broadway's Cort Theatre, *Freak* garnered two 1998 Antoinette Perry Award (nicknamed the Tony Award) nominations—for Best Play and Best Actor. A book-version of *Freak,* published by Putnam in 1997, received positive reviews, as did the HBO broadcast of the show, directed by Spike Lee.

An undisputed success on the stage, Leguizamo hopes someday to find his voice in film. "Theater is so far the medi-

"There's a whole city of people inside this young man's slender frame." –*New York Times* critic Ben Brantley, in a review of Leguizamo's Broadway show, *Freak*

um I've been able to express myself in to the fullest of my creative ability," he told TNT. "My goal in life is to be able to do that on film."

John Leguizamo proudly displays the two Tony Award nominations he received for his one-person play Freak. *(AP/Wide World)*

Sources

Brantley, Ben. "*Freak*: A One-Man Melting Pot Bubbling Over With Demons." *The New York Times,* February 13, 1998.

"The Editorial Play." *The New Republic,* December 7, 1992, pp. 32 ff.

Feingold, Michael. "Spanishing Acts." *The Village Voice,* February 24, 1998, pp. 147 ff.

Goldstein, Richard. "Proto Tipico." *The Village Voice,* February 10, 1998.

McNeil, Alex. *Total Television.* New York: Penguin Books, 1996.

Menard, Valerie. "In Latin color." *Hispanic,* May 1995, pp. 16 ff.

Mills, Nancy. "John Leguizamo interview." *Cosmopolitan,* July 1996, p. 88.

"The Official John Leguizamo Web Site." Celebsite. [Online] Available http://www.celebsites.com (February 18, 1999).

Poland, David. "Send in the Clown." TNT Rough Cut, August 1, 1997. [On-line] Available http://www.roughcut.com/. (February 18, 1999).

Reece, Doug. "New releases will have retail rolling in the aisle." *Billboard,* April 5, 1997, p. 20.

Time, October 28, 1991, p. 85.

Stone, Laurie. "Escape artist." *The Nation,* April 6, 1998, pp. 34-35.

Vellela, Tony. "HBO Freaks on John Leguizamo." *Hispanic,* October 1998, pp. 14-16.

Jennifer Lopez

Born July 24, 1970
New York, New York

Actress, singer, dancer

"I've had a career, I swear, like no other actress—Latina or not," Jennifer Lopez once told *Vibe* magazine. "When I think of who I've worked with—Jack Nicholson, Francis Ford Coppola, Sean Penn—I freak out." From the time she was a young child, she wanted to be a star—in spite of the near absence of Latina role models in Hollywood. Driven and ambitious, Lopez worked hard to be taken seriously as a leading lady and struggled to overcome the barrier of being typecast in ethnic roles. "There aren't a lot of parts for [Latinas], and we're not generally considered for other roles that aren't race specific," she explained to Jeffrey Ressner of *Time* magazine. "It's starting to change a little bit, but we're still treated like foreigners who just got here because we're not white." Now the most handsomely paid Latina in Hollywood history, Lopez has put a great deal of thought into making the right career choices. "I've been careful with what I've selected," she explained in an E! Online interview. "There were projects I could've done for the money because I was broke, but I always felt I had a chance at a better, longer career."

"I want everything. I want family. I want to do good work. I want to love. I want to be comfortable. I want it all."

(Archive Photos)

149

From fly girl to elephant woman

Jennifer Lopez was born on July 24, 1970 in the Bronx, New York (one of the five boroughs of New York City). Both of her parents—David, a computer specialist for an insurance company, and Guadalupe ("Lupe"), a teacher—are Puerto Rican. The second of three children, she has an older sister, Leslie, and a younger sister, Lynda. After graduating from Holy Family School—where her mother teaches kindergarten—she enrolled in Baruch College in New York City. Having decided to pursue a career in dance, she dropped out after one semester. Hoping eventually to appear in Broadway shows, she studied ballet and jazz dance. Lopez appeared in two productions that toured abroad (*Golden Musicals of Broadway,* which toured in Europe, and *Synchronicity,* which toured in Japan) prior to winning a spot in 1990 as one of Rosie Perez's "fly girl" dancers on the Fox comedy *In Living Color.* After being awarded the part—for which she competed with over two thousand other performers—Lopez moved to Los Angeles, California. In a later interview with *Women's Wire,* Lopez said of the experience, "That was cool, but I didn't like to be anyone's backup."

Although she never expected to remain in Los Angeles, Lopez enjoyed good fortune in her new home. Shortly after becoming a "fly girl," she was cast in *South Central,* a television pilot written and directed by the husband of one of her fellow dancers. Although the series failed, Lopez had begun to attract the attention of other producers. In 1992 she appeared on *The Tonight Show* with Jay Leno. The following year she played the role of Melinda Lopez on the television series, *Second Chances,* and portrayed Rosie in the made-for-television movie, *Nurses on the Line: The Crash of Flight 7.* She also had a part in the short-lived television series, *Hotel Malibu,* before making her big-screen debut in 1995, as Maria Sanchez, a Mexican American mother, in *My Family.* The sprawling story of a series of generations of a Latino family, the movie also starred Jimmy Smits (who is perhaps best known for his role as Bobby Simone in the successful television series, *NYPD Blue*).

Next Lopez was cast as Grace Santiago, a New York City transit cop, in the 1995 action comedy, *Money Train.* The following year, she played Miss Marquez, a sweet fifth-grade teacher, in *Jack,* directed by Francis Ford Coppola and starring Robin Williams. In 1997 she played the role of Gabriela in *Blood* and Wine, a thriller starring Jack Nicholson. Although critics took little notice of Lopez's role in the Bob Rafelson film, Henri Behar wrote in *Film Scouts Interviews* that "her swishing hips all but stole a couple of scenes from Jack Nicholson and Stephen Dorff . . . " Also that year Lopez played Terri Flores, a first-time filmmaker, in the action thriller *Anaconda*. *Rolling Stone* reporter Peter Travers referred to her role as doing "hard screen time dodging snakes." The role proved to be physically demanding, and Lopez enjoyed the challenge. "I'm tough that way," she explained to *Cosmopolitan* reporter Dennis Hensley. "Some actresses are like, 'Get my stunt double, I don't want to have to run.' But I'll do anything. . . . I was like the Elephant Woman from the hips down. It was a major bruise movie." The movie was bruising in more ways than one: it took a beating at the box office and from the critics.

The new Queen of Tejano

Lopez's biggest break came when she landed the title role in *Selena*, written and directed by Gregory Nava (whose previous credits included *My Family*). The movie portrays the brief life of Mexican American singer Selena Quintanilla Perez, the so-called Queen of Tejano music, who was shot and killed in 1995 at the age of twenty-three by the president of her fan club. (Tejano—pronounced *tay-HA-no*—is a form of music, originated in the borderland between Texas and Mexico, that combines traditional Mexican folk music with polkas, country-and-western, and even rock-and-roll.) Out of a field of 22,000 women who auditioned for the title role, seven were chosen for a final screen test.

"When I started preparing for the audition and really learning about Selena, I really wanted to play her," Lopez explained in *Vibe*. After winning the part, she moved to Corpus Christi, Texas, where she lived with Selena's sister, Suzette, and she watched tapes of the Tejano artist's performances and

Life Imitates Art

In one of the most memorable scenes in *Money Train*—a 1995 action comedy starring Lopez, Wesley Snipes, and Woody Harrelson— a pyromaniac [someone who has an uncontrollable urge to start fires] squirts a flammable liquid [something that ignites easily] into a subway token booth and lights it, with the occupant trapped inside. Four days after *Money Train* opened on November 22, 1995, someone used exactly that method to attack a clerk in a Brooklyn subway station. The clerk suffered life-threatening burns. A few days later, another clerk was attacked—although unsuccessfully. Sometime later, Bob Dole, the Senate Majority Leader, delivered a speech before the Senate in which he urged Americans to boycott the film. Lopez, who plays a tough transit cop in the movie, told *People* magazine that the film was not responsible for the criminals' actions. She said, "[People] see so many violent movies. Why would they pick that scene from *Money Train?*" The incidents did, however, cause her to look seriously at the power of the printed image. "It just made me more conscious of what I would do in other movies," she explained. "You have such an influence over people, it's kinda scary."

Jennifer Lopez accepts the 1997 American Latino Media Arts (ALMA) Award for Best Actress for her portrayal of the Tejano singer Selena. (AP/Wide World)

studied her every move. She spoke to family and friends in an attempt to learn more about the private side of the popular singer's life. "I didn't want to merely impersonate or caricature her," Lopez told *Time* reporter Jeffrey Ressner. "I wanted to capture her personality, down to the tiniest details—even the way she rubbed her nose." In order to look like the flamboyant singer, Lopez spent two hours every day having make-up applied. The colorful costumes she wore (50 in all) were sewn by Selena's seamstress—from the original patterns. On the advice of the singer's sister, she even wore Selena's favorite nail polish, L'Oreal Sangria.

Not everyone was pleased that Lopez—a New Yorker of Puerto Rican descent—had been cast as a Mexican American. Some charged that Warner Brothers (the studio producing the film) had used the talent search, which included non-professional actresses, to generate publicity. Some even suggested that Lopez, who had previously appeared in a film by director Nava, had never even auditioned for the part. Lopez took the pressure in stride. "I had to do a good job not just for me, but for Selena, her family, her fans, and her legacy," she explained in *Vibe*. "It was a big responsibility, and I took that on without thinking twice."

Although *Selena* received lukewarm reviews, the critics praised Lopez's turn as Selena. Richard Corliss, writing in *Time*, noted that Lopez "Gives a feisty, buoyant performance that could set her on a star path similar to the singer's." Behar wrote in *Film Scouts*, "Nothing quite prepares you for what she does as Selena in Gregory Nava's film. Beyond getting the deceased singer's moves right, she creates a character on whose shoulders the entire film practically rests." Based on her portrayal, Lopez won the Imagen Foundation Lasting Image Award, the Lone Star Film & Television Award, and an ALMA Award, which recognizes Latino contributions to the television and movie industry. She was nominated for a Golden Globe and MTV Movie Award. And she reportedly became the first Latina actress to earn $1 million for one role.

Marriage and other u-turns

With the completion of *Selena* came another turning point in Lopez's life. At a party to celebrate the completion of the movie, her boyfriend, Ojani Noa, proposed. The two had met while he was waiting tables in Miami. "All of a sudden Ojani takes the mike," she told *Cosmopolitan* reporter Dennis Hensley, "and I'm thinking he's going to say something about how hard I worked. He comes up to my table and in Spanish he says, 'I just want to say one thing: Jennifer, will you marry

---

Crossing Over

Like the character she portrayed in *Selena*, Lopez has been hailed as a crossover artist. It is a label she prefers not to embrace. "I was born in the Bronx," she explained in a *Film Scouts* interview. "'Crossover' is when you cross over from one market to another. I've always been in this market. . . . if it's convenient for [the media] to say I'm doing the crossover thing, so be it. I prefer to say I'm Latin, I'm an actor, and I'm having some success."

me?" Everybody just burst out in applause. I started crying. Then he gets down on one knee and puts the ring on my finger. It was very, very romantic." The couple was married about a year later, in February of 1997, but were divorced sometime in 1998.

Taking no break after filming *Selena*, Lopez flew to a new location to begin work on Oliver Stone's *U-Turn*, starring Nick Nolte and Sean Penn. (Stone had to rearrange the production schedule in order to cast Lopez in the film.) "I didn't expect it to happen like this, wrapping one film and flying out to do a new one the next day," she told E! Online. "But I'm fresh enough and ambitious enough to stay up all night for the sake of a job. I'm not gonna take it easy. I want to do so much more when I'm getting these great opportunities." As it turned out, *U-Turn* was a box-office failure. It did, however, allow Lopez to work with some of the best names in Hollywood, which, for a young, up-and-coming star, is an invaluable opportunity and learning experience.

Beyond out of sight

Lopez—who provided the voice of Azteca in the 1998 animated movie, *Antz*— was a hit co-starring with George Clooney in the 1998 crime story *Out of Sight*. In the role of Karen Sisco, a U.S. marshal, Lopez is kidnapped by bank robber Jack Foley (Clooney)—a nonviolent and gentlemanly crook who resorts to kidnapping only after Sisco interferes with his jail-escape plan. The unlikely duo develops a romantic attraction. As the tough but sexy federal officer, Lopez impressed the critics. Janet Maslin, for example, wrote in *The New York Times*, "Ms. Lopez has her best movie role thus far, and she brings it both seductiveness and grit. If it was hard to imagine a hardworking, pistol-packing bombshell on the page [in the original Elmore Leonard novel], it couldn't be easier here."

In spite of her apparent success, Lopez confided in Knight Ridder reporter Rene Rodriquez (printed in the *Arizona Republic*) that being Latina is still an issue in casting for some directors — and that it poses a constant barrier with which she must contend. *Out of Sight* director Steven Soderbergh, however, claimed that he did not take into account Lopez's background. "I just thought she was the best actress for that part," he explained. "Jennifer is really unique, because she can do just about anything, and it's not often you find someone with that kind of range."

Lopez followed her role in *Out of Sight* with a series of other projects. In 1999 she released her first album, *On the 6*, and appeared in *Thieves, Impostor,* and *The Hollow Man.* Written by Andrew Marlowe (who wrote the screenplay for *Air Force One*), and directed by Paul Verhoeven (whose other efforts include *Total Recall* and *Basic Instinct*), *The Hollow Man* concerns the struggles of a man who has become invisible. Lopez plays a scientist. Already the highest paid Latina actress in history, the actress was reportedly offered a $5-million salary to co-star in *Pluto Nash,* a gangster-science-fiction-comedy in which Eddie Murphy plays a bar owner on the moon in the year 2087.

Lopez attributes her success in Hollywood to hard work and preparation. "[It's] about being prepared when your opportunity comes, about being able to perform under pressure," she told Rodriguez. "If you're going in to audition for Oliver Stone or Francis Ford Coppola, are you gonna choke? If you have a good day that day, then it's not luck. It's because you made it happen."

> "I'm aware that I'm becoming more known, and I want to set a good example for my people. Being a role model is okay with me — you have that responsibility when you're in the public eye." –Lopez, *Vibe*

Sources

Altman, Sheryl. "Marshaling In." Women's Wire. [Online] Available http://www.womenswire.com (December 27, 1998).

"Back in Sight," "Crowning Diva Moment," "Jennifer Lopez," "Out of Sight." Entertainment Weekly Online. [Online] Available http://cgi.pathfinder.com/ew/ (December 27, 1998).

Behar, Henri. "Jennifer Lopez on 'Selena.' Film Scouts Interviews. [Online] Available http://filmscouts.com (December 27, 1998).

"Butter Pecan Rican Jennifer Lopez," *Vibe* Online. [Online] Available http://www.vibe.com (December 27, 1998).

Corliss, Richard. "¡Viva Selana!" *Time,* March 24, 1997.

Duggan, Dennis. "A rising Latina star wows them in the Bronx." *Newsday,* March 20, 1997.

"Feeling the Heat," "U-Turn." People Online. [Online] Available http://www.people.com (December 27, 1998).

Fitzpatrick, Eileen. "Selena." *Billboard,* April 5, 1997.

Handelman, David. "A diva is born." *Mirabella,* July/August 1998, pp. 82-84.

Hensley, Dennis. "How do you say 'hot' in Spanish? Jennifer Lopez." *Cosmopolitan,* April 1997.

"Lopez's Big Raise," Mr. Showbiz, December 16, 1998. [Online] Available http://www.mrshowbiz.com (December 27, 1998).

Maslin, Janet. "'Out of Sight': A thief, a marshall, an item." *The New York Times,* June 26, 1998.

Ressner, Jeffrey. "Born to play the Tejano Queen." *Time,* March 24, 1998.

Rodriguez, Rene. "*Too Latin* Jennifer Lopez answers with her talent." *Arizona Republic,* June 26, 1998.

Sessums, Kevin. "Bronx belle." *Vanity Fair,* July 1998.

Travers, Peter. "Selena." *Rolling Stone,* April 17, 1997.

USA Weekend, June 21, 1998.

Wuntch, Philip. "*Out of Sight* review." *Dallas Morning News,* June 26, 1998.

Madonna

Born August 16, 1958
Bay City, Michigan

Singer, actress

UPDATE

"The fascinating thing about Madonna is that she is all-real and all-fake —in other words, pure show biz," *Time* critic Richard Corliss once wrote. Born in Bay City, Michigan, Madonna—born Madonna Louise Veronica Ciccone —has managed to exert a very real influence on the popular culture of her generation. Since the 1985 release of her second, platinum-selling album, *Like A Virgin,* she has been virtually unrivaled on the concert scene, the pop charts, and the music-video airwaves. Revealing a genius for reinventing herself, Madonna produced a string of popular and critically acclaimed albums, including *True Blue, Like A Prayer,* and *I'm Breathless.* In 1993, she launched the wildly popular "Girlie Show" tour, which sold out in nearly every city where it played. **(See original entry on Madonna in *Performing Artists,* Volume 2.)**

Motherhood and movie stardom

Madonna followed the success of her "Girlie Show" tour with an entirely new—and less public—role. The performer and her then-boyfriend, Carlos Leon—a personal trainer she met in

"It's pointless to compare yourself to others. Accepting that idea has been incredibly liberating — especially as an artist."

(AP/Wide World)

1994—decided to take on the challenges of parenthood. On October 14, 1996, Madonna gave birth to a daughter, Lourdes Maria Ciccone Leon, whose name refers in part to Lourdes, France, known as the "village of miracles." (Thousands of religious pilgrims continue to flock to the French town where the Virgin Mary (also called the Madonna, the mother of Jesus in the Catholic religion) was said to have appeared in 1858.)

Madonna—who is also known for her ability continually to recapture the public's interest—insisted that her decision to take on motherhood had nothing to do with publicity-seeking. "My having a child is not for public consumption," she told *USA Today* (quoted in Mr. Showbiz online). "It's not a performance to be judged and rated. Nor is my role as a mother." Determined to raise her child far from the limelight, she cites Jackie Onassis (1929–94), wife of former president John F. Kennedy (1917–63), as a role model. "Look at John Kennedy, Jr.," she told *USA Today*. "He's been photographed since he was two, and he turned out okay. He had a very strong, intelligent mother." Madonna, who lost her own mother as a young child (her mother, also named Madonna Ciccone, died of breast cancer when her daughter was six years old), professes to take motherhood very seriously. "I feel very inspired to give my daughter everything my mother couldn't give me," she told talk show host Oprah Winfrey.

Also in 1996, Madonna appeared in the title role of the wildly popular *Evita*, a musical film about the rise of Juan Peron's (1895-1974) dictatorship in Argentina. Evita Peron, Juan's wife, was a role Madonna felt she was born to play. Although a tremendous hit with audiences, the film—and Madonna's acting—received mixed reviews. *New York Times* critic Janet Maslin called the film Madonna's "most colossal [enormous] music video." Others considered Madonna's performance as the Argentine icon to be a revelation. For the role of Evita, the Hollywood Foreign Press Association awarded the former "Material Girl's" performance with a Golden Globe for Best Actress in a Musical or Comedy. The announcement of Oscar nominees for the 1997 Academy Awards, however, provoked some public outcry: Madonna was not among the five women nominated for the Best Actress award.

A kinder, gentler Madonna

In 1998—nearly fifteen years after she first appeared on *Billboard* magazine's "Hot 100" with her surprise hit, "Holiday"—

Madonna collected a Grammy Award for Best Pop Album for *Ray of Light,* her first studio release since *Bedtime Stories* appeared in 1994. "My intention was to make a record that I'd enjoy listening to," she told *Billboard.* "This album is reflective of where I am in my life right now—in terms of my musical interests and in terms of my personal beliefs." A moody and self-reflective collection of thirteen songs, *Ray* was touted as the work of a "spiritually enlightened" Madonna.

The title song *Ray of Light* was the forty-year-old singer's highest-debuting single ever: it climbed to fifth position on *Billboard's* Hot 100 pop chart when it was released in March 1998. It was the *fortieth* Madonna single to earn a spot on that list. Racking up impressive sales, the album sold more than 2.3 million units in the United States by the end of the year. It

Madonna's performance in **Evita** *earned her a 1997 Golden Globe Award for Best Actress in a Musical or Comedy. (The Kobal Collection)*

For the Record

When *Ray of Light* appeared in March 1998, there was no guarantee that the public would take to singer Madonna's kinder, gentler image. The forty-year-old performer's first studio release in four years, the album featured soul-searching and confessional lyrics. Apparently, the time was ripe for a spiritually enlightened Madonna. *Ray of Light* posted staggering sales results and garnered critical raves as well. What's more, the album's success brings the singer closer to besting a number of performance records. Having released her first chart-making hit ("Holiday") in 1984, Madonna posted her 37th Top 40 hit with *Ray of Light*. Only one female artist has produced more Top 40 hits: Aretha Franklin, whose "A Rose Is Still A Rose" most recently made that list, has a total of 43 Top 40 songs. Madonna, who now has 32 Top 10 hits (including *Ray*), is just two Top 10 hits shy of the Beatles' total. And if she continues to produce A-list singles, she could someday surpass rock-and-roll legend Elvis Presley's claim to 38 hit singles.

also garnered six MTV Video Music Awards that year: the title song won five awards, including best video of the year, while the video for "Frozen" received top honors for special effects. *Ray of Light* fared well at the 1998 MTV Europe Music Awards, as well: it collected the award for Best Album, while Madonna was recognized as that year's Best Female Artist. The album's success also earned Madonna a spot to perform on the 1998 Billboard Music Awards.

Ray of Light represented more than artistic success for Madonna. Produced by the Maverick division of Time Warner—a label Madonna heads with longtime manager Freddy DeMann—it marked a commercial (business) success as well. Once an insignificant label, Maverick, under Madonna's guidance, had blossomed into a successful studio that featured such best-selling artists as Prodigy, a British techno band, and Alanis Morissette.

One of the world's wealthiest women, Madonna followed her latest album's colossal success with a number of other projects. Signed as a model for Procter & Gamble's Max Factor makeup line, she reportedly stood to gain $6 million from the deal. Having been absent from Hollywood during her pregnancy and first years of motherhood, she lined up a number of film projects, including a starring role in *The Next Best Thing,* with Rupert Everett. Seemingly destined to live in the limelight, Madonna once commented on her position in the public eye: "How could I have been anything else but what I am, having been named Madonna. I would either have ended up a nun or this."

Sources

Bronson, Fred. "With 'Light,' Madonna's life begins at 40." *Billboard,* July 11, 1998, p. 94.

"Fact Sheet." E! Online. [Online] Available http://www.eonline.com/ (March 8, 1999).

Flick, Larry. "Maverick's Madonna to 'Light' up awards show." *Billboard,* December 5, 1998, p. 87.

Frankel, Daniel. "Madonna, Everett to Do "Best Thing." E! Online, May 6, 1998. [Online] Available http://www.eonline.com/. (March 8, 1999).

Lycos Celebrity Guide. [Online] Available http://www-blockbusternet.lycos.com/ (March 8, 1999).

"Madonna Biography." Mr. Showbiz. [Online] Available http://mrshowbiz.go.com/ (March 8, 1999).

"Madonna Dishes With Oprah." Mr. Showbiz. [Online] December 13, 1996. Available http://mrshowbiz.go.com/. (March 8, 1999).

"Madonna Says Child Is Not a Career Move." Mr. Showbiz. [Online] December 11, 1996. [Online] Available http://mrshowbiz.go.com/. (March 8, 1999).

"Madonna to the Max." Mr. Showbiz. [Online] Available http://mrshowbiz.go.com/ (March 8, 1999).

Maslin, Janet. Review of *Evita*. *The New York Times,* December 25, 1996.

Dennis Miller

Born November 3, 1953
Philadelphia, Pennsylvania

Comedian, actor

"You know a sense of humor is exactly that—a sense. Not a fact, not etched in stone, not an empirical math equation, but just what the word intones—a sense of what you find funny."

(The Kobal Collection)

After having gotten into stand-up comedy on a whim, Dennis Miller spent six successful years as a member of the cast of *Saturday Night Live*. Venturing out on his own, the former "Weekend Update" anchor met with failure on his short-lived comedy, *The Dennis Miller Show*. Silenced only briefly, Miller came back with HBO's *Dennis Miller Live*, which soon garnered an Emmy Award for its biting and topical humor. Intelligent, well-read, and articulate (well-spoken), Miller once summarized his comic style simply as: "I vent, therefore I am."

A natural-born comic

Born on November 3, 1953, in Philadelphia, Pennsylvania, Dennis Miller—and his younger brother, Jimmy—were raised by their mother, a dietitian. Miller's father, who left his family, died when his sons were still young. As a high school student, the aspiring comedian discovered that comedy had the power to win friends and influence people. "In study hall, I sat next to the biggest football player in school, who never acknowledged my existence," he recalled in a Mr. Showbiz interview. "I could have self-immolated [self-destructed] right in front of him and he wouldn't have thrown water. But one day, I made fun of the teacher with something sarcastic under my breath. This guy laughed so hard. He said, 'I'm going to my next class. You wanna walk with me?'"

After graduating from high school, Miller enrolled in Point Park College in Pittsburgh. Having seen actor Robert Redford portray a journalist in *All the President's Men* (1976), he decided to major in journalism. After graduating, however, he discovered that journalism was not the well-paying career path he had hoped it would be. Faced with the prospect of being paid by the newspaper-column-inch, he decided to look elsewhere for work. Miller tried a number of odd jobs—including selling storm windows, driving a delivery truck, and working at a dairy and grocery store—before discovering where his real talent lay. "One night I saw a comedian at a bar who was so horrific, I thought, '[Hey], *I* can be that bad,'" he told Mr. Showbiz. "So I went up to the owner and asked if I could fill the place with my friends on his slowest night, just to see whether I could do this stuff. He said, 'Yeah, sure,' if he got all the drink money. So I jumped in and found what I was meant to do."

Soon, Miller took his act to New York and Los Angeles—both of which enjoyed thriving comedy circuits. Performing at a number of popular clubs, he quickly made a name for himself. By virtue of his reputation as a comedian, he landed a job with *PM Magazine* in 1980, which involved writing and producing comic interludes. He also hosted *Punchline,* a weekend program aimed at a teenaged audience.

Shortly thereafter—in the early 1980s—Miller moved to Los Angeles, California. There, he caught the eye of *Saturday Night Live* producer Lorne Michaels who often scouted for talent in the city's numerous comedy clubs. After seeing Miller's act at The Comedy Store in Los Angeles, Michaels asked the young comic to join the cast of the popular NBC comedy show.

An infamous anchorman

Although he appeared in numerous roles during his six-year tenure at SNL, Miller is best remembered for his role as the anchorman for the "Weekend Update" segment—a position previously filled by former SNL cast members Chevy Chase, Dan

Aykroyd, and Jane Curtin. Well-spoken, well-informed, and more than a little cynical, Miller was suited to the role of snarky commentator. His unique take on current events, politics, and pop culture struck a chord with both viewers and critics, and his stint as anchor is remembered as one of the show's most memorable segments.

Although he looks back at his days at *Saturday Night Live* with mixed feelings, Miller learned to be a disciplined comedian during his time with the live television show. "I used to whine a lot there because I was new to the whole showbiz thannng," he told a Hollywood Online reporter. "But I did find that round about Friday afternoon at 4:30 p.m., when I began to think in terms of being canned if I wasn't funny, a wonderful transformation would happen. A warrior inside me—amidst the cacophony [noise] of whining—would step forward out of the din and say, "You little Ewoks have to go back into the cave now, I'm going to write jokes, funny jokes. You can come out again and whine on Sunday." In 1988, while still a member of the SNL cast, Miller married Ali Espely, an Irish-born former model. (The couple has two sons, Holden and Marlon.) While meeting the demands of weekly live taping sessions, he managed to fit in numerous emceeing appearances and several Miller Lite commercials.

The angry prophet of the airwaves

Eager to host his own show, Miller quit *Saturday Night Live* in 1990. In January 1992, he launched *The Dennis Miller Show,* a late-night talk show that claimed to have "the smartest monologue on television." "This is a program worth tuning in any night," raved *People* critic David Hiltbrand. "[Miller] throws out pop-culture references . . . with the flashy assurance of a casino blackjack dealer flipping cards." Although warmly received by television critics, the show suffered poor ratings and was canceled after just six months. Disappointed, Miller remained philosophical about the show's failure. "If the worst thing that happens is your TV show gets taken off," he later told Mr. Showbiz, "well, thank God that you were there to *have* your TV show canceled."

After *The Dennis Miller Show* failed, however, Miller seemed to have lost his Hollywood marketability. At first, he could not interest producers in another topical Miller-hosted comedy show. Eventually, however, HBO's Michael Fuchs arranged for

the comedian to vent his wit on cable television. Miller looks back on HBO's willingness to support him with gratitude. "[W]hen I looked up and saw nothing but Road Runner dust clouds wafting into the distance, HBO were the only people who would touch me," he told Hollywood Online. *Dennis Miller Live,* which debuted in 1994, soon paid off handsomely. The comic announced the program's mission during the first show:

"We will strive to be in the vanguard [forefront] of the movement to irresponsibly blur the line between news and entertainment." Miller's blurred mix of news and entertainment was a critical and popular success. Dubbed "the angry prophet of the airwaves" by *Time* magazine, Miller was congratulated for venturing boldly into the political arena. Impressively, the show garnered an Emmy Award in its first season. "In the space of thirteen months," Miller told Mr. Showbiz, "I'd been canceled and then won an Emmy."

The show's format allowed Miller to do what he did best: rant. Each program opened with a monologue in which the comedian vented his gripes about politics and current events. His ranting sessions—always well-seasoned with pop-culture references—were followed by a one-on-one session with a special guest and phone calls from viewers. Each show concluded with a tongue-in-cheek (joking) wrap-up of the week's news events—much like SNL's "Weekend Update."

Ranting and raving

Encouraged by the popularity of his rants, Miller published *The Rants* (1996), a collection of diatribes [rants] taken mostly from his HBO show. Some critics complained that the written word paled in comparison to Miller's impassioned live performances. "[W]hile Miller's run-on monologues are marvels of lung power when performed," wrote *People* critic Alex Tresniowski, "reading them is like looking at still photos of Michael Jordan—you're just not getting the full effect." Even so, *The Rants* became a best-seller. Miller followed the success of his first book with *Ranting Again,* published in 1998. This time, *People* enthused: "Dennis Miller . . . may be the consummate [perfect] '90s funnyman: cynical, obscene, consumed with pop culture, and by turns, smugly self-congratulatory and refreshingly self-effacing [modest]." The review concluded: "Bottom Line: He's ranting—and we're raving."

Film critics weren't raving, however, about Miller's turn in the movies. His appearances in flimsy movies such as *Broken Highway, Madhouse,* and *The Quest* did little to improve his box-office appeal. And his roles in *Disclosure* (1994) and *The Net* (1995), were too brief to merit notice. When he finally landed a leading role—as investigator Rafe Guttman in the 1996 vampire satire *Bordello of Blood*—the "Tales From the Crypt" presentation failed to highlight his talent. Next came a role in *Murder at 1600* (1997), opposite Wesley Snipes. In spite of his occasional forays into Hollywood, Miller is not intent on pursuing a career in the movies. "I'm not hung up on being a movie star," he told Mr. Showbiz. "It's not what I burn to do; I burn to do my show."

Although burning to perform, Miller maintains a realistic perspective on his show business occupation. "I'm in it primarily to make a living," he told a Hollywood Online interviewer. "It's a really great job. Don't get me wrong, I'm tenacious [persistent] when I sit down to write a joke. I don't take the first one in my head. I work on it. But, that said, I'm just a father who is trying to provide for his wife and two sons. I think it is best to keep it that linear [straightforward]. It keeps you sane."

> "I'm not hung up on being a movie star. It's not what I burn to do; I burn to do my show."

Sources

"Celebrity chat transcript for Dennis Miller." Hollywood Online. [Online] Available http://chat.hollywood.com/reeltoreal/celeb/dmiller/transdmiller1.html (February 18, 1999).

"Comedically Incorrect." *Time,* May 30, 1994, p. 67.

"Dennis Miller Star Bio." Celebsite. [Online] Available http://www.celebsite.com/people/dennismiller/index.html (February 18, 1999).

Fields-Meyer, Thomas. Review of *Ranting Again. People,* June 22, 1998, p. 39.

Hiltbrand, David. Review of *Dennis Miller. People,* February 10, 1992, p. 11.

James, Caryn. "Emmy Awards Show: Familiar Faces in Familiar Format." *The New York Times,* September 10, 1996.

Miller, Dennis. *The Rants.* New York: Doubleday, 1996.

Rusoff, Jane Wollman. "The bing-bang mind of Dennis Miller." Mr. Showbiz. [Online] Available www.mrshowbiz.com/ (February 18, 1999).

Tresniowski, Alex. Review of *The Rants. People,* April 1, 1996, p. 36.

Van Gelder, Lawrence. "*Bordello of Blood:* Juvenile Junk Food." *The New York Times,* August 16, 1996.

Awadagin Pratt

Born March 6, 1966
Pittsburgh, Pennsylvania

Pianist, violinist, conductor

> "I want to leave an audience with a sense of what these pieces of music are all about, why the composers were so moved, they had to write it down on paper."

Once faced with a choice between tennis and music, Awadagin (pronounced ah-wah-DAH-jin) Pratt decided music was the one thing he couldn't give up. An accomplished pianist, violinist, and conductor, he has been labeled a "triple threat" on the classical music circuit. Considered by some to be somewhat eccentric (odd or unusual)—like his idol, pianist Glenn Gould — he has collected numerous awards, including *Ebony* magazine's designation as one of the fifty leaders of tomorrow (in 1992). Noted for his passionate involvement with the music he performs, Pratt was the first African American musician to garner the prestigious Naumburg award. Said Robert Mann, founder and first violinist of the Juilliard String Quartet—a Naumburg juror—"His playing is spectacularly involving. Everybody just goes berserk over it—not just the way he plays the surface things, but the degree of musical involvement he brings to it."

A disciplined upbringing

Awadagin Pratt's father, Theodore Pratt, was born in the African nation of Sierra Leone. After traveling to the United

States to continue his education, he met Mildred Sirls, a native of Henderson, Texas, in Pittsburgh, Pennsylvania. Pratt, a professor of nuclear physics, and Sirls, a professor of social work, married and had two children—Awadagin and his younger sister, Menah.

Born in Pittsburgh, Pennsylvania, on March 6, 1966, Awadagin expressed an interest in music at a very young age. He revealed in an interview, cited in the musician's website: "My parents listened to classical music and I, at some age like four or five, was running around conducting the music and told my parents I wanted to become a conductor. Presumably after they had remarked that I was conducting—when I was six—my piano lessons began and I was sorely disappointed that I wasn't having my conducting lessons." Pratt received his first piano lesson as a six-year-old—a group lesson with about 12 other children at a local music store. (His parents bought the family's first piano—a beat-up used upright—for Christmas one year.) Three years after his first piano lesson—about the time his family moved to Normal, Illinois—Pratt began to study the violin. Listening to the local classical radio station, he was exposed to a wide variety of orchestral music, but little piano music. Drawn to classical, he was surprisingly free of influence from pop music. "I started listening to a little bit of popular music when I was 16 or 17," he recalled in *American Visions,* "and I've listened to it a little bit more. But all I listened to growing up was classical music."

The Pratt children were raised in a strict and disciplined environment. "We felt a sense of responsibility about raising black children," Pratt's mother said. "They have to be as prepared as possible to face life and to learn that to be considered as good as others they have to be better." For Awadagin and his sister, most days started at six in the morning with a two-hour session of tennis drills. When they returned home from a full day at school, they returned to the tennis courts for more drills. Both children received music lessons each week. Studying both violin and piano, they were required to practice one hour each day—on each instrument. As a public school student, Pratt participated in drama productions, debates, and other extra-curricular activities. A member of the tennis and basketball teams at Normal Community High School, he also competed in a number of local sports tournaments.

Music scores over tennis

Having graduated from high school by the age of sixteen, Pratt faced a crossroads. A gifted tennis player (both he and his sister were regionally ranked), Pratt had been offered a tennis scholarship to attend Kalamazoo College, a highly rated Division III school in Kalamazoo, Michigan. After weighing his options, he decided that music, not tennis, was something he could not live without. He recalled: "I can't remember exactly what I was thinking, but I think it was an emotional rather than an intellectual decision. The emotional fulfillment I felt that I got out of music surpassed the others. And I definitely made the right choice. I've never second-guessed that decision." Accepting a violin scholarship, Pratt enrolled in the University of Illinois at Urbana.

As a college student, Pratt played violin for one season in the Springfield Symphony Orchestra (now the Illinois Symphony Orchestra). Increasingly confident of his ability, he began to set his sights on a career as a professional musician. Having decided to transfer to a music conservatory, he considered the New England Conservatory, the Cleveland Institute, and the Peabody Conservatory of Music, in Baltimore, Maryland. Only Peabody—which belonged to the Johns Hopkins University system—accepted his application as a student of both piano *and* violin. Pratt packed his bags and headed for Baltimore.

From the start, Pratt made a positive impression at Peabody. Robert Weirich recalled the young musician's piano audition to be accepted at the prestigious conservatory: "It was fearless and for someone that age, remarkable. You can't tell most piano students apart at that age. Awadagin was already Awadagin. In his years with me, he was always experimenting—things went crazy sometimes, but they were never dull. When he plays, he's one of these very rare people who make you hear a piece as if for the first time." Enrolled on a scholarship, Pratt shared first prize in the annual Peabody concerto competition in his *first year.* (Pratt shared first prize with pianist Kevin Kenner.) He graduated in 1989 with performance diplomas in both violin and piano. When he received a graduate performing diploma in conducting in 1992, he became the first Peabody student ever to earn three performance diplomas. Frederick Prausnitz, one of Pratt's mentors at Peabody, was immediately convinced of his student's gift for conducting. "I knew he was special the first time he got in front of an orchestra," he recalled. "From the moment he got up there, he made the musicians make music. He's got the two things a conductor needs: a tremendous mind for music and a tremendous gift for people."

Far from Normal

The same year he earned a graduate degree in conducting, Pratt entered the prestigious Naumburg International competition in New York. Competing against six other finalists, he won first prize in the 1992 competition—becoming the first African American classical musician to receive the Naumburg's top honor. (The competition's previous winners included internationally renowned musicians Stephen Hough, Eugene Istomin, William Kapell, and Abby Simon.) The Naumburg, which is considered to be a better measure of talent than the more high-profile Van Cliburn Competition, brought Pratt a monetary award of $5,000—and a wealth of critical recognition. Ursula Oppens, a highly regarded pianist who served as one of the competition's judges, said, "His best playing was some of the most spectacular I've ever heard. If he keeps developing, he'll be one of the most exciting pianists in the world."

The first year after winning the Naumburg competition, Pratt gave more than forty performances. The following year, his hectic schedule included over seventy solo piano performances. Having created a stir on the concert circuit, Pratt was awarded the prestigious Avery Fisher Career Grant in 1994, which brought a $10,000 cash prize for career development. Also that year, he performed on a PBS television concert honoring Mystislav Rostropovitch, broadcast live from the Kennedy Center in Washington, D.C., and made his first appearance with the New York Philharmonic at Avery Fisher Hall in New York's Lincoln Center—an impressive milestone for a young concert pianist. A concert appearance at the White House, at the invitation of President Bill Clinton and his wife, Hillary, followed. That year also saw the release of Pratt's debut recital disc, *A Long Way from Normal,* featuring works by Brahms, Bach, Franck, and Liszt. The CD was warmly received by critics. *Stereo Review,* for example, enthused: "Pratt seems to be a rare bird among competition winners: He's at home in the virtuoso repertory [works for technically gifted performers] but comes across best in more introspective [in-

"I was never one of those high-powered young music students who were always practicing hours and hours a day. I simply liked the music. I had evident talent, but not, at any time, was it like the priority. I was no prodigy type. I didn't practice that much. Most of my energy was devoted to tennis." –Pratt, "Ask Awadagin"

Dreadlocks and Penguin Suits

Pratt's unorthodox (non-traditional) appearance has attracted a great deal of attention among concert-goers and music critics. As Kevin Nance, a journalist for the *Lexington Herald-Leader*, wrote, "the classical music concert hall is hardly known as a refuge for soloists (especially of the male variety) of unconventional appearance. Concert tails [formal tuxedos] are the norm—white shirts, black ties, that sort of thing. We like our soloists to look like penguins, not rock stars."

White shirts and black ties have never been Pratt's chosen attire. Having never donned a tuxedo for a piano recital, he opts instead for comfortable clothing that lets him focus on his performance. Further, he reasons, "if the soloist or recitalist is coming out less dressed-up, then some people will feel more comfortable coming. I think it's an important thing that particularly helps bring in younger people." Adding to Pratt's unorthodox image is his hair style: as a student at the Peabody Conservatory of Music, he grew dreadlocks (having first admired them on French tennis player Yannick Noah). The dreadlocks have become a part of the musician's signature. "I don't know what my style does for people," he told the *Kalamazoo Gazette*. "It's a by-product of who I am and how I am, so it's important. I'd need to be the way I am if nobody liked it or if everybody liked it."

ward-looking] works that require genuine artistry. Though it remains to be seen if he has the depth of repertory, the technique, and the stamina to sustain a major career, this is a wonderfully satisfying and promising debut album."

More record deals

Having appeared with symphony orchestras nationwide during the 1994–95 concert season, Pratt began to enjoy an international reputation. In 1995 he made his recital debut in Germany and Cape Town, South Africa. An enthusiastic world traveler, Pratt was impressed by his visit to the South African capital in December of that year. "It's a place of tremendous potential," he told *American Visions*. "In Cape Town you can walk down a single block and hear every conceivable point of view. Nothing is swept under the rug." The trip provided the material for Pratt's third album, *Live from South Africa,* released in January of 1997. Unlike the musician's second album, devoted exclusively to Beethoven sonatas, the CD features a varied selection of works for piano. Pratt's first non-solo recording, the album received mixed reviews. While *American Record Guide* called *Live from South Africa* "impressively thoughtful and serious and well worth hearing," *Stereo Review* faulted Pratt's choice of programming and lack of contrast, concluding that "everything tends to sound pretty much like everything else."

Pratt's choice of repertoire (body of works) has been exceptionally broad. A devotee (fan) of composer Ludwig Von Beethoven (1770–1827) since his youth, he features the works of Romantic and French nineteenth century composers, as well. "I do seek pieces that communicate something other than my ability to play the piano," Pratt explained. "I think that art has the capacity to effect change, induce people to look further inside of themselves, so that they may be able to eventually see further away from themselves, and develop a kind of global conscience. It is perhaps too big a burden for all of art—some does exist to entertain—but I do think that some has this power and it would be really good for the world that, when exposed to this music, we do take it fully into our being."

Sources

"Ask Awadagin," "Awadagin Pratt biography." [Online] Available http://www.awadagin.com (January 6, 1999).

"Collections —*A Long Way from Normal* by Awadagin Pratt." *Stereo Review,* September 1994, p. 109.

Freed, Richard. "Awadagin Pratt: Live from South Africa." *Stereo Review,* June 1997, pp. 92-93.

Mah, Linda S. "The hair, the clothes, the stool—Pratt stands out from the rest." *The Kalamazoo Gazette,* May 1, 1998. [Online] Available http://mlive.com/gilmore/stories/pratt.html. (January 6, 1999).

Morin, Alexander. "Awadagin Pratt, piano." *American Record Guide,* May/June 1997, p. 60.

Nance, Kevin. "Pianist casual about appearance but not his music." *Lexington Herald-Leader,* December 1, 1996.

Shepard, T. Brooks. "Classical romance from Awadagin Pratt." *American Visions,* February/March, 1998, pp. 39-40.

Queen Latifah

Born March 18, 1970
East Orange, New Jersey

Singer, actress

> "To get to the point of true contentment with who I am, I had to go through a whole bunch of being something other than myself."

UPDATE

One of the most popular rap artists in the industry, Queen Latifah has displayed a genius for intelligent lyrics that promote female self-respect, African American cultural pride, and the virtues of being positive. Born in New Jersey on March 18, 1970, she released her first single by the age of eighteen, and has enjoyed an increasingly successful career as a singer, actress, and recording producer since then. Initially known simply as a rap artist, Latifah (whose given name is Dana Owens) has successfully broadened her repertoire (body of work) to include other musical genres—including jazz. A convincing actor, she starred for five seasons in the successful Fox comedy series, *Living Single,* and has become increasingly sought-after to play feature film roles. **(See original entry on Queen Latifah in *Performing Artists,* Volume 3.)**

Black Reign and bank heists

Black Reign, a rhythm-and-blues-flavored album released by Motown Records in 1993, proved to be Latifah's most successful album to date. It sold 500,000 copies, earning Latifah gold-record status, while the album's single, "U.N.I.T.Y.", garnered a Grammy Award for Best Rap Solo Performance. The rapper's journey into television also began in 1993, when she took on the role of Kadijah James, editor of *Flavor* magazine, on the popular sitcom *Living Single*. The show's cast regulars also included Kim Fields Freeman, Kim Coles, Erika Alexander, John Henton, and T.C. Carson.

Having appeared in a number of small film roles, Latifah landed a major part in the 1996 crime drama, *Set It Off*. The story of four female bank robbers, the film was popular with both audiences and critics. Co-starring with Kimberly Elise, Vivica A. Fox, and Jada Pinkett, Latifah played the role of Cleo, who finds bank robbery especially appealing. "In a performance of explosive emotional heat, the popular rap star makes this potentially unsympathetic character the most endearing of the four," *New York Times* critic Stephen Holden wrote. "As Cleo takes a wild anarchic [lawless] pleasure in robbing. banks, she also becomes the quartet's fierce mother hen, a protective, self-sacrificing warrior."

Latifah later revealed in her autobiography that the role had been a challenge to her. "I'm not afraid to do roles like Cleo, the hard-core, from-the-hood, down-and-down" bank robber in *Set It Off*. " . . . I worked that role and I played her to a T. It was one of my most challenging parts . . . But it seemed that when that movie came out, everyone wanted to know, 'How much of Cleo is really you?'" Latifah's portrayal of Cleo, who happens to be a lesbian, sparked rumors about her sexuality. "There's still all kinds of speculation about my sexuality, and quite frankly, I'm getting a little tired of it," she explained. " . . . It's insulting when someone asks, 'Are you gay?' A woman cannot be strong, outspoken, competent at running her own business, handle herself physically, play a very convincing role in a movie, know what she wants—and go for it—without being gay? Come on."

The spirit of Sarah Vaughn

Other movie roles followed. Her part in the successful science fiction thriller *Sphere* (1998)—starring Dustin Hoffman, Sharon Stone, and Samuel L. Jackson—was minor, and came to a stinging conclusion. (As *New York Times* critic Janet Maslin noted, "Queen Latifah plays the backup crew member who picks the wrong moment to go on jellyfish patrol.") More substantial was

her role in the 1998 romantic drama *Living Out Loud,* as jazz singer Liz Bailey. Some critics noted that Latifah's performance of such standards as "Lush Life" and "Going Out of My Head" called to mind jazz greats such as Ella Fitzgerald (1918–96) and Sarah Vaughn (b. 1924). "You know, actually I called [on the spirit of Sarah Vaughn]," she told People Online, "and told her, 'Look, if you're feeling this, help me out with it girl. 'Cause you know I don't want to do you any injustice." Most critics agreed that Latifah had done Vaughn justice. Maslin, for instance, raved that the singer ended up "stealing every scene she's in," and that "she becomes the film's most attention-getting figure." Latifah's role as Liz Bailey may not be her last venture into jazz music: she told *Entertainment Weekly* that, if the *Living Out Loud* soundtrack, which contains three of her songs, performs well, she may consider compiling an all-jazz album.

Royal Advice

"I am not a psychologist or a sociologist. I don't have any degrees, and I'm not an expert on life. What I am is a young black woman from the inner city who is making it, despite the odds, despite the obstacles I've had to face.

I have lived in the projects and in fine homes. I have hung out with drug dealers and Presidents. I have had to clean bathrooms for a living and I've had my own maid. I have sold millions of records and won a Grammy. I've made movies that have bombed. I've had to bury my big brother. And I've also wanted to die myself. I've felt like the absolute lowest piece of scum on Earth and I've also felt on top of the world.

Through it all, though, I never forgot who I am. It's what kept me going.
I am a queen."

—from Queen Latifah's autobiography, *Ladies First: Revelations of A Strong Woman*

Life after *Living Single*

Latifah's television career, meanwhile, was cut short. After five successful seasons, *Living Single* was canceled. The actress was both disappointed and puzzled by the Fox executives' decision. "I don't feel that there's another *Living Single*-quality show out of any black shows on TV right now," she explained to People Online. "[*Living Single*] was the number one show among blacks and Latinos when we were *canceled*. So that didn't make sense to me. But you can't control the powers that be." In spite of her disappointment, she took the cancellation in stride. "There's always going to be life after *Living Single*," she told *Jet*. "Life is not about *Living Single*. That was just one part, one thing, one venture that I undertook for my life and it was successful. But it was not the first thing that I've done and it won't be the last."

True to her word, she started work on a new album, *Order in the Court,* shortly after the series went off the air. Released in 1998, the album—which includes hip-hop and rhythm-and-blues tracks—garnered critical raves. *Ebony* critic Lynn Norment wrote that "Queen Latifah shows that she still rules the rap queendom." Similarly, *Entertainment Weekly* reviewer Marc Weingarten said that the album "[reminds] her royal subjects exactly who reigns supreme." Meanwhile, Flavor Unit Entertainment, Latifah's record label and management company, continued to flourish, managing such hot properties as LL Cool J, Outkast, and N.E.X.T.

Also in 1998, Latifah published her autobiography *Ladies First: Revelations of A Strong Woman,* in which she discusses her humble beginnings and troubled past. "This uplifting if somewhat superficial [shallow] book tells the tale of a strong, young African-American who grew up around poverty, drugs and prejudice and followed her head and heart to become a successful and humane woman," wrote *People* critic Mark Bautz. "Less an autobiography than a motivational tract," *Publishers Weekly* noted, "this book attempts to impart the philosophy behind Latifah's image, and in so doing, "let every woman know that she, too . . . is royalty."

Candid about the fact that she once sold and used drugs, among other problems, Latifah urges readers to learn from their mistakes. "A queen uses her mistakes as a stepladder to climb higher," she wrote. "And I've had a long way to climb."

Sources

Bautz, Mark. Review of *Ladies First. People Weekly,* January 18, 1999, p. 37.

Bing, Jonathon, et al. Review of *Ladies First. Publishers Weekly,* December 14, 1998, p. 69.

Holden, Stephen. "*Set It Off:* Just Trying to Get Even While They Get Rich." *The New York Times,* November 6, 1996.

Maslin, Janet. "*Living Out Loud:* Yada Yada as a Way of Getting Another Life." *The New York Times,* October 30, 1998.

Maslin, Janet. "*Sphere:* Solid, Showy Thriller." *The New York Times,* February 13, 1998.

Norment, Lynn. "Sounding Off." *Ebony,* September 1998, pp. 22 ff.

"Q&A with . . . Queen Latifah," "Queen for a day." People Online. [Online] Available http://www.pathfinder.com/people/ (March 20, 1999).

Queen Latifah. "How to really rule your own life." *Cosmopolitan,* February 1999, pp. 176-179.

"Queen Latifah." alt.culture. [Online] Available http://www.altculture.com/ (March 20, 1999).

Queen Latifah with Karen Hunter. *Ladies First: Revelations of A Strong Woman.* New York: Morrow, 1998.

"Queen Latifah." Lycos Celebrity Guide. [Online] Available http://www-spry. lycos.com/ (March 20, 1999).

"Queen Latifah says 'there's life after *Living Single.*'" *Jet,* July 20, 1998, pp. 34-38.

Review of *Ladies First. Jet,* January 25, 1999, pp. 58 ff.

Weingarten, Marc. Review of *Order in the Court.* EW Online. [Online] Available http://cgi.pathfinder.com/ew/daily/ (March 20, 1999).

Wolk, Josh. "Jazz You Like It." EW Online. [Online] Available http://cgi. pathfinder.com/ew/daily/ (March 20, 1999).

Robert Rodriguez

Born July 20, 1968
San Antonio, Texas

Director, writer, producer

Director Robert Rodriguez burst onto the scene with a super-low budget first feature, *El Mariachi*, which immediately became a hit with critics and film-goers. Next came an equally successful sequel, *Desperado*. Marked by their high energy and confident style reminiscent of Hong Kong action movies, Rodriguez's films soon gathered an impressive cult following and earned the director a reputation as one of the industry's up-and-coming young talents.

A Lonestar loner

Born in San Antonio, Texas, on July 20, 1968, Robert Rodriguez was the third of ten children (five girls and five boys) born to Cecilio and Rebecca Rodriguez. A film fanatic since youth, he saw John Carpenter's *Escape From New York* (1981) when he was in the eighth grade. The film inspired him to shoot his own movies on his father's old Super 8 camera. Soon, he began using a video camera—a much cheaper means of shooting footage. Using his nine siblings as cast and crew, the young director edited his movies using two VCRs.

"It is such a pleasure to watch the way Rodriguez moves the camera, directs actors and cuts and then ties it all together with a brilliant soundtrack. The film whooshes around you."
—Louis Black in the *Austin Chronicle*

(The Kobal Collection)

Interested in both filmmaking and cartooning throughout high school, Rodriguez felt like an outcast. "[A]ll the time growing up I was making little movies or drawings and I didn't know anyone else who was doing the same thing, and you want so desperately to meet somebody else who does the same thing as you," he explained in a Sony interview. "Because you're such a small percentage of the regular population, you feel like such an oddball, an outcast because you do strange things."

Taking the bull by the horns

After graduating from high school, Rodriguez decided to attend the University of Texas at Austin. While taking lower-level classes, he started a comic strip, *Los Hooligans*—whose characters were based on his younger brothers and sisters. The comic strip ran in the *Daily Texan* newspaper for three years, and made the young cartoonist somewhat of a campus celebrity. Having been refused admission to the school's film department because of poor grades, Rodriguez continued to make his own home movies on borrowed Super 8 and video equipment, still using his brothers and sisters as cast and crew. "I felt I had to be very focused and determined at an early age," he explained to *Profiles* magazine. "I didn't want to be in my 20s, without a job and living at home. I knew that if I was going to get anywhere, I had to take the bull by the horns in my early years, when I had the time and energy."

When Rodriguez entered his videotaped movie, *Austin Stories,* in a regional film competition, the judges were dumbfounded (amazed). Louis Black, one of the judges for the film competition, recalled in the *Austin Chronicle:* "We spent the day watching generic [average] film school output—editing and camera movement galore but precious little articulated [well-defined] camerawork (in which the visual exercises actually have something to do with the content of the film). At the end of the day, having watched many, many high production value yet relatively boring films, we watched this video. Homemade, almost an anti-graduate-student-work, it blew everything else away. Robert Rodriguez's *Austin Stories,* three vignettes [short stories] starring brothers and sisters, shot with the family video camera and edited on the family's two antiquated [outdated] video decks, didn't just win, it hands-down beat everything else."

Having beaten university film students in the competition, Rodriguez approached Steven Mims, a professor of film at the University of Texas, to suggest that the department reconsider admitting him. Rodriguez was admitted into the university's Film One project, and soon produced his first 16 millimeter short film (edited on video for just $800). *Bedhead*—a continuation of the humorous family drama, *Austin Stories*— was a smashing success. The eight-minute short was aired on PBS (public television) and garnered numerous awards nationwide, including top honors at the Marin County Film Festival, the ninth annual Third Coast Film Festival, the Atlanta Film and Video Competition, the 11th Annual Edison Black Maria Film Festival, and the Charlotte Film Festival. *Bedhead* also captured awards in prestigious international competitions, including the Melbourne International Film Festival.

El Mariachi

While still in film school, Rodriguez entered a month-long drug research program to earn extra money—and to set aside time to write a script for a low-budget feature film. Using a list of what was available to him as a filmmaker—automatic weapons, guitars, a bulldog, a jail, and buses—he produced the screenplay for *El Mariachi*. He then traveled (during summer break) with his best friend, Carlos Gallardo to Acuna, Mexico, where he had previously shot short films on video. Funding production costs with the money from the drug test, and using Gallardo as his leading man, Rodriguez shot *El Mariachi*.

The story of a guitar player who is transformed into a gun-carrying hero, *El Mariachi* was intended for the Mexican home video market. On a visit to Los Angeles, however, Rodriguez stopped by the office of Robert Newman, a representative of the prestigious ICM talent agency, to give him a trailer (preview) for *El Mariachi* and a copy of *Bedhead*. Newman agreed to represent the film, which Sony's Columbia Pictures purchased for approximately $1 million. Released worldwide, *El Mariachi*—which had been shot on a shoestring budget of $7,000—became the lowest budget movie ever released by a major studio. It also marked the first American release of a Spanish-language film.

Next Rodriguez signed a two-year writing and directing deal with Columbia, which sent him on a tour of international film festivals. The first-time feature filmmaker made the rounds

"I didn't want to be in my 20s, without a job and living at home. I knew that if I was going to get anywhere, I had to take the bull by the horns in my early years, when I had the time and energy."

from Berlin, Germany (where *El Mariachi* captured the Panorama award) to the Uybari Film Festival in Japan (where it was voted Most Entertaining Film). Rodriguez also traveled to festivals in Munich, Germany and Edinburgh, Scotland, as well as the prestigious North American film fests at Telluride, Colorado, Toronto, Canada, and Sundance, in California (where his film captured the audience award for best dramatic film).

More gunplay

Rodriguez soon followed cult favorite *El Mariachi* with a sequel, *Desperado.* "*El Mariachi* was a movie that I originally conceived to be a part of three pictures," he said in a Sony Interview. "I was going to make three movies about the Mariachi, which is why the first one ended the way it did—kind of open-ended with him changing as far as a person, he was no longer going to be able to play the guitar and he was going to go on to be almost like an action hero." As the legendary Mariachi in *Desperado,* Antonio Banderas portrays a guitar player who carries guns in his guitar case and wreaks vengeance on drug dealers. "It's a beautiful character," Rodriguez told Sony. "What I really love about him is he's not like an ex-cop or something turned vigilante. . . . he's an artist who can no longer express himself creatively. So what happens is that he bottles up all his emotions and ultimately explodes. That's kind of what I want people to see."

Road Racers, Four Rooms, and *From Dusk Till Dawn*

Having completed his second feature $200,000 under budget, Rodriguez had earned a reputation as a fast and efficient worker. At the last minute, Columbia put him in charge of a teen-rebel movie for cable television, *Road Racers.* Part of Showtime's *Rebel Highway* series, the $1.3 million movie solidified Rodriguez's reputation as a no-nonsense worker: filming required more than 75 camera set-ups in a day (20 is about average). He also wrote, directed and edited a segment of the film *Four Rooms,* a collection of vignettes that take place in a Los Angeles hotel on New Year's Eve. Of the film's four seg-

ments—directed by independent film directors Allison Anders,
Alexandre Rockwell, Quentin Tarantino, and Rodriguez—*New
York Times* critic Maslin claimed that the young Texan's was
"the only watchable *Rooms* segment."

Rodriguez teamed again with Tarantino on *From Dusk Till
Dawn* (1995), directed by Rodriguez and written by Tarantino.
A genre-bending vampire western, the story revolves around
two escaped convicts (Tarantino and George Clooney) who pick
up an ex-preacher (Harvey Keitel) and his two kids (Juliette
Lewis and Ernest Liu) en route to their meeting place in Mexico—which happens to be a motorcycle joint that's run by vam-
pires. Unapologetically violent, the movie was not to everyone's
taste. *Tucson Weekly* critic Stacey Richter wrote, "This is goofy,
fun entertainment, at least as long as it doesn't make you

Robert Rodriguez's 10-Minute Film School

In "Robert Rodriguez's 10-Minute Film School," the director offers some helpful suggestions for aspiring filmmakers. Says Rodriguez: "You can previsualise your movie and draw it out, but what you should really do is make a blank screen for yourself and watch your movie. Close your eyes and stare at this. Imagine a screen, imagine your movie. Shot for shot, cut for cut. Sit there, close your eyes and get rid of everybody, get rid of all your thoughts in your head except your movie and watch your movie. Is it too slow? Is it too fast? Is it funny? Does it make sense? Watch it and then write down what you see. Write down the shots that you see. And then just go get those shots."

sick." *New York Times* critic Janet Maslin suggested that Rodriguez is capable of better: "Rodriguez demonstrates his talents more clearly than ever—he's visually inventive, quick-witted and a fabulous editor—while still hampering himself with sophomoric [immature] material."

A monster-thriller with Kevin Williamson

Rodriguez next directed *The Faculty* (1998), written by *Scream* screenwriter/director Kevin Williamson. A science fiction-horror film about a high school in Ohio that is being taken over by space aliens, *The Faculty* was generally dismissed by critics as unoriginal, although many noted that Rodriguez's energetic direction provided the film with much of its liveliness.

From his humble beginnings, Rodriguez has proved himself to be a successful director and family man (he and his wife, co-producer Elizabeth Avellán, have a son, Rocket Valentino). Asked what distinguishes a Robert Rodriguez film, the director replied, "Energy." He told a *Profile* reporter: "The crew is small, fast and we shoot with the camera on, so the film looks rougher, more fluid. I grew up in a family of ten. I'm used to seeing everything rushing around. That's why my movies are so frantic. It's very much the way I see things."

Sources

Black, Louis. "Cozying Up to *The Faculty*." *The Austin Chronicle,* December 27, 1998. [Online] Available http://www.opus1.com/~tw/WW/12-27-98/austin_screens_feature1.html (February 3, 1999).

Byerley, Jim. Review of *Desperado*. HBO Film Reviews. [Online] Available http://www.hbo.com/Filmreviews/reviews/desperado.shtml (February 3, 1999).

Corliss, Richard. "The Indie 500." *Time,* August 28, 1995. [Online] Available http://cgi.pathfinder.com/time/magazine (February 3, 1999).

"Info 'bout Robert Rodriguez." [Online] Available http://www.geomatics.kth.se/sjoberg/homepage/robert.htm (February 3, 1999).

Interview of Robert Rodriguez. *Profiles* (Continental Airlines), November 1995. [Online] Available http://www.geomatics.kth.se/sjoberg/homepage/pro-int.htm (February 3, 1999).

Lavin, John A. Review of *Desperado*. *Movie Magazine International,* August, 23, 1995. [Online] Available http://www.shoestring.org/mmi_revs/desperado.html (February 3, 1999).

Maslin, Janet. "Guitarist's Repertory of Songs and Gunfire." *The New York Times,* August 25, 1995.

Maslin, Janet. Review of *From Dusk Till Dawn*. *The New York Times,* January 19, 1996.

Meek, Tom. Review of *The Faculty*. *The Boston Phoenix*. [Online] Available http://www.exposure.co.uk/makers/rodrigez.html (February 3, 1999).

Richter, Stacey. Review of *From Dusk Till Dawn*. *The Tucson Weekly,* January 25, 1996. [Online] Available http://www.opus1.com/~tw/filmvault/tw/f/FromDuskTillDawn_f.html (February 3, 1999).

"Robert Rodriguez: Guerrilla Film-maker." [Online] Available http://www.exposure.co.uk/makers/rodrigez.html (February 3, 1999).

"Robert Rodriguez's 10-Minute Film School." [Online] Available http://www.exposure.co.uk/makers/minute.html#books (February 3, 1999).

"Sony Interview with Robert Rodriguez." [Online] Available http://www.geomatics.kth.se/sjoberg/homepage/sony-int.htm (February 3, 1999).

Adam Sandler

Born September 9, 1966
New York, New York

Actor, comedian, musician

> "I'm the funniest guy in my bathtub. I know that for sure."

(AP/Wide World)

Whether as class clown, stand-up comic, *Saturday Night Live* performer, or movie star, Adam Sandler has perfected a unique brand of brainless humor that dumbfounds critics while smashing box-office expectations. While many find his comedy tasteless and humorless, Sandler has won a large and loyal following. His first comedy album broke sales records and was nominated for a Grammy Award. And thanks to movies such as *The Waterboy,* which broke box office records, the former class clown has earned blockbuster status in Hollywood. Sandler's amazing rise to celebrity has left more than a few people scratching their heads in disbelief. "I can't believe he's making all that money for things he was being punished for here [in high school]," Isabel Pellerin, the official disciplinarian at Sandler's high school, told *People.* "I thought he would grow up. Instead he grew rich."

A born performer

Born in Brooklyn, New York (one of the five boroughs of New York City), Adam Sandler was the youngest son of Stan, an engineer, and Judy, a homemaker. Even as a child, the aspiring comic was "perpetually performing," his mother told *People*. Sandler first stepped onto a stage at the age of eleven, when his mother coaxed him into singing at his sister's wedding. Encouraged by the audience's response to his performance of Ringo Starr's "You're Sixteen," he decided to sing another song. "It went over so well, I sang another one," he told *Edmonton Sun* reporter Steve Tilley. "And after the second one, [the audience] was like, 'All right, get off. You're boring us.'"

Raised in Manchester, New Hampshire, he was neither a top student nor an accomplished athlete. A self-described misfit, he was often disciplined in school for clowning around in class. "Teachers would ask him to leave the class," Sandler's high school principal Bob Schiavone told *Scholastic Scope,* "but they were laughing while they asked."

In spite of his undisputed title as class clown, Sandler did not originally consider pursuing a career as a comic. "[M]y brother is the one who said, 'You should go be a comedian,'" he told E! Online. Seventeen years old and uncertain about his future, he decided to give stand-up comedy a try. His first experience—a spontaneous performance at a club in Boston—did not go well. But Sandler was hooked. "[I]t was the first time in my life where I said, 'All right. I think I can.' I became kind of obsessed with getting good at comedy. Growing up, I wasn't great at anything."

After graduating from Manchester Central High School in 1984, Sandler enrolled in New York University to pursue a degree in fine arts. Not all of his attention was focused on his studies. As a freshman he landed a recurring role on the popular NBC series, *The Cosby Show*—as Theo Huxtable's friend, Smitty. He also spent several nights a week performing at Manhattan comedy clubs. Not every performance was a hit. "Some nights I had absolutely no laughs," he told *Toronto Sun* reporter Bob Thompson. "There would be a lot of angry energy, but I was too young to notice." In no time, the young comic struck a chord with audiences. A former doorman for the Comic Strip, where Sandler once performed, told *People:* "He was onstage for 15 minutes, and he had only told two jokes, and the audience was laughing hysterically. All he was doing was standing there." Sandler graduated from NYU with a bachelor's degree in fine arts in 1991.

"With Adam it was never about the material. He was just so likable." –Lucien Hold, talent coordinator for Manhattan's Comic Strip, where Sandler performed as a young comic

Live, on Saturday Night

After performing at numerous New York clubs and universities, Sandler took his act to Los Angeles, California, where he worked the local comedy club circuit. During one performance at L.A.'s Improv, he caught the eye of comic Dennis Miller. The former *Saturday Night Live* cast member convinced producer Lorne Michaels to take a look at the young comedian. Soon, Sandler had a spot on the NBC show that had launched many comedic careers.

Joining SNL during the 1990–91 season, Sandler worked primarily as a writer. His occasional performances, however, soon attracted the notice of critics and viewers—for better or worse. One critic called Sandler "The most talentless, juvenile, and offensive member of the current cast." But Sandler's outrageous performances as Cajunman, Canteen Boy, Iraqi Pete, and Opera Man soon attracted legions of loyal fans.

Two years into his five-year stint at SNL, Sandler released his first album of comedy material. Primarily a collection of adolescent humor, *they're all gonna laugh at you!* was nominated for a Grammy Award and spent more than one hundred weeks on *Billboard* magazine's Heatseakers charts. Also during his time at SNL, he ventured into films, taking small parts in unmemorable productions such as *Airheads, Coneheads, Mixed Nuts,* and *Shakes the Clown.*

A yen to re-live the third grade

Having co-written the script for *Billy Madison* (1994), Sandler took the lead role in the flimsy story of a wealthy kid who has six months to repeat grades one through twelve in order to earn his inheritance. Although popular with Sandler's die-hard fans, the film was dismissed by critics. *New York Times* critic Janet Maslin wrote: "This *Saturday Night Live* regular is at his most bearable in *Billy Madison,* which is to say that the random idiocies and squeaky-voiced singing are kept under control. . . . If you've ever had a yen to relive the third grade, this must be the next best thing."

Faint praise aside, *Billy Madison* performed well enough to encourage Sandler to quit SNL in 1995 to pursue a film career. Next came *Happy Gilmore,* the story of a hockey player who discovers a unique flair for playing golf. "Sandler's second starring vehicle is better than his first (last year's pinbrained

Billy Madison)," wrote *People* critic Tom Gliatto, "but we're talking about increments [degrees] barely visible to the human eye." Further, he wrote, "Sandler's appeal remains a mystery."

But Sandler's appeal could not be denied. Poor reviews or not, audiences were flocking to the comic's films. In its first weekend, *Happy Gilmore* earned $10.1 million, beating out the popular children's movie, *Muppet Treasure Island*. The newly appointed film star joked, "Give Kermit my humblest apologies, but I need the money more than he does." Peter Travers explained the comedian's mystifying appeal in *Rolling Stone:* "It's a love/hate thing with Adam Sandler. Critics don't send him valentines. 'Mindless,' 'inane' [silly] and 'remarkably juvenile' are the kinder blurbs his comedy has elicited. But in the hearts that beat in adolescents of all ages . . . Sandler is king."

Not quite bullet-proof

Having produced a surprise hit during the 1995 holiday season— *Hanukkah Song,* a musical spoof of the Jewish holiday— Sandler released his second album, *What the Hell Happened to Me?* the following year. (The album included the popular Hanukkah tune, which had become one of the most-requested songs ever on major radio stations across the country.) Following the album with a twelve-city comedy and music tour, he played to sold-out crowds of hard-core fans.

Also in 1996, Sandler co-starred with Damon Wayons in *Bulletproof,* an action-comedy in which a policeman attempts to escort a drug dealer from Arizona to Los Angeles. While the film was considered a failure, *Village Voice* critic Frank Ruscitti admitted that Sandler had his funny moments. "Adam Sandler steals the movie as the drug connection, his singing shower scene ranking with the one in [Jim Carrey's] *Ace Ventura: Pet Detective*." Similarly, *New York Times* critic Stephen Holden referred to Sandler's singing shower scene as "one of the few moments in *Bulletproof* to capture the spirit of goofy playfulness that is painfully absent throughout much of the rest of this blood-drenched action comedy."

The king of dumb comedy

After releasing a third, profanity-filled album titled *What's Your Name?* in 1997, Sandler next teamed with Drew Barrymore in the romantic comedy, *The Wedding Singer*. As Robbie Hart, he portrays a good-natured lead singer for a band that plays at weddings. After being dumped by his fianceé, he begins to fall in love with a sweet banquet waitress who is engaged to a sleazy Wall Street trader. "The ultimate goal was to make people laugh, but my character had to be believably in love," the actor told E! Online. "You have to believe that this guy wants to be with this woman and that he's got some pain because he can't be with her. I didn't want to only make fun of that. I could relate to Robbie Hart. I'm working on being him." *The Wedding Singer* was a box-office smash that prompted some film reviewers to take a second look at Sandler. Peter

Travers, for example, urged: "For those who've written Sandler off as a taste not worth acquiring, *The Wedding Singer* offers a strong case for reconsideration."

When *The Waterboy* was released at the end of 1998, film critics—again—had few kind words to spare. "Like other dumb comedies," the Mr. Showbiz review announced, "Adam Sandler movies are best seen in their trailer [movie preview] form. . . .If you've seen the trailer, you've already seen the film at its best." Yet again, in spite of scathing critical reviews, audiences flocked to theaters—this time to watch Sandler's portrayal of Bobby Boucher, "former water distribution engineer." So successful was the movie that it raked in an amazing $39.4 million in ticket sales in its opening weekend. (It cost just $19 million to make.) The most successful film ever to open in November or December (summer releases typically perform better at the box office), *The Waterboy* edged out Jim Carrey's wildly popular 1995 comedy, *Ace Ventura: When Nature Calls,* which yielded $37.8 million. Having proved his box-office potential, Sandler became one of a handful of actors under the age of forty who command a $20 million salary per film. (The $20 Million Club includes actors Jim Carrey, Tom Cruise, and Will Smith, among others.) Just months after the film's release, the actor announced his engagement to model Jackie Titone.

In 1999's *Big Daddy,* Sandler plays the part of a single man who adopts a young son to impress his girlfriend. While comedic at times, the role is a serious one as his character slowly realizes that he loves the boy—and not just as a ploy to win back his girlfriend. The role is an extreme break-away from his usual goofy characters, but Sandler does not worry about picking the right roles. "I don't think people say, 'I wonder what Adam's next movie is going to be,'" he told E! Online. "My movies just kind of sneak up on you. I don't have to worry too much about what everybody is going to say. Anyway, I really don't pay attention to what the world says about my movies. I just care about what my buddies think."

Not An Early Bird

In *Happy Gilmore,* Sandler plays a former hockey player who turns to golf. Portraying a golfer wasn't much of a stretch for the Brooklyn-born comic. "I was raised in New Hampshire around a lot of hockey nuts, but I never played myself because I couldn't get up early enough for practice. I chose to play golf instead because I could set my own tee time."

Sources

"Adam Sandler: Opera man...waterboy...funny guy!" *Scholastic Scope,* January 25, 1999, p. 22.

"Adam Sandler Star Bio." Celebsite. [Online] Available http://www.expressnet.lycos.com/ (February 18, 1999).

"Adam Sandler to Tie the Knot." Mr. Showbiz, January 15, 1999. [Online] Available www.mrshowbiz.com/. (February 18, 1999).

Adams, Kathleen et al. "Real news stories this week that could become plots for Adam Sandler's next movie." *Time,* November 23, 1998, p. 39.

Braunstein, Peter. "Everybody pays the fool." *The Village Voice,* November 24, 1998, p. 65.

Bruno, Mary. "Adam Sandler hits the road." Mr. Showbiz. [Online] Available www.mrshowbiz.com/ (February 18, 1999).

Corliss, Richard. "Sandler happens." *Time,* November 23, 1998, p. 102.

Gliatto, Tom. Review of *Billy Madison. People,* February 27, 1995, p. 18.

Gliatto, Tom. Review of *Happy Gilmore. People,* February 26, 1996, p. 17.

Holden, Stephen. *"Bulletproof:* Blood-Drenched Comedy." *The New York Times,* September 6, 1996.

Maslin, Janet. "Haphazardly Repeating Grades 1-12." *The New York Times,* February 11, 1995.

"Q&A: Adam Sandler." E! Online. [Online] Available http://www.eonline.com/ (February 18, 1999).

Review of *The Waterboy.* Mr. Showbiz. [Online] Available www.mrshowbiz.com/ (February 18, 1999).

Rozen, Leah. Review of *The Waterboy. People,* November 16, 1998, p. 32.

Ruscitti, Frank. Review of *Bulletproof. The Village Voice,* September 17, 1996, p. 80.

Schneider, Karen S. "Last laugh." *People,* November 30, 1998, pp. 73-76.

Thompson, Bob. "The Adam Family." *Toronto Sun,* February 8, 1998 [Online] Available http://www.canoe.ca/JamMoviesArtistsS/sandler_adam.html (February 18, 1999).

Tilley, Steve. "Sandler's High Note." *The Edmonton Sun,* February 4, 1998. [Online] Available http://www.canoe.ca/JamMoviesArtistsS/sandler_adam.html (February 18, 1999).

Travers, Peter. Review of *The Wedding Singer. Rolling Stone,* March 5, 1998, pp. 73-74.

"The Waterboy floods B.O." Mr. Showbiz, November 9, 1998. [Online] Available www.mrshowbiz.com/ (February 18, 1999).

Jerry Seinfeld

Born April 29, 1954
New York, New York

Comedian, actor

UPDATE

Having ventured into the comedy circuit after college, Jerry Seinfeld soon became a stand-out performer in the stand-up arena. By 1990, he had become a true comedic star, landing frequent appearances on *The Tonight Show* and *Late Night with David Letterman,* among others. But it was not until 1990, with the debut of his NBC sitcom, that the name Seinfeld became a household name. *Seinfeld,* which debuted as a mid-season replacement show, immediately earned critical raves along with a large and die-hard popular following. Peopled with believable characters and set in a recognizable Manhattan apartment, the show was celebrated for its outrageous plots—plots that, ironically, revolved around *nothing.* **(See original entry on Seinfeld in *Performing Artists,* Volume 3.)**

A period of national mourning

"I'm hardly interested in my own life," Jerry Seinfeld once complained to a reporter from the *New York Post* (cited in *Time*). "I don't know how you could be interested." But interest in Sein-

> "I would like to be considered a great comedian. I don't think I'm there yet."

(AP/Wide World)

193

Lucrative Laughter

In 1998—the fateful year when *Seinfeld* aired its final episode—comedian Jerry Seinfeld earned the top spot on *Forbes* magazine's annual ranking of the nation's highest-paid entertainers. According to that magazine, Seinfeld earned $225 million *in 1998 alone*. Second on the list was Larry David—the *Seinfeld* co-creator who wrote the series' final episode. And that's not all: *Forbes* estimated that *Seinfeld,* the series, was the single most profitable piece of entertainment in history.

feld's life—no matter how uneventful—seems to be a fact of life, even in the wake of his self-canceled television show.

By the end of its final season *Seinfeld* and cast had collected a slew of awards, including an American Comedy Award for Funniest TV Series Actor (1992), an Emmy for Outstanding Comedy Series (1993), a Golden Globe for Best Television Series, Comedy or Musical (1993), a Screen Actors Guild Award for Outstanding Performance by an Ensemble in a Comedy Series (1994, 1996, and 1997), and a People's Choice Award for Favorite TV Comedy Series (1998). Although some critics complained that the show experienced too-frequent rough spots during its final years, viewers continued to tune in to the series—and in impressive numbers. The decision to stop the show was not made by NBC, but by Jerry Seinfeld and the rest of the cast. After eight years, they wanted to go out on top, while they were still producing quality television. When the plan to cancel the successful sitcom was announced in late 1997, *Seinfeld,* then approaching its ninth season, was the nation's top-rated sitcom.

So popular was the show that it had become somewhat of a cultural phenomenon. And news of its cancellation was widely mourned like a death in the family. "The run-up to the show's final episode was a period of national mourning," reported *Time* Asia, "filled with high-flown elegies [poems lamenting the dead] and exhaustive studies of the Seinfeld canon [body of works]." The cover to the following week's *People* magazine pleaded, "SAY IT AIN'T SO!," adding, "A stunned nation prepares for life without *Seinfeld.*"

Shot over a nine-day period under a veil of secrecy, the final episode aired on May 14, 1998. Preceded by months of hoopla, the seventy-five minute farewell was harshly criticized as a tremendous let-down. Many found the finale—in which the four friends are carted off to jail—to be too dark and disturbing. In spite of mixed reactions to the final episode, the series remains a lucrative (profitable) phenomenon. Two weeks after the finale aired, *Rolling Stone* magazine reported that a second run of syndication (reruns) was expected to generate $1.5 billion.

Journey to the center of the universe

Having completed work on the sitcom, Seinfeld—who had been living in Hollywood Hills, near Los Angeles, California—returned to his native New York. "I really don't dislike Los Angeles," he explained to *Rolling Stone*. "I just love New York. That's where I belong. . . . For me, New York is the only place. It is the center of the humor universe, New York. That is where all humor is born. Everything else is just imitating that."

Once re-established in New York, Seinfeld spent his "retirement" preparing to return to his career roots—as a stand-up comedian. Many applauded the former television star's return to his comedic roots. Former stand-up comic David Spade, for instance, told *Time,* "It's nice that someone still cares about stand-up and doesn't just see it as a stepping-stone." Seinfeld launched his return to stand-up with a month-long world tour, which started in Australia and ventured to Sweden and Iceland. Arriving in London, England—land of the soccer-crazed—in the midst of the World Cup finals, the comedian still managed to pack theaters to capacity. Next he launched a U.S. tour that started in San Antonio, Texas, and finished . . . in the center of the humor universe, on Broadway, in New York City's theater district. Tickets to all ten performances sold out in one day.

Seinfeld proved that he hadn't lost his stand-up savvy. "[His] stand-up act is terrific, better than the final episode, and better, in fact, than many episodes from [the 1997–98] season," wrote *Newsweek*'s Yahlin Chang. ". . . . [his] humor remains more innocent than cutting-edge—but with his perfect timing, flawless delivery and sheer good nature, who cares?" Those who weren't able to land a $60 ticket to one of Seinfeld's performances were able to catch the performance on cable television. Seinfeld's August 9, 1998, show was broadcast live as an HBO special called "I'm Telling You for the Last Time."

As to the question whether he intends to do another sitcom, Seinfeld lays the issue to rest. "Not on your life," he insisted during a question-and-answer session at the end of his

---

Life after *Seinfeld*

Soon after the last episode of *Seinfeld* aired, the series' namesake was back on stage performing his stand-up routine. As for the other cast members, life after the much-heralded sitcom held a diverse assortment of projects. Jason Alexander (George) starred as Boris Badenov in a 1999 live-action *Rocky and Bullwinkle* movie; Julia Louis-Dreyfus (Elaine) was heard in the animated movie *A Bug's Life* as the voice of the princess; and Michael Richards (Kramer) appeared as Mr. Micawber in TNT's production of *David Copperfield*.

Broadway run. "What happened to [*Seinfeld*] was crazy. This [stand-up comedy] is my actual profession. The sitcom was just a weird hobby. This is what I like, coming to talk to people."

Sources

"The Best People of 1998." *Time* Asia, December 21, 1998. [Online] Available http://cgi.pathfinder.com/time/asia/magazine/ (March 17, 1999).

Chang, Yahlin. "Still a stand-up guy." *Newsweek,* August 3, 1998, pp. 70 ff.

"Fact Sheet—Jerry Seinfeld." E! Online. [Online] Available http://www.eonline. com/Facts/People/ (March 17, 1999).

Handy, Bruce. "It's All About Timing." *Time,* January 12, 1998. [Online] Available http://cgi.pathfinder.com/time/magazine/ (March 17, 1999).

Heath, Chris. "The end." *Rolling Stone,* May 28, 1998, pp. 64 ff.

McDowell, Jeanne. "Seinfeld: The Retirement Years." *Time,* December 28, 1998-January 4, 1999, p. 154.

Ressner, Jeffrey. "As for The Old Master . . . " *Time,* August 10, 1998, p. 81.

Silverman, Stephen M. "Seinfeld Laughs All the Way to the Bank." Time Daily, September 8, 1998. [Online] Available http://cgi.pathfinder. com/time/daily/ (March 17, 1999).

Jada Pinkett Smith

Born September 18, 1971
Baltimore, Maryland

Actress

Asked if there were someone whose career she would like to pattern hers after, Jada Pinkett Smith told E! Online, "I want people to look at me how they look at [Academy Award-winning actress] Glenn Close. You look at her body of work, and I swear, it's just like, 'God! How does she do all these things?' She can do anything." During her short but active film career, Pinkett Smith, too, has proved she can do anything. Playing roles in everything from action and horror movies to romantic comedies, she has avoided being typecast (repeatedly being cast in the same type of role). "I can only work with people who can appreciate my input and what I have to say," she said. "I'm not a puppet. I'm not just gonna be on somebody's string to dangle around. I just refuse to do that." Already a media darling, the self-confident and glamorous Pinkett Smith saw her star-appeal skyrocket when she began dating handsome television and film star Will Smith, whom she married in 1997. Smith told *Ebony*, "Jada is an intellectual goddess. She just understands life . . . the parameters of living."

"I want people to look at my body of work and say, 'Do you see all the stuff this woman did? She went from horror to action to comedy to drama. I mean, goodness gracious! How did she do all this?'"

(AP/Wide World)

An independent child

Robsol Pinkett, Jr., a contractor, and Adrienne Banfield, a nurse, divorced after they were married less than one year—around the time their daughter, Jada, was born. Raised by her mother and grandmother, Marion Banfield, Pinkett Smith grew up in Pimlico, a tough neighborhood in northwest Baltimore, Maryland. "Being raised by a single parent forced me to be independent," Pinkett Smith told *Cosmopolitan* reporter Kevin Maynard. "I had to learn how to dress and feed myself early on." Marion Banfield, a social worker, instilled in her grandchild a sense of self-confidence and personal ambition. "She taught me that I can achieve whatever I want to achieve," the actress told *People* reporter Shelley Levitt. "Grandma wanted her grandchildren to have every possible experience—ballet, tap dancing, piano lessons, gymnastics. She didn't ever want us to ever think we were deprived."

From a very young age, Pinkett Smith wanted to be a performer. She was just five years old when she first appeared on stage. "I played the Wicked Witch of the West," she explained in the *Virginian Pilot*. "Or is it the East? Anyway, I never got over it." By her teens, she had become serious about acting. At the age of 14 she entered the Baltimore School for the Arts, where she studied music and dance. There she became friends with fellow student Tupac Shakur, who enjoyed a successful career as a rapper and actor before being killed in 1996. Although she never got into serious trouble as a teenager, Pinkett Smith admitted to *Interview* reporter Karen Brailsford that she "barely graduated" from high school. Nevertheless, she enrolled in college at the North Carolina School for the Arts in Winston-Salem. After her first year, the nineteen-year-old aspiring actress decided to move to Los Angeles, California, to try her luck in Hollywood.

A menace to Hollywood

Early during her stay in Los Angeles, Pinkett Smith met actor Keenen Ivory Wayans at a party. Although she had no professional experience, she asked Wayans—creator of the successful Fox television comedy *In Living Color*— for a job as a choreographer (dance arranger) on his show. Wayans did not offer her a job; but he did offer her some advice. Pinkett Smith explained to *Entertainment Weekly* reporter Heather Keets, "He encouraged me to get off my lazy tail, get an agent, and do something."

She followed his advice—and within six months of her arrival in L.A., landed her first part. After fifteen auditions, she won the role of Lena James, a tough college student from Baltimore, on the popular NBC television sitcom, *A Different World*. During her two years on the show, Pinkett Smith matured as an actress, and eventually attracted the notice of two aspiring filmmakers. Allen and Albert Hughes, teenaged twin brothers who had previously directed music videos, had managed to put together $2 million to produce an independent film called *Menace II Society*. The Hugheses wanted Pinkett Smith to play a single mother in their big-screen debut. At first, she was not interested in the part because of the movie's uncompromising violence. After discussing the project with the brothers, however, she decided to accept the role. "When I started to look at my character, Ronnie, I realized that for the first time you're seeing a young, responsible single mother," she told *Interview*. " . . . Most of the time black women within that element are drug addicts, hookers, loudmouths, what have you. I had to give the [Hughes] brothers props." The story of African American teenagers lost in the inner-city hell of south central Los Angeles, *Menace II Society* (1993) garnered critical acclaim and numerous awards, including an Independent Spirit Award for Best Cinematography and an MTV Movie Award for Best Film.

More than a horror queen

Teaming with the Hughes brothers had been a wise move. Widely admired for her performance in the low-budget drama, Pinkett Smith next took a part in the 1994 comedy-drama *The Inkwell*. The actress described her character, in *Interview*, as "a snooty don't-know nothing." Also that year she played the role of Lyric, a soul-food waitress, in *Jason's Lyric*. Marred by a weak story focused on violence, the film did not fare well at the box office—or among critics. *A Low Down Dirty Shame*—in which Pinkett Smith played Peaches, the wisecracking secretary of a private detective—received no more praise from crit-

Pam Grier Blazes the Trail

Ernest R. Dickerson's *Tales from the Crypt: Demon Knight* (1995)—which features Pinkett Smith as a platinum blonde enemy of evil—marks the first appearance of a female African American action hero in nearly twenty years. In the 1970s, Pam Grier (b. 1949) became a box-office phenomenon playing strong, resourceful women in a series of low-budget black action films including *Coffy, Foxy Brown,* and *Sheba, Baby.* "Foxy and Coffy and the rest were heroines of the women's movement," Grier later told *The New York Times.* "They showed women how to be assertive and self-sufficient, not passive victims." (Although entertaining, these movies were hardly examples of high art: filled with scantily clad women and laughable dialogue, they belonged to a low-budget genre of urban dramas known as "blaxploitation" movies.)

Grier's career slowed after the 1970s. She played small film roles in *Fort Apache, the Bronx* (1981), *Above the Law* (1988), and *Mars Attacks!* (1996). She also appeared in television shows such as *Miami Vice* and *Martin.* But it was not until 1997 that she regained her former celebrity, appearing in the title role of Quentin Tarantino's *Jackie Brown.* Also in 1997, Grier worked with Pinkett Smith in the romantic comedy, *Woo.* Diagnosed with cancer in 1988, Grier was given 18 months to live. She beat the odds, however. "It was such an unbelievable roller coaster," she told *The New York Times.* "But since 1990 I've been healthy and I realize what a miracle it is to be here."

ics. Even so, Pinkett Smith managed to impress film critics while co-starring with her friend Wayans.

In 1995's *Tales from the Crypt: Demon Knight,* Pinkett Smith played Jeryline—Hollywood's first female African American action hero since the 1970s, when Pam Grier earned cult celebrity status as an action hero. The actress decided to dye her hair platinum blonde for the part: "It was something I thought would really work for my character," she told Brailsford in *Interview.* It was not the first time Pinkett Smith had colored her hair: she told E! Online, "Even when I was in high school, I was like, 'I'll rip up my jeans and just dye my hair fuchsia.' It was just wanting to show the difference between me and the rest of the world."

After *Tales from the Crypt,* Pinkett Smith was offered a part in *Vampire in Brooklyn,* with Eddie Murphy. She chose not to take the role. "[Murphy] wanted me to do *Vampire in Brooklyn* with him," she explained to *Jet.* "But, I couldn't because I'd just finished *Demon Night* which was also a horror film. And I didn't want to become a horror queen. And Angela Bassett did 100 percent better than I could have ever done. I loved the character, a female lead that was full and had something to do." Instead, Pinkett Smith accepted a less significant

part, as timid college professor Carla Purdy, in *The Nutty Professor*, also starring Murphy. "I wanted to work with Eddie," she explained to *Jet*. "But I knew that on the page Carla Purdy wasn't about anything. I did the project because I wanted to work with him. . . .[the part] was very difficult for me because I had to play straight, innocent, vulnerable. And that was something audiences hadn't seen me do before. I think critics and people were surprisingly pleased to see that side of me." The film grossed $130 million, substantially increasing the actress's box-office clout [influence]. *Cosmopolitan* observed, "*The Nutty Professor* propelled her film career into high gear."

As Cleo, a member of a team of women bank robbers in *Set It Off*, Pinkett Smith again showed audiences something they hadn't seen before. She told *Entertainment Weekly*, "I thought

Jada Pinkett Smith plays it straight opposite funny-man Eddie Murphy in The Nutty Professor. *(The Kobal Collection)*

A Short Scream

"You know, African Americans aren't in horror movies very much, and if they are, they're the first to be killed," Pinkett Smith told the *Virginian Pilot*. As Maureen in *Scream 2*, Pinkett Smith was, in fact, one of the first to be killed—but she still received top billing for her few minutes of screen time.

it would be hilarious to have this little short girl play this macho lesbian." *Set It Off* also featured Queen Latifah, Vivica A. Fox, Blair Underwood, and Kimberly Elise. Also that year she appeared in *If These Walls Could Talk*, a three-part made-for-cable movie which aired on HBO. Focused on the topic of abortion, the trilogy is set in three different eras: 1952, 1974, and 1996.

A wide range of roles

In 1997, Pinkett Smith returned to the horror genre—one of her personal favorites. "I love horror flicks," she told the *Virginian Pilot*. "*Nightmare on Elm Street* is my favorite. I love to yell at the screen. You yell 'Don't go back in that room. You're crazy,' and, of course, she goes right back into the room." As Maureen in *Scream 2*—a character she describes as "just a little college missy"—Pinkett Smith was wildly popular with audiences, even though she had doubts about her performance. "Wes Craven was very cool in directing [*Scream 2*]," she explained in the *Virginian Pilot*. " . . . I think Wes and the actors did a lot to shape it. I said 'Wes, you're the man. Tell me what to do. I'll do anything.' I really got into it. I thought I went over the top, but Wes kept saying, 'More. I want more.'" Film critics deemed Pinkett Smith's performance good—but brief: she plays a skeptical moviegoer who is killed off just as the film gets under way.

The following year Pinkett Smith appeared in *Return to Paradise,* a drama about three friends (played by Vince Vaughn, Joaquin Phoenix, and David Conrad) who are torn apart when one is arrested for drug possession in Malaysia. The film, based on a 1989 French thriller called *Force Majeure,* did little to further Pinkett Smith's career. In a lukewarm review, a *People* reviewer wrote, "*Paradise* has several rough patches (particularly a subplot involving Pinkett Smith as an interfering reporter)." Also that year Pinkett Smith assumed her first starring role as Darlene "Woo" Bates in *Woo,* a romantic comedy about a blind date gone wrong. Tommy Davidson (a former *In Living Color* cast member) co-stars as the law student who falls for the sassy young woman. "Woo is a very extreme version of who I was at 17," the actress explained to E! Online. "Woo is, basically, a very energetic, self-centered young woman with a lot of charisma. She's exploring the world, trying to find herself. She has no idea what she wants, what she needs or what she's doing." The movie was panned by critics, although some recognized Pinkett Smith's misused ability. Melanie McFarland wrote in the *Seattle Times,* for instance, that "Pinkett Smith deserves better; she's proved her dramatic mettle [strength] in past work and is capable of working the same box-office magic as her husband, Will."

The fresh princess

The actress met rapper and actor Will Smith in 1990, while auditioning for the part of his girlfriend on the sitcom *Fresh Prince of Bel Air.* Pinkett Smith did not win the part: the show's producers thought that she was too short, at five feet tall, to play opposite the 6'2" rap artist. She never dreamed that Smith—who was at that time married to Sheree Zampino — would become a romantic interest in her life. "I perceived Will Smith as the goofy Fresh Prince on the show," she told *Ebony.* "Every time I'd see him, that's the way he was acting." Marriage, fatherhood (his first marriage produced one son, Willard C. Smith II, known as Trey), and eventually divorce helped him to mature, she said. When Smith's marriage ended in 1995, the two began to spend time together. "I helped him understand what happened in his marriage," she told *People.* "He's become my best friend."

Asked when they planned to tie the knot, Pinkett Smith repeatedly told reporters that she was in no hurry to pronounce marriage vows. "I'm not in any rush to get married," she told *Jet* in 1996. "The only time I'm going to get married is when I have kids. . . . I think people don't think about the concept of marriage. People fantasize and romanticize about it, but it's a very, very serious situation. And I think people take it way too light today. That's why you have people getting married and divorced at the drop of a hat. I'm not going to be one of those people. When I decide to get married, that is going to be the man I spend my life with."

After living together for two and a half years, the couple were married in front of family and friends on New Years Eve, 1997, at the elegant Cloister's Mansion outside of Baltimore. (The couple had already been secretly wed at a private ceremony in Mexico.) The following July, their first child, Jaden, was born. When a *Virginian Pilot* reporter asked what qualities

"I'm extremely ambitious. I won't sell my soul to the devil, but I do want success and I don't think that's bad." –Pinkett Smith, *Cosmopolitan*

she would most like her baby to have, she answered, "Self esteem, and the ability to make decisions—quick."

Sources

Brailsford, Karen V. "The sass of '94." *Interview,* September 1994, p. 136.

Collier, Alore D. "What Jada wants, Jada gets." *Ebony,* December 1996, p. 144.

Entertainment Weekly, October 7, 1994; December 9, 1994; December 23, 1994; February 24, 1995; May 19, 1995; November 8, 1996; November 15, 1996; May 2, 1997.

Gerston, Jill. "Pam Grier finally escapes the 1970s." *The New York Times,* December 21, 1997.

"Jada Pinkett talks about her movie career, Will Smith, and the future." *Jet,* October 21, 1996, p. 36.

"Jada Said It." Delores Darling. [Online] Available http://www.deloresdarling.com (December 28, 1998).

Maynard, Kevin. "Jada Pinkett—Mrs. Smith is one hot babe!" *Cosmopolitan,* June 1998, pp. 204-205.

McFarland, Melanie, *Seattle Times,* May 8, 1998, "Woo's world is one to be easily missed." [Online] Available http://www.seattletimes.com (December 28, 1998).

Mills, Nancy. "Jada Pinkett interview." *Cosmopolitan,* December 1996, p. 114.

Norment, Lynn. "Will Smith & Jada Pinkett: Making superstardom and love work." *Ebony,* September, 1997, pp. 132-136.

People Weekly, July 29, 1996, p. 96; November 18, 1996, p. 21; January 19, 1998, p.52.

Rozen, Leah. "Return to Paradise." People Online. [Online] Available http://www.pathfinder.com (December 28, 1998).

Vincent, Mal. "Jada Pinkett makes a good (but quick) impression in Scream 2." *The Virginian Pilot.* [Online] Available http://www.newstimes.com (December 28, 1998).

"Will and Jada Smith had secret marriage," *Jet,* April 6, 1998, p. 26.

"Will Smith and Jada Pinkett Expecting First Child," "Mrs. Smith goes on the record about wooing Will," E! Online. [Online] Available http://www.eonline.com (December 28, 1998).

Will Smith

Born September 25, 1968
Philadelphia, Pennsylvania

Actor, rap artist

UPDATE

Raised in Philadelphia, Pennsylvania, Will Smith began his career as a rap musician and soon branched out as an actor. Starring in the popular NBC sitcom, *Fresh Prince of Bel Air,* he was nominated for a Golden Globe award for Best Comedy Actor in 1993, and shortly thereafter made his first film appearance in *Made in America.* Although his role was small, it marked the first in a series of successful—and increasingly significant—movie roles the rapper-turned-actor would make his own. **(See original entry on Smith in *Performing Artists,* Volume 3.)**

Lights, camera, ACTION!

One of a few rap artists to work successfully in both hip-hop and film, Will Smith now commands between $12 million and $20 million for a feature film appearance. His most successful album, *Big Willie Style,* produced spectacular sales results on its way to becoming a *quadruple* platinum release (over four million units sold; an album achieves "platinum" status when it sells one million copies.) While his meteoric rise to celebrity may seem as ef-

"I feel very little external pressure to achieve or do anything at all. I'm much more comfortable with failure than with not attempting something."

(The Kobal Collection)

205

fortless as his lyrics, Smith—who earned a prestigious NAACP (National Association for the Advancement of Colored People) image award in 1999—insists that it is the result of hard work and determination. "It may look like I walk into things and just do 'em," he told *Premiere*. "And there's probably a part of me that wants it to look like that. It's a psychological advantage to look as if you're not trying too hard. But the truth is, while other people are out playing around, out at the club and hanging out, I'm reading the script again. It's the same thing with making music. While other people are out trying to see what kind of car they want to buy, I'm in the studio."

Careful in the management of his career, Smith decided—before taking on *Bad Boys* (1995)—that it was time to add an action film to his repertoire (body of work). He explained to *Premiere* that "the way to be the greatest movie star ever would be to combine Eddie Murphy, Tom Hanks, and Arnold Schwarzenegger." Six seasons playing the lead role in the popular television series *Fresh Prince of Bel-Air* had established both Smith's comic and regular-guy appeal. But he had yet to prove himself as an action hero. That soon changed. "Just that one scene [in *Bad Boys*], where I'm running down the street with a gun, my shirt open, you know, just pure testosterone. That was the missing piece." In spite of lukewarm reviews, the film—which paired Smith with comedian-actor Martin Lawrence as two policemen who become unlikely buddies— became a surprise hit at the box office and earned Smith the 1996 Blockbuster Entertainment Award for Male Newcomer, Theatrical.

Seemingly overnight, action films became Smith's claim to fame. *Independence Day,* an alien-disaster film released in 1996, featured Smith in a role as military pilot Captain Steven Hiller. *New York Times* critic Janet Maslin listed two reasons why the exceptionally popular movie was impossible to resist: the film's "cartoonish" dialogue—and the ever-likable Smith. Clearly, Smith had arrived as an action hero.

Next Smith donned dark glasses to appear with veteran actor Tommy Lee Jones in *Men in Black* (1997), a science fiction comedy about immigration agents who police space aliens. Adapted from the Marvel comic book, the special effects-laden movie was a box-office sensation. Returning to his musical roots, Smith contributed the single "Men in Black" to the movie's soundtrack, which also included tracks from De La

> "If I set my mind to it, within the next 15 years, I would be the President of the United States."
> —Smith, *Vibe*

Soul, Jermaine Dupri, and Snoop Dogg. "I guess music is the most personally satisfying of all the things I do, because it's a part of me," Smith once confided to E! Online. "With television and film, you're living out someone else's dreams, rather than realizing your own."

With the 1998 release of *Big Willie Style,* Smith undoubtedly realized dreams of his own. The multiplatinum album was the rapper's most successful musical effort to date, and the single, "Gettin' Jiggy Wit It," won the 1999 Grammy Award for Best Rap Solo. Also included on the album is a rap version of "Just the Two of Us," written for Smith's son Trey, by his first marriage. Divorced from first wife Sheree Zampino in 1995, the actor married Jada Pinkett Smith on New Year's Eve, 1997. The couple has one child together: a son, Jaden, born in July 1998.

Will Smith and Tommy Lee Jones fight the forces of alien evil in Men in Black. *(The Kobal Collection)*

Wild, Wild West

Wild, Wild West, released in June 1999, is based on a popular 1960s television show by the same name. The CBS series, which ran from September 1965 to September 1969, featured actor Robert Conrad as James West, a special agent whom President Ulysses S. Grant (1822–85) had assigned to the frontier. Together with sidekick Artemus Gordon (played by Ross Martin), West fought an endless parade of devious villains and evil scientists—aided by an arsenal of unusual devices. Conrad and Martin reunited to film the 1979 made-for-TV movie, *The Wild, Wild West Revisited*, which was followed in 1980 by *More Wild, Wild West*.

Like the television series, the 1999 *Wild, Wild West*, directed by Barry Sonnenfeld, is set in a fantasy version of the Old West. As special agent James West, actor Will Smith is called on to save the world from an evil genius (played by Kenneth Brannagh), with the assistance of his faithful sidekick, Artemus Gordon (played by Kevin Kline).

A terminator

Enemy of the State, an action thriller released in 1998, presented a new challenge to Smith. "There's not that eye-candy appeal of a special-effects film," he told *People*. "It's like I'm saying, 'Come see me act.' It's scary." The role of Robert Clayton Dean, a young attorney who is framed for the murder of a United States congressman, required Smith to create a persona the public had not yet seen. "It's not as if people won't recognize him," director Tony Scott told *Premiere*. "He plays an affable [likeable] guy with a sense of humor. But they'll also see him playing some tough, strong, emotional moments—doing things that, as an actor, he's never been asked to do before." In spite of disappointing reviews, the film was a resounding commercial success, earning $20 million in the first week of its release.

In mid-1999 Smith appeared in the film *Wild, Wild West*, directed by Barry Sonnenfeld (who also directed *Men in Black*), and later appeared in *Love for Hire*, based on a script he co-wrote with wife Pinkett Smith. Having produced an uninterrupted string of blockbuster hits, he seems to guarantee the success of every movie in which he appears. Success is something that the rapper-actor takes for granted. "I guess I never really expected anything else," he told *Premiere*. "It's what I came here for, you know? . . . I see people all the time who are better rappers than me, better actors than me, better-looking and stronger than me. But my ace in the hole is my dangerously obsessive drive, you know? I'm a terminator. I absolutely, positively will not stop until I win."

Sources

Maslin, Janet. *"Enemy of the State*: The Walls Have Ears and Eyes." *The New York Times*, November 20, 1998.

Maslin, Janet. *"Independence Day*: Space Aliens and Chance to Save Planet." *The New York Times*, July 2, 1996.

"Q & A—Will Smith." E! Online. [Online] Available http://www.eonline.com/ (March 17, 1999).

Rhodes, Joe. "Iron Will." *Premiere*, November 1998, pp. 91 ff.

Tomashoff, Craig. "Talking with . . . Will Smith." *People,* December 7, 1998, p. 36.

"Will Smith Biography," "Will Smith May Be Re-Born." Mr. Showbiz. [Online] Available http://mrshowbiz.go.com/ (March 17, 1999).

"Will Smith On Trading Acting Tips with L.L. Cool J," "Will Smith To Return To Rap." MTV News Gallery. [Online] Available http://www-mtv-d. mtvnodn.com/ (March 17, 1999).

"Will Smith runs for his life in action thriller *Enemy of the State.*" *Jet,* November 23, 1998, pp. 58-61.

David Spade

Born July 22, 1964
Birmingham, Michigan

Comedian, actor

> "My goal in life is to be a wussy like Barney Fife on the old *Andy Griffith Show*. He was kind of a fake tough guy. Deep down, he was a wimp."

(AP/Wide World)

Having grown up watching the NBC comedy show, *Saturday Night Live*, David Spade later made a name for himself as a member of the cast of that show. A fan of former SNL'ers Dan Ackroyd, Chevy Chase, Eddie Murphy, and Bill Murray, he won legions of young fans with his amusing impersonations and less-than-flattering celebrity lampoons (poking fun of someone). "It's just easier to make fun and cut down," Spade once told *The Washington Post*. "It's kind of a way of life in America. So if you can make that an art form, where people want to hear what you're going to say about something, it can be cruel and funny."

A scrawny kid in the West's Most Western Town

The youngest of three sons born to Wayne "Sam" Spade and Judy Todd, David Wayne Spade was born in Birmingham, Michigan, on July 22, 1964. When David was four, his father, an advertising copywriter, moved his family to the small mining town of Casa Grande, Arizona, near the Mexican border. Shortly thereafter, he abandoned his wife and children. "My dad just took off," Spade told *Washington Post* reporter Lloyd Grove. "It was one of those divorces, he split one day and then he'd show up once a year and give me a Nerf football for Christmas, and thought he was my hero again." Raising three children on her own, Spade's mother had to work two jobs. "It was hard for her," Spade told a Mr. Showbiz interviewer, "but she kept it from us."

A bright student who was placed in advanced math and reading classes, Spade was not popular in elementary school. "In grade school I was smart, but I didn't have any friends," he told Mr. Showbiz. Slight of build as a child (and as an adult—he stands five feet seven feet tall and weighs one hundred and thirty pounds), he was bullied in Little League. When Spade was twelve, he moved with his mother and stepfather to Scottsdale, Arizona—a town that advertises itself as "The West's Most Western Town."

A stand-up guy

Spade was more popular in high school, where he benefited from the popularity of his older brothers Bryan and Andrew. ". . . I was suddenly cool by association," he told *Washington Post* reporter Grove. "And I totally dusted all my old math friends. I was, like, 'Hey, nerds, why don't you go do some flashcards?'" A fan of *Saturday Night Live,* he "borrowed" material from the show to guarantee laughs at talent show performances. After graduating from Suguaro High School in Scottsdale, Spade enrolled in business courses at Arizona State University, a local school. But comedy soon overshadowed his desire to study business. "At ASU the [training] wheels came off, because I started trying to do stand-up," he told Grove. "Once I found something I liked, I didn't care about all that other stuff and school started to suck. . . ." After dropping out of college in 1985, the aspiring comic supported himself by working at a variety of jobs—including working as a busboy, valet parker, and clerking in a skateboard shop.

Two tragic events in Spade's life strengthened his commitment to making a name for himself as a comic. Shortly after his stepfather—a doctor and war veteran—committed suicide, his best friend died in a motorcycle crash. "When my stepfather died, I just kind of fell apart," he told Mr. Showbiz. "I felt pretty vulnerable, like there literally could be no tomorrow—that while I was doing a lot of talking, everything could end. So I figured if I don't go after it now, I might never get to do it."

Eighteen years old when he ventured into stand-up comedy, Spade struggled before moving to California to try his luck at the Los Angeles-area comedy clubs. After touring the United States performing at nightclubs and on the college circuit, he won a spot to perform at Los Angeles's celebrated Improv—not, he claimed, because he was talented, but because he was different from the other comics, whose ranks included Richard Belzer, Paul Reiser, and Jerry Seinfeld. It wasn't long before the comic attracted the notice of an agent, who later cast Spade in the 1987 movie *Police Academy 4: Citizens on Patrol,* with Steve Guttenberg, Bobcat Goldthwait, and Sharon Stone. Although the picture was a dismal failure, Spade was soon offered a month-long stint as guest host for Fox television's "Joan Rivers Show." He turned down the offer. "That was my lesson in not getting too greedy and not biting off too much," he told Grove. ". . .to host the show, I had no idea what I was doing. I was, like, 22. It could have gone the wrong way and hurt me more than helped me."

Six years at *Saturday Night*

Spade's appearance on an HBO special in 1989 marked a turning point in his career. A showcase to feature six up-and-coming comics, the *13th Annual Young Comedians Show* was hosted by veteran comedian Dennis Miller, who was at that time a popular member of the cast of *Saturday Night Live.* Miller convinced Lorne Michaels, the producer of SNL, to let Spade audition for a spot on the show. In April 1990, the young comic joined SNL as a writer and performer.

Signing a contract to appear on *Saturday Night Live* did not bring instant celebrity. With only three on-camera appearances during his first year at SNL, Spade grew frustrated. Because of his physical similarity to slight, blond-haired cast member Dana Carvey (best known as "Garth" from *Wayne's World),* Spade found that he lost many parts to the better-known comedian. "I was a writer-performer, but they didn't want me to perform because Dana Carvey was there," he told Mr. Showbiz. "Also, they wanted me to pay my dues."

While dues-paying, Spade cemented a friendship with fellow cast member Chris Farley, who was also new to the show.

"Basically, I'm not really cool, it's more of an optical illusion. But if it works, I'll take it." –Spade, Mr. Showbiz

Eventually, Spade moved into the spotlight thanks to the biting humor of his "Hollywood Minute" sketches, in which he lampooned celebrities with funny—and often cruel—humor. "It was a weird dynamic," he told Grove. "I was just going to gun people down. It was going to be a bloodbath, because that's the only way I was going to get on [camera]." Not everyone enjoyed Spade's blood-letting brand of humor. "David had to apologize lots of times to people who had no fear of calling him up and yelling at him, like Eddie Murphy," said SNL producer Michaels. (In one "Hollywood Minute" segment, Spade poked fun at Murphy, whose movie career had stalled, saying, "Look kids, a falling star! . . . Make a wish!")

During his run on the show, Spade created a number of popular characters—such as the receptionist for rock-and-roll icon Dick Clark (who repeatedly asks well-known celebrities to identify themselves with the line, "And you are...?"). He also popularized the dismissive "buh-bye" in the role of a flight attendant in one of the show's more popular skits. Having become a celebrity in his own right, he grew uncomfortable with ridiculing other performers. "I'm trying to get away from being smart-assy, because I don't want to get laughs by being mean to people," he explained to a Mr. Showbiz interviewer. "When I was a nobody blindsiding stars, it was funny. But I'm kind of one of them now, so it doesn't make as much sense." During the 1995–96 season the comedian introduced "Spade in America," in which his toned-down commentaries—although still biting—were somewhat broader and gentler.

Spade left SNL in 1996, after having spent six seasons on the show. "When I leave, it will be to ease the pressure, not to be a movie star," the comedian earlier confessed to Mr. Showbiz. "You can't stay there forever—it kills you inside. It ages you in dog years. It's a tough place."

Spade says "buh-bye" to SNL

While still a cast member of SNL, Spade appeared in several small movie roles (in such films as *Light Sleeper, The Coneheads,* and *PCU*) during breaks from taping. In 1995 he was awarded his first significant role—as Richard Hayden, opposite

On Chris Farley

When his good friend, fellow *Saturday Night Live* alumnus Chris Farley died in 1997 of a drug overdose at the age of 33, Spade was devastated. He refused to discuss the death with reporters and did not attend the comedian's funeral. "A death like this is something you go through with your close friends," he later told E! Online. "It isn't necessarily for public consumption."

good friend Chris Farley—in *Tommy Boy,* a film produced by Lorne Michaels. As the straight-man for the overweight Farley, Spade described the movie's comedy as "the age-old secret of fatty and skinny." Although critically panned, the movie fared well at the box office, prompting the 1996 Spade/Farley comedy *Black Sheep.* (In between the two flicks with Farley, Spade appeared in an uncredited cameo [small role] as a hair stylist in *A Very Brady Sequel.*)

Just Shoot Him

Spade enjoys an unusual amount of creative influence in *Just Shoot Me,* the NBC television comedy in which he plays a smart-mouthed office manager. The comedian's contract allows him to suggest lines for his character and provides him the final say in the shooting of at least one take per episode.

Shortly after his departure from *Saturday Night Live,* Spade was offered—and declined—his own TV show. Offered a part in *Just Shoot Me,* an NBC comedy produced by award-winning writer/producer Steven Levitan (whose credits include *Frasier* and *The Larry Sanders Show*), Spade did not accept at first. "David was hesitant," Levitan told *ET Weekly,* "but it was never an issue of 'I want tons of screen time.' It was about 'I wanna be funny.'" Spade decided to accept a role in the witty comedy, set at the New York headquarters of a fictional women's magazine. In the role of wisecracking office manager Dennis Finch, Spade joined an ensemble (group) cast that included Enrico Colantoni, Wendie Malick, Laura San Giacomo, and George Segal.

While *Just Shoot Me* has enjoyed popular and critical acclaim, Spade's other projects have been less successful. The movies *8 Heads in a Duffel Bag* (1997), starring Joe Pesci, and *Senseless* (1998), with Marlon Wayons, did little to further his reputation as box-office bait. He enjoyed more success when he returned to his stand-up roots as host of the 1997 Billboard Music Awards and as the headline act of the HBO special *David Spade: Take the Hit.* Having done a number of voice-only projects, the comedian was heard in Disney's animated feature *Kingdom of the Sun* (1999). Among his other projects, he co-wrote (and starred in) 1999's *Lost and Found,* in which a young man kidnaps a beautiful neighbor's dog so that he can appear as a hero to her when he "finds" the animal.

Having earned a spot on Hollywood's A-list, Spade remains level-headed about fame. "You can't get a big head about it," he told E! Online. "Hey, a lot of people would recognize [notorious

The cast of NBC's Just Shoot Me. *(The Kobal Collection)*

German leader Adolph] Hitler if you showed them his glossy [photograph]. It doesn't necessarily mean they like you."

Sources

"David Spade's Recent Career." ET Weekly. [Online] Available http://www.lycos.com (February 17, 1999).

"David Spade Star Bio." Celebsite. [Online] Available http://www.celebsite.com/people/davidspade/content/bio.html (February 17, 1999).

Grove, Lloyd. "David Spade's Best Digs." *The Washington Post*. [Online] Available http://www.lycos.com (February 17, 1999).

"The Hot Spot: Q&A with David Spade." E! Online. [Online] Available http://www.eonline.net/Hot/Qa/Spade/interview.html (February 17, 1999).

"NBC: Just Shoot Me." NBC. [Online] Available http://www.nbc.com/NBCtvcentral/promo/promotional-stars.nbc?bio+justshootme/new_spade (February 17, 1999).

Rusoff, Jane Wollman. "Noted wiseass David Spade is more than Chris Farley's little buddy." Mr. Showbiz. [Online] Available http://www.mrshowbiz.com/ (February 17, 1999).

"Trivia for David Spade." Internet Movie Database. [Online] Available http://us.imdb.com/BPublicity?Spade,+David (February 17, 1999).

James Stewart

Born May 20, 1908
Indiana, Pennsylvania

Died July 2, 1997
Beverly Hills, California

Actor

Having produced eighty-one films in a career that spanned nearly fifty years, Jimmy Stewart earned every major award bestowed on actors—including the American Film Institute's eighth life-achievement award (1980), a Kennedy Center Honor for lifetime contributions to the performing arts (1983), a Special Academy Award for "50 years of meaningful performances, for his high ideals, both on and off the screen" (1984), and the highest civilian (non-military) honor, the Presidential Medal of Freedom (1985). Probably best remembered for his favorite role—as decent, down-to-earth banker George Bailey in Frank Capra's 1946 classic, *It's a Wonderful Life*—Stewart won one Oscar (Academy Award) and four other nominations during his career. Although the characters he portrayed ranged from wide-eyed young idealists to wizened men-of-the-world, Stewart always conveyed sincerity. He enjoyed quoting an expression from fellow actor Laurence Olivier: "I always play myself, with deference [respect] to the character."

"It's been a wonderful experience for me, making movies. I've had the feeling for a long time that I was in something that was important to the public."

(Archive Photos)

A small-town boy

Born on May 20, 1908, James Maitland Stewart was raised in Indiana, Pennsylvania, a small town in the western part of that state. His parents, Alexander Maitland and Elizabeth Ruth Jackson Stewart, were of Scots-Irish descent. Both attended college—something that few women of Ruth's generation could claim. James—who was called "Jimsey" or "Jimbo" by his parents—had three siblings: an older brother, Alex (called Alec), and two sisters, Mary and Virginia. Strict Presbyterians, the Stewarts taught their children the value of responsibility. All were expected to help out at the family's business—a hardware store that had been owned and operated by the Stewart family for some fifty years. The actor later explained to *McCall's* magazine (cited in *James Stewart, A biography*), " . . . the Stewart Hardware Store seemed the center of the universe. It was a three-story structure full to the rafters with everything needed to build a house, hunt a deer, plant a garden and harvest it, repair a car, or make a scrapbook. I could conceive of no human need that could not be satisfied in that store. Even after I grew up and moved away and saw larger sights, the store remained with me."

As a boy, Stewart enjoyed playing the accordion and staging plays he had written himself. Donald Dewey noted the actor's first "performance" in *James Stewart, A Biography:* "His public debut was not particularly auspicious [favorable]: at the age of five, he sneaked a couple of hand puppets into church on Sunday and spent the service in a lot of animated muttering." After graduating from the Model School, which ended in the ninth grade, Stewart enrolled in Mercersburg Academy, a college preparatory school, to improve his chances of being accepted at Princeton University in New Jersey. His father, who had earned his college degree at Princeton, was determined that his sons would attend his alma mater.

Popular with other students, Stewart often entertained his classmates in his dorm room by playing the accordion. The high point of his days at Mercersburg came when he was cast in the drama society's production of *The Wolves,* a little-known French play by Romain Rolland. As Buquet, a commoner who rises to a position of power, Stewart showed little of the promise of his later career. "Jimmy Stewart was about as clumsy a young adolescent as a play coach ever had to work with," the drama club's faculty advisor, Carl Cass said (quoted in *Pieces of Time*). "He was a long-legged kid who looked funny in any kind of clothes he wore. I had to find a role in which he wouldn't have to wear neat-fitting clothes. And he had to be coached so that he wouldn't fall when he walked onstage."

In front of the footlights

After entering Princeton University in 1928, Stewart became a member of the Princeton Triangle Club, and was soon featured as a lead performer in a number of the drama club's musicals. His drama experience would serve him well. Graduating with a bachelor's degree in architecture in 1932, during the hard economic times of the Great Depression (1929–39), he found it difficult to find work. Joshua Logan—a director Stewart had befriended at Princeton (and who would eventually earn a prestigious reputation for directing musicals such as *Annie Get Your Gun* and *Paint Your Wagon*)—convinced the young actor to return to the stage. Stewart soon moved to Falmouth, Massachusetts, to appear in summer stock theater with the University Players. (There he met fellow actor Henry Fonda, 1905–82, who would become a lifelong friend.)

In October 1932, Stewart made his first appearance in New York's prestigious Broadway Theater, in an unsuccessful staging of *Carry Nation*. Two months later, he appeared as the chauffeur in *Goodbye Again*—but the two lines he was allotted allowed him little time to impress the critics. His first substantial Broadway role came in 1934, when he played Sergeant O'Hara in *Yellow Jack*, the story of Walter Reed's battle against yellow fever [an infectious disease transmitted by the mosquito]. Although the play was not a hit, Stewart drew positive reviews. Then, when he played a youth shocked by his mother's adultery in *Divided by Three*, he impressed *New York Times* critic Brooks Atkinson, who called the young actor's performance "a minor masterpiece."

Mr. Stewart goes to Hollywood

After a number of other stage appearances, Stewart headed to Hollywood, where he roomed with Fonda, who had moved there earlier. There, Billy Grady, a talent scout for the powerful MGM movie studio, cast him to play an inexperienced reporter in a 1935 crime melodrama called *Murder Man*. Stewart impressed the film's leading man, Spencer Tracy (1900–67). When the veteran actor noted the younger man's tenseness, he told him to ignore the cameras. "That was all he needed," Tracy said (quoted in *The New York Times*). "In his very first scene he showed he had all the good things." Noted for his modesty, Stewart later said that his debut performance in a feature film was awful.

Neither studio executives nor audiences agreed with Stewart's self-assessment. Over the next five years, he made twenty-four movies, including the 1938 screwball comedy, *You Can't Take It With You*. Directed by the legendary Frank Capra, the film won Academy Awards for Best Director and Best Picture. For his portrayal of an idealistic young senator in *Mr. Smith Goes to Washington* (1939), Stewart received the New York Film Critics best actor award. Nominated for an Academy Award for that role, many considered him to be the favorite to win; that year's award, however, went to Robert Donat for *Goodbye, Mr. Chips*. The following year, Stewart won the Academy Award for Best Actor for his performance in *The Philadelphia Story*. He also won the respect of his celebrated co-stars, Katharine Hepburn (1907–) and Cary Grant (1904–86). Grant later commented (quoted in *Jimmy Stewart: A Life in Film*), "I was absolutely fascinated by him. When you watch him you can see how *good* he is in the film. I think the reason Jimmy stood out from other actors was that he had the ability to talk naturally." Stewart sent his Oscar home to Pennsylvania, where his father displayed it in a case in the family hardware store, next to photographs, medals, and paintings by Stewart's sister.

A military man

At the risk of losing his box-office popularity, Stewart took an extended break from film-making—to enlist in the army. He logged 300 hours of flying to ensure that he would be accepted as a combat pilot, and he tried desperately to gain weight, so that he would not be turned down for failing to meet the military's minimum standards. (Stewart—who stood 6'3½" and weighed about 140 pounds—was turned down for being underweight in his first attempt to enlist. He reportedly gained ten pounds and met the minimum weight standard with only one ounce to spare.)

In March 1941—just nine months before the Japanese attack on Pearl Harbor and the United States' entry in to World War II (1939–45)—Stewart was admitted into the military. Qualifying as a pilot, he moved from operations officer to chief of staff and squadron commander. Responsible for training and supervising new crews, Stewart demonstrated a gift for leadership. Walter Matthau (1920–)—who later became a celebrated actor—was among the young recruits trained by Stewart. Matthau later said (quoted in *Jimmy Stewart: A Life in Film*): "I used to go to the briefings just to listen to him, just to hear him do his Jimmy Stewart. I watched the way the new crews would relate to him. They used to relate to him as though he were a movie star for a while then they'd forget about all that and realize he was one of the boys. He was marvelous to watch."

Having led some twenty bombing missions over Germany, Stewart won numerous decorations, including two Distinguished Flying Crosses and the Air Medal. When the war ended, he was discharged as a colonel and remained in the Air Force Reserve. When, in 1959, the Senate approved his promotion to brigadier general, he became the highest-ranking entertainer in the American military.

"Hearth fires and holocausts"

In one scene in *Philadelphia Story*, Stewart was required to take Katharine Hepburn (1907–) in his arms, gaze into her eyes, and utter some very flowery lines. A simple-spoken man, the young actor had trouble coming to terms with his lovelorn lines. Hepburn recalled in *Jimmy Stewart, A Life in Film*: "It did really cause him the most terrible distress. He had to say: 'There's a magnificence in you Tracy, a magnificence that comes out of your eyes, that's in your voice, in the way you stand. . . . You've got fires banked down in you, hearth fires and holocausts.' Well, it was not exactly a Jimmy Stewart line.

Jimmy rehearsed the scene with me and he nearly died. George Cukor [the director] said: 'Jimmy, you're not running away to the circus so don't paw the ground with your foot. Just say it.' And Jimmy took a deep breath and he said it. He was magnificent."

A wonderful life

In 1946, Stewart made his first movie since leaving Hollywood for the military. The experience led to a crisis of self-confidence. "I felt when I got back to pictures that I had lost all sense of judgment," he later said (as quoted in *Up Front*). "I couldn't tell if it was good or bad." Stewart's performance as George Bailey, in Frank Capra's *It's a Wonderful Life,* would ultimately come to be recognized as the actor's signature role. After seeing the film, President Harry S Truman (1884–1972) announced (as quoted in *The New York Times*), "If Bess [Truman's wife] and I had a son, we'd want him to be just like Jimmy Stewart." Although *It's a Wonderful Life* was not at first a success at the box office, it later became one of the most

A scene from the Christmas classic It's A Wonderful Life. *(The Kobal Collection)*

popular movies ever made (thanks, in part, to its status as a Christmas classic on television).

One of Hollywood's most eligible bachelors, Stewart married Gloria Hatrick McLean in 1949. Married for 45 years, the couple's family included four children—sons Ronald and Michael, from his wife's first marriage, and twin girls, Judy and Kelly, born in 1951. The couple remained happily married until 1994, when Gloria Stewart passed away.

Later roles

As Stewart grew older, he developed a more mature, confident, and complex screen personality. He took on a broad range of roles in a succession of films that were both critically acclaimed and popular successes. His long list of film credits includes: *Call*

Northside 777 (1948) a docudrama based on a true story about the investigation into the killing of a policeman; *Harvey* (1950), in which Stewart plays a lovable drunk who is accompanied by an invisible six-foot rabbit (for which Stewart was nominated for an Academy Award for best actor); *The Glenn Miller Story* (1953), a biographical film about the legendary Big Band leader; *The Spirit of St. Louis* (1957), about pilot Charles Lindbergh; *Vertigo* (1958), a classic Alfred Hitchcock thriller; and *Anatomy of a Murder* (1959), for which he won awards from the New York Film Critics and Venice Film Festival for his portrayal of a defense attorney. Stewart also appeared in a number of well-received Westerns, which he once claimed (cited in *The New York Times*) were his favorite type of movie because they "give people a feeling of hope, an affirmative [positive] statement of living." He appeared in *Winchester '73* (1950), *Bend of the River* (1952), *The Man From Laramie* (1955), and *The Man Who Shot Liberty Valance* (1962). Still a favorite among audiences, Stewart made his last feature film appearance in 1978 in *The Magic of Lassie,* followed by a 1983 television movie with legendary actress Bette Davis (1908–89), called *Right of Way,* and a voice-part in the animated film, *An American Tail: Fievel Goes West* (1991).

Asked, as he neared his eightieth birthday, how he wanted to be remembered, the actor responded (as quoted in *The New York Times*) that he wished to be known as someone who "believed in hard work and love of country, love of family and love of community." On July 2, 1997, Stewart died at home, from a blood clot in his lung. "America lost a national treasure today," said President Bill Clinton. "Jimmy Stewart was a great actor, a gentleman, and a patriot."

"I've had many people tell me that they remember certain little things I did in pictures. I think it's wonderful to have been able to give people little pieces of time they can remember." –Stewart, *Pieces of Time*

Sources

Dewey, Donald. *James Stewart, A Biography*. Atlanta: Turner Publishing, 1996.

Fishgall, Gary. *Pieces of Time, The Life of Jimmy Stewart*. New York: Scribner, 1997.

"James Stewart, the Hesitant Hero, Dies at 89." Obituary. *The New York Times,* July 3, 1997, p. A1 ff.

"Jimmy Stewart Dead at 89." E! Online. [Online] Available http:// www.eonline. com/News/Items/0,1,1380,00.html (January 22, 1999).

"Jimmy's Page." [Online] Available http://www.skynet.co.uk/~goddard/ homepage.htm (January 22, 1999).

"Online NewsHour: Remembering Jimmy Stewart." [Online] Available http:// www.pbs.org/newshour/bb/remember/1997/stewart_7-2.html (January 22, 1999).

Pickard, Roy. *Jimmy Stewart, A Life in Film*. New York: St. Martin's Press, 1992.

"Up Front." [Online] Available http://www.pathfinder.com/people/970721/features/stewart4.html (January 22, 1999).

Chris Tucker

Born October 31, 1973
Atlanta, Georgia

Actor, comedian

A comedian since childhood, Chris Tucker gave up a job in his family's cleaning business to pursue a career in stand-up comedy. A fan of movies such as *Scarface, The Fugitive,* and Eddie Murphy's *48 Hours,* Tucker soon transformed his machine-gun style verbal comedy into a thriving movie career. Appearing first in small roles in small films, he eventually landed a breakthrough part co-starring with Jackie Chan in the blockbuster action-comedy *Rush Hour.*

Survival of the funniest

Born in Atlanta, Georgia, Chris Tucker discovered a knack for comedy at a young age. The youngest of six children, he used humor as a defense against his older brothers. "I had to become the family clown," he told *Calgary Sun* writer Louis Hobson. "Being the youngest, my brothers beat on me and their friends beat on me. Out of necessity, I learned to make them laugh. If I did, they'd stop beating on me."

A class clown in school, Tucker often found himself in trouble with teachers and administrators. "I was that horrible

"Unfiltered Chris Tucker is dangerous for patients with high blood pressure. The fast-talking, slang-spewing young comic. . . does not brake for children, animals, or fussbudgets. . . ."
—EW Online

(AP/Wide World)

225

kid who'd call teachers by their first names and get the whole class a detention," he told the *Calgary Sun*. "I'd do whatever it took to distract the teacher. She'd say turn to page ten, and I'd yell out, 'Turn to page 15!,'" he told the *Toronto Sun*. Eventually, Tucker encountered a school principal who challenged him to put his talent to use. After one of his teachers complained to the principal that the aspiring comic's shenanigans (silly, disruptive behavior) were funny—but inappropriate in the classroom—the principal dared Tucker to entertain *all* his classmates . . . in the school talent show. Tucker accepted the challenge, and hosted the talent show before 1,000 of his peers. "I got a big response," he told Hollywood Online, "and that feeling! I'll never forget that feeling! At that moment I said I'm going to do this the rest of my life."

Before he was old enough to purchase a drink in a bar, Tucker was entertaining bar patrons with his stand-up routines. "Stand-up comedy was my classroom," he told the *Toronto Sun*. "It really hones [sharpens] your skills. You take the crowd up and you take them down."

By the age of 19, Tucker—who had been working for his parents' carpet-cleaning business—began appearing regularly as a professional stand-up comedian in the Atlanta area. A featured performer at Atlanta's Comedy Act Theatre, among others, he later toured with the Def Jam comedy act and starred at the Comedy Store in Los Angeles, California. One night, a veteran stand-up performer caught his act. "Richard Pryor came to see me one night and told me I was funny," he told the *Calgary Sun*. "That was the coolest thing that's ever happened to me." Tucker's mother, however, was not pleased with her son's choice of profession. A religious woman, she disapproved of her son's swearing onstage, and encouraged him to settle for a job in the family's cleaning business.

On the big screen

Tucker had other plans for his career. In 1994 he made his movie debut with a brief, but memorable, appearance in the hip-hop movie *House Party III*. A reviewer for EW Online wrote that Tucker's small role as party promoter Johnny Booze "carried far more voltage than his few minutes on the screen might suggest."

Still touring with his stand-up comedy routine, Tucker next appeared in *Friday*, a 1995 comedy-drama written by rapper Ice

> As a child, Tucker used comedy as a way to avoid being beat up by his older brothers. "My brothers claim I should be supporting them, too," he told the *Calgary Sun*, "because if it wasn't for them, I'd never have become a comedian."

Cube. "When we did *Friday* we were just all hungry to do a movie," he said (quoted in "Chris Talks" online). "I was on the road traveling so much that I needed to get out there a little more [in the public eye]. I was ready to make a movie and make sure it was good." While Tucker's appearance in *Friday* succeeded in placing him in the public eye, film critics had little good to say about the movie—or the comic's performance. *New York Times* critic Caryn James complained, "This is a ruder, cruder version of the hip-hop movie *House Party*." As Smokey, a marijuana-smoking loafer, Tucker played opposite rapper Ice Cube (in the role of a 22-year-old who has recently lost his job). James wrote, ". . . . The film's weakness is Mr. Tucker, whose exaggerated expressions and line readings become annoying."

Noted for his high-pitched voice and non-stop verbal assaults, Tucker made a number of other small—high-impact—appearances. Some—critics and audience members, alike—found him fresh and energetic. Others found his style offensive. As DJ Ruby Rhod in Luc Besson's futuristic *The Fifth Element* (released in 1997, starring Bruce Willis), Tucker "made a strong if not entirely favorable impression," according to *People* magazine. *New York Times* critic Janet Maslin was more to the point: "As a yammering, swishy talk show host, Chris Tucker is flat-out incomprehensible."

Next Tucker appeared in *Dead Presidents*, the second feature film of Albert and Allen Hughes, whose *Menace II Society* (1993) had drawn critical accolades. Tucker played Skip, the comic sidekick of Anthony, played by Larenz Tate (who also appeared in the Hughes brothers' first feature). A Vietnam War-era (1964–75) coming-of-age tale, *Dead Presidents* disappointed critics.

Money Talks and *Jackie Brown*

Starring opposite Charlie Sheen as a fast-talking petty hustler from Los Angeles in *Money Talks*, Tucker began to cross over to mainstream Hollywood movies—and to draw positive press for his comic personality. "Anyone who devoutly follows North American stand-up," wrote Bruce Kirkland of the *Toronto Sun*, "already knows that this motor-mouthing, eye-popping, manic 24-year-old is a rising star of cutting-edge comedy." Released in 1997, the film was advertised with a tag-line that boasted "This ain't no buddy movie." But the film—which pits together two unlikely companions, one accused of murders he didn't commit and the other a polished television crime reporter—is, without question, a buddy movie. "We want to be like Gene Wilder and Richard Pryor," Tucker told the *Toronto Sun,* referring to that duo's successful pairing in the 1976 buddy movie, *Silver Streak,* and 1980's *Stir Crazy.* Tucker's friendship with veteran actor Sheen was not simply a Hollywood fiction: the two became buddies offscreen as well. "I was aware instantly of his wealth of talent and his absence of fear," Sheen told the *Toronto Sun.* "He's not ego driven. He just went completely insane. I just became a fan." While *Money Talks* was a critical failure, Tucker's devoted fan base continued to grow.

As Beaumont Livingstone in Quentin Tarantino's *Jackie Brown* (1997), Tucker once again made a brief but powerful impression. Tucker found working with the *Pulp Fiction* director and the movie's critically acclaimed cast to be an important learning experience. "I have this jail scene with Samuel L. Jackson," he explained to the *Toronto Sun.* "I just worked two days, but being directed by Quentin and working with Sam was like being in an acting class. They taught me so much about this acting thing. Until then, I'd just been flying by the seat of my pants."

Starring roles

Appearing in *Rush Hour* (1998), an action comedy co-starring Hong Kong sensation Jackie Chan, Tucker hoped to broaden his audience—much as *Beverly Hills Cop* had done for comedian/actor Eddie Murphy. *Rush Hour* is the story of two mismatched cops involved in a high-profile case concerning the kidnapping of the Chinese consulate's daughter. Called in by the FBI (Federal Bureau of Investigations), Los Angeles Police Detective James Carter (Tucker) is assigned to keep Hong Kong Detective Inspector Lee (Chan) out of the FBI's investigation. At first reluctant partners, the two develop a close bond.

The Tucker-Chan pairing—billed as "The fastest hands in the East versus the biggest mouth in the West"—was a hit with audiences. "Putting the two of them together was like lightning in a bottle," New Line Cinema production head

Chris Tucker and Jackie Chan ham
it up in the action-packed *Rush
Hour*. *(The Kobal Collection)*

Michael De Luca told the *Los Angeles Times*. The film grossed
$84 million in the first three weeks of its release. With a PG-13
rating, the movie aimed to appeal to a wider audience than
Tucker's previous efforts, which were rated R. "We did two
things that were very conscious," director Brett Ratner told
Hollywood Online. "Since *Money Talks* [also directed by Ratner]
was an R-rated movie, we went for a PG-13. And that meant no
cursing, which tends to alienate middle America. The other
thing was we focused it on the characters and a real dilem-
ma—saving a young girl's life." Like *Beverly Hills Cop*, both
characters in *Rush Hour* are on the right side of the law—
which also serves to make the movie more appealing to general audiences. As *See Magazine* critic Cynthia Amsden noted,
Rush Hour is "a buddy cop flick that resurrects the *Beverly
Hills Cop* idea and goes it one better."

Next came Tucker's biggest starring role, as William Soul, a James Bond-style secret agent in the spy comedy, *Double-O-Soul*. "[It's] an action-comedy, but it's not a spoof of the Bond movies," Tucker told the *Calgary Sun*. "It's no black Austin Powers [the spy character created by Mike Myers]." The film co-stars singer Mariah Carey, in her film debut, as Tucker's love interest. The comic—who earned less than $1 million for his role in *Money Talks*— reportedly collected a $7 million paycheck for his role in *Double-O-Soul*.

Concerning future projects, Tucker hopes to branch out into dramatic roles. "I've already done my action movies with the best," he told the *Toronto Sun*. "Now it's time to move on." Further, he said, "I want to do something like *Forrest Gump* or *The Color Purple*, one of those good five-hankie movies."

Sources

Amsden, Cynthia. "On Screen: Preview, *Rush Hour*." *SEE Magazine*, September 17, 1998. [Online] Available http://www.greatwest.ca/SEE/Issues/1998/0917/ screen1.html (January 22, 1999).

"Chris Tucker." [Online] Available http://www.acmi.canoe.ca/ JamMovies ArtistsT/tucker_chris.html (January 22, 1999).

"Chris Tucker—Funniest Guy Alive & You Know This, Man!" [Online] Available http://angelfire.com/fl/kellykeith/chris.html (January 22, 1999).

Eller, Claudia. "Studios Were in Passing Lane for *Rush Hour*." *The Los Angeles Times*, October 6, 1998 [Online] Available http://sofla.hollywood. com/news/topstories/10-06-98/html/2-1.html (January 22, 1999).

"Interview: Chris Tucker." Hollywood Online. [Online] Available http://www. hollywood.com/movietalk/celebrities/ctucker/html/sound.html (January 22, 1999).

James, Caryn. "Evolution of a Very Confused Young Man." *The New York Times*, September 29, 1995.

James, Caryn. "Replacing Rap's Anger With a Sense of Humor." *The New York Times*, April 26, 1995.

Maslin, Janet. "*Fifth Element*: World Saved by a Nude Babe? Cool!" *The New York Times*, May 9, 1997.

Maslin, Janet. "*Rush Hour*: Kicks, Swivels and Wisecracks on Hollywood Boulevard." *The New York Times*, September 18, 1998.

Natale, Richard. "Movies: Cross-Cultural Buddies Cash In." *The Los Angeles Times*, September 22, 1998 [Online] Available http://sofla. hollywood.com/news/topstories/09-22-98/html/1-2.html (January 22, 1999).

Review of *Friday*. People Online. [Online] Available http://www.pathfinder. com/people/movie_reviews/95/friday.html (January 22, 1999).

Review of *Money Talks*. People Online. [Online] Available http://st3.yahoo. com/bre/moneytalks.html (January 22, 1999).

Review of *Rush Hour*. EW Online. [Online] Available http://www.eonline. com/Reviews/Movies/Leaves/0,20,802,00.html (January 22. 1999).

Liv Tyler

Born July 1, 1978
New York, New York

Actress, former model

The product of an unusual upbringing, Liv Tyler had become a "former model"—whose ranks include her mother—by the tender age of fifteen. Next turning to acting, she soon caught the eye of movie-goers, critics, and well-respected directors. In just a few years' time, she established a varied and successful film career—and did so well before her twentieth birthday. The biological daughter of Aerosmith frontman Steven Tyler, whose substance abuse has included, according to his daughter, "everything possible known to man," the actress enjoys a reputation as a mature and well-grounded young woman who is exceptionally comfortable in front of the camera, and who makes thoughtful decisions about her career. "What she inherited from me," Tyler's father once boasted to *Time,* "was just the great art of being herself."

An unconventional upbringing

Liv Tyler was born at Mount Sinai Hospital in New York City on July 1, 1978. From the start, she was surrounded by famous people: Rolling Stones musicians Mick Jagger and Ron Wood

"The thing about Liv is that she's really smart about the choices she's making. This is an *extremely* well-grounded girl."
— Tom Hanks, Tyler's director in *That Thing You Do*

(The Kobal Collection)

were the first to visit her in the hospital. Her mother, Bebe Buell, was a model—and a backstage regular during the 1970s rock era. Born Liv Rundgren, Tyler grew up believing that musician Todd Rundgren, leader of the rock group Utopia, was her father. She had no reason to believe otherwise: Rundgren had been a father to Tyler from the time he cut her umbilical cord at the hospital.

Tyler's upbringing was not exactly conventional (traditional). She lived in an all-American setting—in a large house in Maine, with her mother, aunt, uncle, and two cousins, surrounded by cow-filled pastures. At the same time, she accompanied her mother—who has been described as a free-spirited party girl—to heavy metal concerts, where she mingled with musicians and roadies. Tyler confides that she never felt a need to rebel against her parents: "My mother would always warn me about things that I would never do—things that she did, but I would never dream of doing, because I had no interest. She had nothing to worry about. I never felt like my parents were the enemy."

Two dads are better than one

When Tyler was eleven, she discovered that Rundgren was not her biological father. She accompanied her mother to Boston, where Rundgren was performing. Backstage after the concert, she met Steven Tyler, lead singer for the band Aerosmith. She was struck by his uncanny physical resemblance to her. Returning to Portland, Maine, where she lived with her mother, Tyler wrote in her diary, "I don't know why, but I feel like Steven is my daddy."

Steven Tyler, a notorious alcohol and drug addict, weaned himself from narcotics before inviting Bebe and Liv to an Aerosmith concert in 1988. There Liv met Tyler's daughter, Mia (whose mother is model Cyrinda Foxe). The two looked like twins. Buell told *GQ* reporter Lucy Kaylin: "It was ridiculously uncanny. That's when Liv said to me, Mommy, that's my father isn't it? Boom. Just like that." Tyler was ecstatic to learn she had a second father. She told her mother, "Wow, this year Christmas is gonna *rock!*" By the time she was twelve, Tyler had taken the last name of her biological father.

Steven Tyler was well aware that Liv was his daughter. Soon after Liv's birth, Buell, who was concerned about the musician's drug addiction, discussed with him her plan to raise the child as Rundgren's daughter. "He'd be in a coma during some of the discussion," she told *GQ*, "but, yeah, we discussed it." She also discussed the matter with Rundgren. " . . . Todd had his points," she explained. "We weren't sure if Steven would be alive in a year's time, because he was having problems with seizures and convulsions." Tyler first met his daughter shortly after she was born. He broke into tears. His failure to be a father to Liv still causes him grief: "I didn't get a chance to change her diapers," he told *GQ*, "and I will cry inside for that the rest of my life."

From modeling to movies

Among Tyler's family's circle of friends was supermodel Paulina Porizkova. Having taken snapshots of the five-foot-ten teenaged beauty, Porizkova circulated the photographs among modeling agents. Agencies were attracted to Tyler's unusual beauty—especially the surprisingly full lips she inherited from her father. After moving to New York, Tyler—who was just fourteen years old—became a much sought-after model, appearing on the cover of such magazines as *Seventeen, Rolling Stone, Inside Edge,* and *Bikini.* She also appeared inside *Mademoiselle, Mirabella,* and the Italian and German *Vogue.*

After just one year, Tyler had had her fill of modeling. "I was modeling a lot," she explained in a Mr. Showbiz online interview, "and I didn't love it, and I definitely didn't want it to be a serious thing to do for the rest of my life." She was intrigued by acting—even though she knew nothing about the craft and hadn't been exposed to great films as a kid. To help Tyler learn about the profession, her grandmother gave her books about acting. Before she could read them, however, she was offered her first part (after a talent agent had seen an article about children of the famous in *The New York Times*).

After just one try-out reading, she was offered a part in *Heavy.* Three weeks later, she was cast in *Silent Fall,* directed by Bruce Beresford, whose previous hits included *Breaker Morant* and *Driving Miss Daisy. Heavy* director James Mangold decided to delay shooting until Tyler was free of her commitment to the Beresford film. Co-starring with Richard Dreyfus in her first feature film, Tyler played Sylvie Warden, the older sister of an autistic boy. *Time* magazine's Ginia Bellafante called the film—which revolves around a grisly double-murder witnessed by the nine-year-old autistic boy—a "little seen, little praised" drama.

Next Tyler played the role of Call, a sweet waitress who befriends a lonely overweight cook, in *Heavy*. "I could really see Liv bonding with this guy," director Mangold explained in *Time*. "She came with this asset of a humongous heart." Although the 1994 film won a special jury prize at the Sundance Film Festival, critics had little positive to say. *Time* magazine's Richard Corliss, for instance, wrote: "the characters shop, eat, sleep, do some world-class moping and, in general, wait for something the hell to happen. And all that happens is Liv."

Looking at Liv

Tyler's next role was a family project: together with actress Alicia Silverstone, she appeared in "Crazy," a music video for Aerosmith. "When I agreed to do it," she explained in a Mr. Showbiz online interview, "I just thought it'd be fun, and I guess I didn't realize the reality of it. I didn't realize that, like, three weeks later it would be all over MTV. I didn't really pay much attention to it. But then whenever I put MTV on, it was there. It was kind of scary." Almost overnight, Tyler became a sex symbol. Although the video is anything but tame, the original was even more risqué. "Steven and I vetoed [rejected] the first script," Tyler's mother told *Entertainment Weekly*. "Omigod, it had some racy stuff in there."

After playing the role of a store clerk named Corey in *Empire Records*—a slow-moving 1995 drama set in a record store—she landed a part in *Stealing Beauty* (1996). Filmed in Italy, the movie was directed by Bernardo Bertolucci, whose critically acclaimed movies such as *The Last Emperor, The Sheltering Sky,* and *Little Buddha* had created a loyal art-house following. Tyler was nervous about meeting the legendary director. "I was so scared," she confided in *Entertainment Weekly*, "my ears were bright red and my stomach was making noises I never knew it could." Bertolucci was impressed with the young actress. "When I first met her," he explained, "I could not make up my mind about her age. One minute she was 13, a little girl. Another minute she was a femme fatale of 25. It was as if she was moving through different ages. And that was very, *very* exciting."

Bertolucci cast Tyler as Lucy Harmon, a 19-year-old American who spends the summer in Tuscany, Italy, with family friends. When Tyler arrived in London for a screen test, she learned that the revised script included a subplot in which her character discovers her true parentage. She was struck by the similarity to her own history. "I tried my damnedest not to think of my own situation," she told *Time* reporter Bellafante, "but at one point, after a take, I just started to cry and cry. I remembered when I found out about my dad."

Stealing Beauty was not one of Bertolucci's better efforts. Richard Corliss, for example, wrote in *Time* that the movie was "all about looking at Liv." He had positive remarks for Tyler, however: ". . . she truly is at ease with herself and the camera. Her allure can seem a come-on, but she's not a flaunter; she doesn't shake her beauty." Even though the film did not fare well, the number of Tyler's admirers continued to increase, not least of all in Europe, where she was nicknamed Liv Taylor—after the famous actress Liz Taylor.

That thing she did, and more

Also in 1996, Tyler took a part in *That Thing You Do,* Tom Hanks' debut movie as a director. The story of a 1950s rock band, the movie was a critical and popular success. But in the role of Faye Dolan, the girlfriend of the lead singer, Tyler, according to *People* reporter Leah Rozen, had "little to do besides squeeze into cigarette pants and tearfully deliver one big speech at the end."

The following year, Tyler appeared in *Inventing the Abbotts,* directed by Patrick O'Connor (whose previous credits include *Circle of Friends*). Adapted from a story by Sue Miller, the movie takes place in a small Midwestern town in the 1950s. A sort of modern-day Romeo and Juliet, it portrays the story of a rich girl who falls for a boy from a poor, rival family—played by Joaquin Phoenix, brother of the late River Phoenix. (The two co-stars became romantically involved during the filming, and lived together for some time

Stealing Liv

Stealing Beauty is the first movie by famed director Bernardo Bertolucci to be promoted by a rock video. (The video, "Rocket Boy," by Liz Phair, features clips of Tyler in the movie.) "It's something new," the director admitted to *Entertainment Weekly*. "I'm used to having my usual audience, people who have seen my movies before. This is the first time kids will be going. In Italy . . . it is a fantastic hit with teenagers. They have stolen something like 250 posters [with Tyler's picture] from the streets of Rome. So this is real exciting."

Liv Tyler and Bruce Willis wave to the crowd at the premiere party for Armageddon. *(AP/Wide World)*

before separating.) Tyler described her experience playing Pamela Abbot in an online interview: "When you do a film, everybody wants you to describe your character, and I never could figure out why it's always been so hard for me. I just realized recently, it's because you don't necessarily verbalize it. I relate to her in all ways: her understanding of the situation around her and not being crippled by the dysfunctional sides of her family, and accepting them and striving to be different from them instead of the same." Although the movie received a lukewarm reception, Tyler won praise from a number of critics. Peter Travers wrote in *Rolling Stone* that "Tyler finds the defiant grace of a girl crashing into womanhood," while *Village Voice* critic Amy Taubin asserted that "Tyler and her costar Joaquin Phoenix are the only reasons to see the picture."

In 1998's *Armageddon,* Tyler played the daughter of Bruce Willis—a deep-core oil driller who must save the world by drilling to the center of an asteroid to plant a nuclear device before it collides with Earth, destroying the planet. Already a veteran of several films, Tyler—who turned 18 while filming *Armageddon*— found the role difficult to grasp. "It was really hard," she explained to *GQ* reporter Kaylin. "My first week was all the emotional stuff in mission control while they're in space, and it's like two-second snaps of me reacting to things. I'd never done that kind of acting before. You just never walked away feeling good about it. I don't think I ever really came to terms with who my character was." Tyler did not allow her unpleasant experience with *Armageddon* director Michael Bay to affect later projects. The following year, she participated in no fewer than three projects, including *Onegin,* co-starring Ralph Fiennes, *The Little Black Book,* and *Cookie's Fortune.*

Tyler once lamented that she was not taken seriously when she first entered the movie business. But things have changed. "Everyone treated me like this kid," she told *People* magazine. "Now my opinion is considered worthy. Finally."

Sources

Bellafante, Ginia. "Living it up!" *Time,* June 17, 1996, pp. 86 ff.

"Biography for Liv Tyler," The Internet Movie Database Ltd. [Online] Available http://us.imdb.com (December 15, 1998).

Corliss, Richard. "One life to Liv—but can she act?" *Time,* June 17, 1996, p. 88.

"Feeling Guilty?" Mr. Showbiz. [Online] Available http://mrshowbiz.go.com (December 15, 1998).

"Inventing Liv." *People.* [Online] Available www.pathfinder.com/people (December 15, 1998).

Kaufmann, Stanley. "Gatherings." *The New Republic,* June 24, 1996, pp. 32 ff.

Kaylin, Lucy. "All you need is Liv." *Gentleman's Quarterly,* August 1998, pp. 156 ff.

"Liv Tyler." *People,* May 12, 1997, p.154.

"Liv Tyler biography page." [Online] Available http://icdweb.cc.purdue/edu (December 15, 1998).

Miller, Samantha. "Tyler too." *People,* August 31, 1998, pp. 81-82.

Rozen, Leah. "Inventing the Abbotts." *People,* April 7, 1997, p. 19.

Rozen, Leah. "That Thing You Do!" *People,* October 7, 1996, p. 19.

Svetkey, Benjamin. *"Liv for the moment." Entertainment Weekly,* June 11, 1996.

Taubin, Amy. "Inventing the Abbotts." *The Village Voice,* April 8, 1997, p. 79.

Travers, Peter. "Inventing the Abbotts." *Rolling Stone,* April 17, 1997, pp. 85-86.

Valdes, Alisa. "Liv on the edge, scenes from the life of a model born into rock and rising fast." *The Boston Globe,* October 13, 1994. [Online] Available http:////www.pns.it/livtyler/articles. (December 15, 1998).

Mark Wahlberg

Born June 5, 1971
Dorchester, Massachusetts

Actor

"It's funny, isn't it? Everybody expects you to (be) so bad that if you do something halfway decent, they think you're amazing."

UPDATE

Raised in a rough neighborhood near Boston, Massachusetts, Mark Wahlberg first earned notice as a member of the teen group New Kids on the Block, which featured the musical abilities of older brother Donnie. Having spent a very brief period with the squeaky-clean New Kids, Wahlberg ventured out on his own, where he soon garnered celebrity as a tough-posing rapper (known as Marky Mark) who had few qualms about baring his biceps, and more. His first album, *Music for the People*, went platinum, selling one million copies. His second album, *You Gotta Believe,* although less successful, spawned a popular tour that drew devoted fans in Japan, France, England, and the United States. Venturing into film acting for the first time in 1994, Wahlberg soon found that his acting ability had eclipsed his musical reputation. **(See original entry on Wahlberg—listed as Marky Mark—in *Performing Artists*, Volume 2.)**

Don't call him Marky

Penny Marshall—who directed Mark Wahlberg in his first feature film appearance, the 1994 comedy, *Renaissance Man*— was one of the first to notice the former rapper's ability to "hold screen." "He's a natural," she told *Time*. "He's got a killer smile, is a good actor and takes direction very well. There's a certain quality of presence that he's used to and that he can give off." Wahlberg, on the other hand, needed to be convinced. Unsure of his ability to act, he was hesitant to enlist in the project. Co-star Danny DeVito was instrumental in boosting the young actor's confidence. "Danny told me that I could act," Wahlberg told *Time Out,* "but I had to let go of all this other [stuff] that I was doing. And that was really it. His faith in me just allowed me to have a little faith in my own ability."

Although *Renaissance Man* received lukewarm reviews, it marked the beginning of what would eventually become an illustrious film career. Next Wahlberg appeared in *The Basketball Diaries,* a harrowing portrait of a teenage athlete's descent into heroin addiction. Released in 1995, the film was based on the 1978 cult memoirs of underground writer/musician Jim Carroll. Cast in the role of Jim's best friend, Mickey, Wahlberg played opposite an up-and-coming young actor—Leonardo DiCaprio. The future *Titanic* star had doubts about the former rapper's acting ability. "I'm working with some of the best character actors that are out there," Wahlberg explained to *Time Out*. "People aren't quick to say, 'This underwear model, he must be a fantastic actor." (During his tenure as rapper Marky Mark, Wahlberg had posed in his underwear for a Calvin Klein advertisement.) But, as *Time* contributor Christopher John Farley noted, "Wahlberg's performance in *The Basketball Diaries* as a drug-addled Catholic school dropout . . . was surprisingly well received."

Here today, here tomorrow

Wahlberg assumed his first starring role in *Fear,* a 1996 thriller directed by James Foley. While the film was universally panned by film critics, Wahlberg, who plays the role of a violent and obsessed boyfriend, received positive reviews. "[Wahlberg] delivers a particularly cogent [convincing] performance as the terrorist-boyfriend," wrote A&E critic Sam Strait. "His gentlemanly psychopath, David, is smarmy, smooth, and intense, and exudes [gives off] soft-spoken menace. A professional singer and erstwhile [former] Calvin [Klein] model, Mr. Wahlberg continues to prove he's worthy of the appellation [title] actor." Director Foley, too, had high praise for his lead-

Mark Wahlberg and Burt Reynolds travel back to the 1970s in Boogie Nights. (The Kobal Collection)

ing man, who was nominated for a 1997 MTV Movie Award as Best Villain: "He seemed to have access to a great deal of emotion with little effort," he told *Time*. "He doesn't wear his intensity on his sleeve. But he is very intense, very serious . . . He's driven to be celebrated for the quality of his work."

While Wahlberg was celebrated for the quality of his work in *Traveller*, a 1996 film about a clan of Southern conmen, the little-seen art-house drama did little to boost his celebrity. It was not until 1997, when *Boogie Nights* was released, that Wahlberg truly came into his own as an actor. An entertaining look at the adult film industry in the 1970s, *Boogie Nights* received critical raves, as did Wahlberg's performance as Dirk Diggler, a busboy-turned adult movie star. "This new movie of his is going to make him a star," predicted DreamWorks executive David Geffen. "He's built a legitimate career for himself, which he did not have as a recording artist. . . .People thought he was here today, gone tomorrow, but he's going to be here today and here tomorrow." Wahlberg, too, saw the movie as a departure from his rap-artist past. " . . . with the roles I've played in the past, people tried to find ways to compare my acting work to my music career," he told Knight-Ridder reporter Rene Rodriguez. "This is the first time that I got to do something that is in no way, shape or form like anything I've ever done before."

Again, Wahlberg had been hesitant to accept the role — which was offered to him only after Leonardo DiCaprio declined. He later explained to Mr. Showbiz that he had once vowed, "There were three things I'd never do in a movie: dancing, singing, and stripping—and that was all in the first thirty pages of the *Boogie Nights* script." Directed by Paul Thomas Anderson, the movie was nominated for several Academy Awards.

After *Boogie Nights*
Wahlberg followed his *Boogie Nights* success with a role as a sympathetic hitman in *The Big Hit,* directed by Kirk Wong. Released in 1998, the dark comedy also featured Lou Diamond Phillips, Christina Applegate, and Antonio Sabato, Jr. Next he took on the role of policeman Danny Wallace in *The Corruptor* (1999), a violent tale of deception and betrayal in New York City's Chinatown. Starring opposite Hong Kong action superstar Chow Yun Fat—who plays Nick Chen, a corrupt New York City policeman—Wahlberg garnered positive press. *New York Times* critic Stephen Holden, for instance, wrote, "Wahlberg's Danny, a pug-faced naif [innocent] who in the movie's surprise revelation turns out not to be as innocent as we thought, is an effective foil for Chow's brooding policeman."

Having matured into a legitimate actor, Wahlberg finds himself sought-after by such heavy-hitters as actor Robert DeNiro, with whom he co-stars in *Out on My Feet,* released in 1999. Concerning the sorts of future projects he would like to participate in, he once told a *News-Times* interviewer, "Stuff that is more . . . human. People are forgetting that there might be a person under this skin and in this body. I have a lot of life experiences that I think can be helpful in my work. As much as I didn't like most of those experiences, I'm still willing to go back there for the good of my profession."

Sources

Farley, Christopher John. "Marky Mark's New Rap." *Time,* October 6, 1997, pp. 86-88.

Hensley, Dennis. "Cosmo Q & A: Mark Wahlberg—The artist formerly known as Marky Mark." *Cosmopolitan,* August 1997, pp. 168 ff.

Holden, Stephen. "'The Corruptor: Gang-Busting Partners in Chinatown." *The New York Times,* March 20, 1999.

"Mark Wahlberg." The Online Movie Club. [Online] Available http://www.sacbee.com/leisure/themovieclub2/spotlight/ (March 16, 1999).

"Mark Wahlberg Biography," and "Mark Wahlberg Interview." Mr. Showbiz. [Online] Available http://mrshowbiz.go.com/ (March 16, 1999).

Paphides, Peter. "'70s special 'Boogie Nights.'" *Time Out,* January 1998. [Online] Available http://www.markymark.com/ (March 16, 1999).

Rodriguez, Rene. "Mark Wahlberg's maturation: from bad boy to 'Boogie' man." The News-Times Movies (Knight-Ridder Newspapers), October 20, 1997. [Online] Available http://www.newstime.com. (March 16, 1999).

Strait, Sam. Review of *Fear.* 99 Lives, The Video Magazine (A&E). [Online] Available http://www.99lives.com/ (March 16, 1999).

Robin Williams

*Born July 21, 1952
Chicago, Illinois*

Actor, comedian

UPDATE

Voted "least likely to succeed" as a student, actor comedian Robin Williams proved his classmates wrong—with a vengeance. Having enjoyed tremendous success as a stand-up comic when he was in his early twenties, he soon landed numerous television appearances that highlighted his comedic ability. Having made an exceptionally popular guest appearance on the well-rated ABC sitcom *Happy Days,* Williams won a lead role in his own series. *Mork and Mindy,* which co-starred Pam Dawber, surpassed even *Happy Days* in popularity, and topped the Nielsen ratings in both 1978 and 1979, averaging 60 million viewers per episode. With Williams' tremendous popularity came numerous offers of film roles. Moviemaking, however, proved to be more of a challenge for the energetic comedian. His first films—including *Popeye, The World According to Garp,* and *Moscow on the Hudson*— were, at best, only moderately successful. Beginning in 1988, however—having put troubles with drug and alcohol abuse behind him—Williams enjoyed a run of successful film appearances, beginning with the critical and commercial success, *Good Morning Vietnam,* for which he was

"You're only given a little madness. You mustn't lose it."

(Corbis Corporation)

243

nominated for an Academy Award for his role as a fast-talking disk jockey. Williams would later receive Oscar nominations for his role in the 1989 prep school drama, *Dead Poets Society* and the 1991 Terry Gilliam drama, *The Fisher King*. **(See original entry on Williams in *Performing Artists*, Volume 3.)**

From The Birdcage to Hamlet

In the two decades since his first leading role in a feature film (*Popeye*, 1980), Robin Williams continued to turn out a staggering number of performances—some successful, some not. Noted for his manic comic energy, he built a film resumé that includes comedies, dramas, and even science fiction and fantasy. Shortly after his successful starring turn in *Mrs. Doubtfire* (1993), he made a relatively rare television appearance in *In Search of Dr. Seuss* (1994). Next came an uncredited appearance as John Jacob Jinglehiemer Schmidt in the 1995 comedy *To Wong Foo, Thanks for Everything, Julie Newmar*, followed by a small, uncredited role in that year's *Nine Months*, a remake of a French film titled "Neuf Mois." Returning to a leading role, he portrayed Alan Parrish in the $65 million science fiction drama *Jumanji*. A special-effects laden story of a jungle-themed board game that sucks players into its alternate universe, the film performed solidly at the box office, in spite of lukewarm critical reviews.

Having appeared in *The Secret Agent* (1996), a poorly received adaptation of a Joseph Conrad novel by the same name, Williams took a lead role in *The Birdcage*, an American remake of a popular 1979 French comedy called *La Cage aux Folles*. Directed by Mike Nichols, the film is about two gay men, Armand (Williams) and Albert (played by Nathan Lane) who have lived together happily for years—until Armand's son, whom the two have raised, decides to marry the daughter of an extremely conservative senator. (The daughter was played by Calista Flockhart, who later earned celebrity status as television's Ally McBeal.) Although plagued by mixed reviews, the film far outperformed studio executives' modest expectations: in the opening weekend, theatergoers purchased some $18 million worth of tickets.

Although studio executives and director Nichols wanted to cast Williams in the flashier role of Albert, the actor chose instead to play the more low-key part of Armand. Williams explained to the *New York Times* that his decision was based, in part, on the fact that he had recently played a part in drag (man in women's clothing) in *Mrs. Doubtfire*. "I thought, 'No, I want to try something different, something more elegant," he told Bernard Weinraub. "People expect me to be the more flamboyant one. I wanted something new." *New York Times* critic Janet Maslin applauded Williams' portrayal. "*The Birdcage* might seem an odd occasion to find Williams playing things straight, but this is one of his most cohesive [connected] and least antic performances. It's also a mischievously funny one: He does a fine job of integrating gag lines with semi-serious acting, all the while modeling a delirious, silky wardrobe with the emphasis on nightmare prints."

Also in 1996, Williams starred in *Jack*, a comedy about a boy whose body ages at four times the normal rate. Directed by respected veteran Francis Ford Coppola (perhaps best known for directing the *Godfather* series), *Jack* again scored well with audiences in spite of poor critical marks. Williams, however, received positive press for his portrayal of a young boy in a man's body. "As might be expected, Williams leaps at the chance to contrast Jack's boyish manner with his middle-aged looks," wrote Maslin. "He mimics a child perfectly when fidgeting or horsing around or wiping his nose on his shirt. And he shows just the right comic embarrassment when trying to masquerade as a grown man, or when marveling at the nose and ear hair on his 40-year-old body." In an abrupt turnaround, Williams completed that year's offerings with an appearance as Osric in a modern adaptation of the tragic Shakespeare drama, *Hamlet*. Directed by Kenneth Branagh, the film was nominated for an Academy Award for Best Adapted Screenplay, among others.

Deconstructing Robin

Williams remained busy in 1997. In Woody Allen's *Deconstructing Harry*, he played a small role as an unfocused actor: when the camera tries to capture him, he appears blurred and fuzzy. In the television series, *Great Minds Think for Themselves*, he was heard as the voice of The Genie. The year also produced two popular but faintly praised comedies: *Father's Day*, which pairs Williams with comedian Billy Crystal, and *Flubber*, a Disney remake of *The Absent-Minded Professor* (1961). Most successful, however, was his supporting role in 1997's surprise hit, *Good Will Hunting*, penned by co-stars Ben Affleck and

Robin Williams as the therapist who befriends Matt Damon's troubled genius in Good Will Hunting. *(The Kobal Collection)*

Matt Damon. As therapist Sean Maguire, who helps a brilliant young South Boston janitor (Damon) come to terms with himself, Williams took on a rare serious role. The gamble paid off. Nominated for his fourth Academy Award, he received his first Oscar, for Best Supporting Actor. Winning the award, however, did have a downside. "It's very strange because then they announce your name and it's real. It's happened," he told ET Spotlight. "Good news, bad news. Good news is you won. Bad news is you have to speak now. Can't I just take it and run? No. Sorry. I mean that's the other side of it."

With an Oscar securely under his belt, Williams showed no signs of slowing in 1998. Continuing in the dramatic genre, he appeared in *What Dreams May Come,* based on a novel by Richard Matheson and directed by New Zealand filmmaker Vincent Ward. The story of a man who is killed in an automobile crash and searches for his wife in the afterlife, the film was most praised for its stunning visual effects, which portray heaven as a strange and magical version of the world left behind. Returning to comedy (with a touch of seriousness) in a big way, Williams played the title role in *Patch Adams,* about an unconventional doctor who uses humor to deal with terminally ill young patients. While the film received dismal reviews, audiences flocked to theaters: within just ten days of its release, *Patch Adams* earned $65.5 million. Williams next wrapped up production on *Jakob the Liar,* a story about a man who looks after a young girl in 1930s Germany. Future projects include *The Interpreter,* about a man who lands in the midst of an international crisis; *Rim,* a computer-age thriller; and *Damien of Molokai,* a biographical tale of a Belgian priest who cared for lepers in Hawaii in the 1800s.

Laughter Is the Best Medicine

In the comedy *Patch Adams,* Williams portrays a real-life doctor who uses humor therapy to help young terminally ill patients cope with their illnesses. Although he isn't a real doctor, Williams is a firm believer in prescribing laughter for whatever ails you. "I think it's [a cleansing] for the soul," he once told an ET Spotlight interviewer. "I think it [laughter] really does help. It releases. There have been studies about it, it's a fact. It allows you to get through painful times."

Sources

de Lisle, Leanda. "Robin, tacos and princesses." *The Spectator,* March 14, 1998, pp. 56 ff.

Halliwell, Leslie. *Halliwell's Filmgoer's and Video Viewer's Companion,* Revised Edition. New York: Perennial Library, 1998.

Holden, Stephen. "*What Dreams May Come:* Apparently, the Afterlife Is Anything but Dead." *The New York Times,* October 2, 1998.

Maslin, Janet. "*Good Will Hunting:* Logorhythms and Biorhythms Test a Young Janitor." *The New York Times,* December 5, 1997.

Maslin, Janet. "*Jack:* One From the Heart." *The New York Times,* August 9, 1996.

Maslin, Janet. "*Patch Adams:* Take Two Giggles, Twice Daily, and Physician, Squeal Thyself." *The New York Times,* December 24, 1998.

"*Patch* Cures B.O. Ills," "Robin Williams Biography." Mr. Showbiz. [Online] Available http://mrshowbiz.go.com/ (March 16, 1999).

"Robin Williams Interview," "What Dreams May Come." ET Spotlight. [Online] Available http://www.etonline.com/ (March 16, 1999).

Simanton, Keith. "*Patch* might be just what the doctor ordered." *The Seattle Times,* December 25, 1998.

Steyn, Mark. "Court jester." *National Review,* May 18, 1998, pp. 38-39.

Weinraub, Bernard. Review of *The Birdcage. The New York Times,* March 12, 1996.

Kevin Williamson

Born March 14, 1965
New Bern, North Carolina

Writer, director

"I'm not Horror Boy. If you look at what my work has in common, it's teenagers."

A fan of horror movies since childhood, Kevin Williamson penned his first screenplay hoping that, if it didn't sell, he'd at least have a writing sample with which he could land work on a teen series such as *Beverly Hills 90210*. That screenplay was made into *Scream*—a critical and popular hit that became one of the highest-grossing films in the history of horror. Following that film with another successful genre-bender, *I Know What You Did Last Summer*, Williamson was credited with breathing new life into the tired horror genre. As *Newsweek* critic N'Gai Croal wrote, "Williamson has single-handedly resurrected a genre that was as lifeless as a Halloween slumber party on Elm Street." Although Williamson's coming-of-age television drama *Dawson's Creek* may seem to be a far cry from his scary-movie roots, his scripts invariably have one thing in common: the trials and tribulations of teenagers.

Growing up in the shadow of *Halloween*

Kevin Williamson grew up in the rural community of Oriental, North Carolina—a quiet fishing community and tourist spot on the state's intercoastal waterway (which happens to be located near the real Dawson's Creek), where his father, Wade, worked as a fisherman. His mother, Faye, is a homemaker and former hotel manager. His older brother, John, now a pharmacist, still lives in the area.

His isolated surroundings did not prevent Williamson from becoming a self-described pop-culture junkie. As a child, he spent hours in front of the television, watching shows such as *Apple's Way* and *James at 15*. He told *TV Guide,* "I slept in front of the TV every night on top of the remote control." Although the nearest movie theater was twenty-five miles away, he managed to find a way to see the latest releases. Having committed much of the movie *Jaws* to memory, he soon became a Steven Spielberg fanatic. "My bedroom was a Spielberg museum, and it began my love affair with the movies," he admitted in the foreword to the *Scream* screenplay.

Growing up during the heyday of horror films that featured the likes of "Freddy Krueger" (*A Nightmare on Elm Street*), "Jason" (*Friday the 13th*), and "Michael Myers" (*Halloween*), Williamson developed a passion for the horror genre. He describes the first time he saw John Carpenter's classic horror film, *Halloween* (1978), as a religious experience. "It was a night I'll never forget," he explained in the foreword. "The movie changed my life. *Halloween* was my revelation. I already knew my love of movies was bordering obsessive but I had no idea of how fixated I was until the experience of *Halloween*. The movie frightened me beyond belief." Williamson was so taken by the movie that he returned to the theater time after time to see it again; once he sat through six straight showings. Just thirteen years old at the time, he had to sneak in to attend the movie without an adult (because of the movie's 'R' rating). After buying a ticket to a general-admission movie in the same theater complex, he'd jump into line to see the movie of his choice. Williamson was impressed by *Halloween*'s ability to move viewers, even if that meant scaring the life out of them.

Talking big

Interested in storytelling since his youth, Williamson made movies with a camera his parents had given him. As a student at Pamlico County High School, he wrote plays for the drama club and contributed reviews for the school newspaper. "I always tried to talk bigger than I was and smarter than I was," he

Halloween brings Williamson Full Circle

A fan of horror movies since childhood, Williamson was particularly taken by John Carpenter's *Halloween*. He was thirteen years old when the soon-to-be classic slasher movie first hit theaters in 1978. "The film definitely had an effect on people," he later wrote in the foreword to *Scream*. "It was a roller-coaster ride from beginning to end. I knew from that first screening that I wanted to affect people like that. I wanted to make them scream and jump and then laugh at themselves for getting so worked up. *Halloween* was the film that opened my eyes."

At a time when horror movies had become formulaic and predictable, Williamson came forward with a new sort of slasher that acknowledged its cinematic heritage. For his role in producing such smart and self-conscious features as *Scream* and *I Know What You Did Last Summer,* he has been called the man who saved the horror genre. Filled with verbal echoes and visual imitations of *Halloween*, both films pay tribute to the John Carpenter trend-setter.

Two decades after Williamson—and the rest of America—first experienced *Halloween*, the young director participated in the production of *Halloween H20* (1998). Although credited as co-executive producer rather than writer, he contributed the original story treatment as well as a number of final revisions. About returning to the source of his inspiration, he told *Sci Fi Entertainment,* "You know, it feels like a full circle thing for me. *Halloween* is the movie that (made me) realize the power of cinema in terms of how people can really go on that roller coaster ride."

confessed to *TV Guide*. He also traveled from crowd to crowd — which served him well later as a writer who focuses on teens. "I hung out with the smokers," he said. "I hung out with the in-crowd. I hung out with the A-students. I am really glad I did because now I have such a huge filing cabinet of information."

Not everyone was impressed by Williamson's early efforts to entertain. In one of his English classes, he had been required to read aloud a story he had written. The story—titled 'Just a Matter of Time,' about a girl who is date-raped by her sports-jock boyfriend—contained some suggestive scenes. "My English teacher said 'Sit down,'" Williamson recalled in *Sci-Fi Entertainment*. "She gave me an F. She said 'You can't write, you're from the sticks of North Carolina, you are illiterate, you're ignorant, and your voice shouldn't be heard.' And so, I believed her for the next ten to twelve years of my life." Although he took his teacher's criticism to heart, it was not long before the aspiring writer had found his revenge.

After graduating from East Carolina University, where he majored in theater arts, Williamson moved to New York City to work as an actor. In 1994, he moved to California, where he enrolled in an extension class in screenwriting at the University of California at Los Angeles (UCLA). While attending the ten-week course, he wrote a screenplay for an offbeat black comedy called *Teaching Mrs. Tingle*—inspired, in part, by the high school teacher who had told him he'd never be a writer. Williamson wrote the screenplay in just two weeks. "You know when you're ready to write, it just pours out of you," he explained to *Sci-Fi Entertainment*. "That's that feeling. I just knew I had a story to tell and it's all about that woman who told me I would never be a writer." The script—which concerned a high school senior who will do anything to graduate at the top of her class—sold to a prominent production company for more than one hundred thousand dollars. "I thought I'd made it," Williamson later told *Writer's Digest*.

With his sudden wealth, Williamson paid off student loans, leased an expensive car, and moved into his own apartment — with no roommates. His script, however, remained unproduced. Having been paid for a script that had not been produced did little to bolster his resumé or reputation. With no produced script to his credit, Williamson soon wound up where he had started—broke and unemployed.

A scary movie

Williamson took a variety of odd jobs to support himself, including dog-walking, word-processing, and house-sitting. One night, while house-sitting in Gainsville, California, he watched a Barbara Walters television special about a series of murders that had taken place in that town. "It was scary as hell and was really spooking me," he recalled in the foreword to *Scream*. "The idea that this man was stalking and killing these college kids in this small, unsuspecting town was very frightening. It reminded me of *Halloween*. Then, suddenly, I heard a noise. It was coming from another room. I went to check it out and discovered an open window. I had been staying in the house for two days and hadn't noticed it had been open. I was starting to lose it. I don't do well in scary situations."

Taking a butcher knife in one hand and a cordless phone in the other, Williamson called a friend while he searched the house for intruders. He checked the shower, closets, under beds, and in the garage. But his friend—instead of lending moral support—teased him. "He kept trying to scare me on the phone," Williamson explained, "saying things like 'Freddy's gonna get you,' and 'Michael's behind you,' [referring to serial killers in popular horror films] and 'Kill, kill, kill, ha, ha, ha.'"

Eventually, the two began to argue about which killer was the most frightening, and what horror movie worked the best. "The conversation turned into a movie debate where we started quizzing each other with our movie knowledge," he said. "Thus, *Scary Movie* was born." Williamson wrote the screenplay for *Scary Movie* in three days during a weekend in Palm Springs, California. "I thought maybe I could come up with something—maybe a direct-to-video movie—that would help me at least pay the phone bill. I was desperate," he recalled. Having found its way to the desktops of Hollywood executives, *Scream*—as *Scary Movie* was renamed—marked the beginning of a new era in the horror film industry.

The slasher movie returns with a vengeance

Williamson was afraid that the script for *Scary Movie* would not sell. Almost overnight, however, the script inspired a bidding war among major movie studios and producers. Fearful that he might sell another script that would never be produced, Williamson decided to sell the rights to Miramax, whose head, Bob Weinstein, promised to make the film right away. (Williamson reportedly earned $500,000 in the deal.) Miramax made very few changes in the script: they asked Williamson to add a scene (in which the school principal dies), and they changed the movie's title to *Scream*.

Miramax considered a number of directors—including Danny Boyle (*Trainspotting*), Anthony Waller (*Mute Witness*), and Robert Rodriguez (*El Mariachi*)—all of whom turned down the project. Wes Craven—known for his role behind the camera in *A Nightmare on Elm Street*—also refused the project. After Williamson spiced up the script with more scary material, however, Craven agreed to direct the film. Williamson thought Craven was the perfect choice for *Scream*. "He knew [horror movies] inside and out and I think quite frankly, he was tired of them," Williamson wrote in the foreword. "I think he saw *Scream* as a challenge. He understood what I had set out to do with the horror genre and he completely concurred [agreed]. He loved the idea of exposing conventions of the genre. Wes gave *Scary Movie* its tone. He brought it to life with a perverse wickedness and I'm forever grateful."

Released in 1996, *Scream* featured a cast of young actors from television and independent films. Aimed primarily at high school and college audiences, the film earned $103 million at the box office (making it one of the top-grossing horror films of all time), and won the MTV Best Picture Award (beating out such blockbusters as *Independence Day* and *Jerry Maguire*). Film critics applauded *Scream* for its fresh approach to horror—a genre that had become very predictable. And Williamson, whose script was filled with humor, pop-culture references, and parodies (imitations) of other horror films—was credited with reinventing the horror movie.

A Hitchcockian Move

Williamson (who, during his brief stint as a struggling actor had appeared on *In Living Color* and the soap opera *Another World*) makes a cameo (brief, usually uncredited) appearance in *Scream 2*, as a talk-show host. He's not the only behind-the-scenes filmmaker to relish brief appearances on camera: famed director Alfred Hitchcock (1899–1980) was renowned for his clever cameo appearances.

More horror

Next Williamson turned to writing a screenplay based on a 1973 novel by Lois Duncan. When studio executives asked him to transform the original morality tale into a teen slasher film, he came up with the story of four teenagers who accidentally hit someone on the road during a joy ride back from the beach. Frightened, they throw the body into the ocean—only to realize that their victim was not yet dead. The following summer, a killer begins to haunt them.

I Know What You Did Last Summer was not well received by film critics, who found it lacking the originality of Williamson's first screenplay. The film did become a hit with young movie-goers, however, thanks in large part to its stars, Jennifer Love Hewitt, Ryan Phillippe, and others.

Unlike many sequels, *Scream 2* was not an afterthought based on the box-office performance of the original. "When I sold *Scream*, I attached a five-page treatment outlining the second and third installments of the story," Williamson wrote in the foreword. "I think that's what makes it so special. . . . *Scream 2* and *Scream 3* have always been a part of the plan . . . " Released in December of 1997, the sequel featured surviving cast members of the original film—Neve Campbell, David Arquette, Courteney Cox, Jamie Kennedy, and Liev Schreiber—as well as Sarah Michelle Gellar, Jada Pinkett Smith, and Jerry O'Connell. Although the film performed well at the box office, many critics felt the screenplay paled in comparison to Williamson's first effort.

Coming of age

Not content to be known simply as a "horror boy," Williamson created the television series *Dawson's Creek,* a coming-of-age story about a young man growing up in a small town. More than a little autobiographical, the series is set a few miles from Williamson's childhood home and revolves around an aspiring writer—who, like the young screenwriter—idolizes Steven Spielberg. "His characters are incredibly honest," James Van Der Beek—who plays the title role of Dawson Leery—told *Time*. "They say things teenagers are thinking but don't necessarily say, especially about sexuality."

At the same time wise and naive (inexperienced), Williamson's characters reflect the difficult transition between childhood and adulthood. "My teenagers are self-aware and smart and they talk like they have ten years of therapy and they have all the answers," he told *TV Guide*. "But their behavior completely contradicts that. Their behavior is that of a 15-year-old, inexperienced and not sure of the next step." Some found Williamson's *Dawson* teens less than convincing. *People* reviewer Terry Kelleher wrote, "They look like college students, they talk like doctoral candidates (in popular culture), but they're just starting 10th grade. . . .They're easy to watch, just a little hard to believe."

Slated to work on the first twenty-two episodes of *Dawson's Creek* for the WB network, Williamson also signed a deal—worth $20 million—with Miramax. Included in the contract is the final installment of the *Scream* trilogy as well as a number of new television projects. (Williamson described the premise for one such television project, *The Wasteland,* in *TV Guide*: "Take these Dawson kids, age them by eight years and move them to L.A. without a clue.) Williamson also made his debut as a director with *Teaching Mrs. Tingle* (1999)—the screenplay he had written in response to the teacher who told him he'd never make it as a writer. (Although he had been scheduled to direct his screenplay of *The Faculty* (1998), he turned the project over to director Robert Rodriguez when *Tingle* became available.) "I sort of feel like I've been unemployed for so long with all these stories to tell and now someone wants to hear all of them," Williamson once told *Entertainment Weekly*. "I feel like it's all going to end one day so I better take advantage of it while I can, because today's hot flavor might be gone tomorrow."

> "I've kind of been labeled 'the teen guy.' It's not a bad rap. If that's my fate, I accept it happily. It's my goal to compliment the youth of today. Not to talk down to, criticize, or ridicule, but to entertain and maybe shed some new light on the experiences so that teens can relate and adults can remember."
> —Williamson, *YM*

Sources

Billen, Andrew. "No sex please, we're American." *New Statesman,* May 8, 1998, p. 43.

Broeske, Pat. "Reinventing a Genre." *Writer's Digest,* November 1997. [Online] Available http://www.h-y-p-e.com/kw/articles/1998/writersdigest.html (January 28, 1999).

Croal, N'Gai. "The Return of the Undead." *Newsweek,* November 3, 1997, p. 84G.

Fretts, Bruce. "High School Confidential: Dawson's Creek." *Entertainment Weekly,* January 9, 1998, pp. 34 ff.

Fretts, Bruce. Review of *Scream. Entertainment Weekly,* June 27, 1997, p. 127 ff.

Gleiberman, Owen. Review of *I Know What You Did Last Summer. Entertainment Weekly,* October 24, 1997, p. 44.

Gliatto, Tom. Review of *Scream 2. People,* December 22, 1997, p. 22.

Johnson, Ted. "Kevin Williamson, who came of age on the real Dawson Creek, stays in touch with his inner teen." *TV Guide,* March 7-13, 1998. [Online] Available http://www.h-y-p-e.com/kw/articles/1998/tvguide.html (January 28, 1999).

Kelleher, Terry. Review of *Dawson's Creek. People,* January 19, 1998, p. 14.

Krantz, Michael. "The Bard of Gen-Y." *Time,* December 15, 1997. [Online] Available http://www.h-y-p-e.com/kw/articles/1998/time.html (January 28, 1999).

Mangels, Andy. "His Voice Should Be Heard." *Sci-Fi Entertainment,* December 1998. [Online] Available http://www.h-y-p-e.com/kw/articles/1998/scifient.html (January 28, 1999).

Marin, Rick. "My So-Called Soap." *Newsweek,* January 19, 1998, p. 68.

Nashawnty, Chris. "With *Scream* and its evil spawn, this screenwriting scaregiver single-handedly saved the choking horror-film genre." *Entertainment Weekly,* December 1997. [Online] Available http://www.h-y-p-e.com/kw/articles/1998/ew97.html (January 28, 1999).

Rozen, Leah. Review of *I Know What You Did Last Summer. People,* November 3, 1997, p. 22.

Tucker, Ken. Review of *Dawson's Creek. Entertainment Weekly,* January 23, 1998, pp. 45 ff.

Williamson, Kevin. "Foreword as printed in *Scream: The Screenplay.*" [Online] Available http://www.h-y-p-e.com/kw/articles/1998/foreword.html (January 28, 1999).

Williamson, Kevin. "Let's Talk." *YM Magazine,* September 1998. [Online] Available http://www.h-y-p-e.com/kw/articles/1998/ym.html (January 28, 1999).

Oprah Winfrey

*Born January 29, 1954
Kosciusko, Mississippi*

Talk show host, actress, producer

UPDATE

"Most of the world is operating on somebody else's definition of what they should be, and all I'm here to do is help people remember: Define yourself."

(AP/Wide World)

Born into poverty, Oprah Winfrey overcame her humble beginnings to become one of the world's highest-paid entertainers. Blessed with an innate (natural) ability to communicate, she assumed her first television post while still in college, at a local television station in Nashville, Tennessee. Having left Nashville for Baltimore, Maryland, she was eventually assigned to co-host a local morning talk show. It was soon apparent that she had found her calling. Ready to stake her claim in big-time broadcasting, she accepted a position on *A.M. Chicago*, a talk show broadcast by an ABC-TV Chicago affiliate. In short order, the show, hosted by Winfrey, beat out the well-established local and national favorite, *The Phil Donahue Show*. A phenomenal success, the show evolved into a one-hour afternoon chat-fest that would soon become a national institution. Popular with a broadly defined audience, *The Oprah Winfrey Show* reportedly grossed $125 million in its 1986 syndication agreement. Already one of the world's highest paid entertainers, Winfrey later established her own company, HARPO Productions, which took over ownership and production of *The Oprah Winfrey Show*. **(See original entry on Winfrey in *Performing Artists*, Volume 3.)**

The queen of daytime—and beyond

One of only three women (including actress Mary Pickford, 1893–1979, and comedian Lucille Ball, 1911–89) to own a major film company, Oprah Winfrey continues to host a talk show that reaches an audience of nearly 20 million people daily. In 1998, *Entertainment Weekly* magazine named her the most powerful person in show business in the magazine's annual list of the 101 most powerful people in the entertainment world. She was the first African American to earn that title. Winfrey's impact on the public is in no small measure quantifiable: her influence has extended to the publishing industry, agricultural markets—and to the way countless television-viewers have begun to think about their lives.

The Oprah Winfrey Show has remained the top-rated talk show since it first aired nationally in September 1986. Produced in Chicago by Winfrey's company, HARPO Productions, Inc., it is carried by 206 television stations nationwide—and in 142 international markets. By its twelfth season, the show had collected 32 prestigious Daytime Emmy Awards, including the 1998 Outstanding Daytime Talk Show honor. The highest-rated talk show in television history, it is contracted to run through the year 2002.

But there was a time when Winfrey considered canceling her popular show. Daytime television featured an overabundance of talk shows—many of which descended into increasingly outrageous exercises in poor taste. Winfrey's duties as producer mounted—as did her interest in acting. More than once, she considered quitting her talk show in order to focus on acting. In 1997, however—while she was in Philadelphia, Pennsylvania, filming a movie—she realized that her talk show was a gift. "I thought, 'You come from a people with no choice, no money, no power, no vision, no vehicle for themselves and their children,'" she later told *USA Weekend*. "You've been *given* this."

In September 1998, Winfrey kicked off her talk show's thirteenth season with a new format. "I believe television can do something it has never done before," she said in a press release. The new concept—which she christened "Change Your

> "I thought, 'You come from a people with no choice, no money, no power, no vision, no vehicle for themselves and their children. You've been *given* this."

Oprah's Book Club

A voracious reader since childhood, Winfrey decided to use her power as a television personality to put books back in the lives of Americans—by featuring a monthly book segment on her popular talk show. "I want to get the country reading," she declared. Improbable as the marriage of television and book-reading may seem, Winfrey's mission has been profoundly successful. "Her one-woman literacy campaign is savvier than any to come out of Washington lately because it suggests that television's power can be used to entice people to read," wrote *New York Times* reporter Caryn James. "This is a revolution," Nobel Prize laureate Toni Morrison told *Life*. She should know: Morrison's *Song of Solomon*—originally published in 1977—is one of eight serious novels that sold nearly 10 million copies based on Winfrey's endorsement. And that was in the book club's first year alone. A publishing industry phenomenon, Oprah's Book Club has demonstrated the power to turn little-read books into overnight bestsellers. James explained the key to the success of Winfrey's efforts: "She does not function as a literary critic, but as a cheerleader for reading, reassuring viewers that books are user-friendly and relevant to their lives."

"The best thing about it," Winfrey told *Redbook*, "is the thousands of letters [she receives] from people who haven't picked up a book in 20 years."

Life TV"—focused on self-help and enlightenment, with each show devoting the final ten minutes to a segment called "Remembering Your Spirit." "I'm trying to get people to relate to the truth of their own lives," she told *USA Weekend*. Also new that season was the show's theme song, "Run On With Oprah," performed by the talk-show diva herself.

In her continuing quest to present quality television, Winfrey, in her role as producer, developed an ongoing series of made-for-television movies under the title of "Oprah Winfrey Presents." Her first made-for-TV film, 1997's *Before Women Had Wings,* which chronicles the relationship between an abusive mother and her two daughters, earned a Golden Globe nomination for co-star Ellen Barkin. (Besides producing, Winfrey co-starred in this film as well.)

A spiritual odyssey

Winfrey did not renew her talk show at the expense of her acting career. Having signed a multi-picture contract with Disney studios, she produced and starred in *Beloved* (1998), directed by Jonathan Demme. Adapted from Toni Morrison's Pulitzer Prize-winning novel, the movie is set in Ohio after the Civil War (1861–65) and follows the story of a woman who escaped slavery but is haunted by its legacy. Winfrey later reported having been profoundly moved by the experience of playing a

former slave. "The whole purpose for life on Earth is to attach yourself to that force which is divine and let yourself be released to that," she said in a press release. "I felt that way about making the movie *Beloved*. It was divine—I know no other word to use."

Asked what she hoped to accomplish through the movie, she told *Good Housekeeping:* "I didn't want to make just a slave story about the haunting of a house by a ghost. It's a spiritual odyssey. And it's a love story. It's about a mother and her children. It's about the depth of love, what a mother is willing to go through to protect her children." The role of Sethe, who does the unimaginable in order to protect her children, was a difficult part to embrace. "I tried to empty myself and let the spirit of Sethe inhabit me," she continued. "I've

Oprah Winfrey, along with Thandie Newton (r) and Kimberly Elise (l), enacted the powerful drama Beloved. *(Archive Photos)*

Mad Cowboy Litigation

Shortly after her April 16, 1996, show on "dangerous foods" aired, Winfrey found herself in the midst of a lawsuit. The show—which featured a segment on mad cow disease—had prompted a group of Texas cattlemen to file a suit against her. The suit claimed that Winfrey and one of her guests, Howard Lyman, a vegetarian activist, had mistakenly suggested that mad cow disease could present a problem among herds of cattle in the United States. "It has just stopped me cold from eating another burger," announced Winfrey on national TV—and scores of her viewers apparently followed. (Mad cow disease is spread amongst cattle, and is fatal to humans that ingest the meat of an infected cow. Cases of the disease were documented in the United Kingdom and some parts of Europe, but not in the United States.) Cattle prices plummeted to a ten-year-low, the cattlemen claimed, costing an estimated $11 million in lost revenue. In February 1998—after five weeks of testimony—a federal jury in Amarillo, Texas, found that Winfrey did not slander [falsely charge] the beef industry with her show about dangerous foods. "Free speech not only lives," the talk-show hostess said outside the courthouse, "it rocks!"

gathered a lot of slave memorabilia. Documents taken from plantations that list slaves by name and age—and price. The names of people are listed along with the cattle, plows, and carriages: Amos, $500. Josiah, $900. Little Anna, $300. During filming, I had several of those documents framed and set up on an altar in my trailer. Every morning, before my scenes, I lit candles and said the names of these slaves. I prayed every day to the ancestors."

Winfrey, who had previously garnered an Academy Award nomination for her role in *The Color Purple* (1985), received mostly positive reviews for her portrayal of Sethe. The film, however, performed poorly at the box office. The film's heavy subject might have been more than audiences were able to bear. CNN movie analyst Martin Grove told *People:* "*Beloved* is just too long, too somber, too depressing."

Failure, however, is not something that Winfrey seems to fear. "If I can't take a risk, nobody can," she told *Vogue* (cited in *People*). "With fame, notoriety, credibility—if you can't have the courage to stand up and speak out for what you truly believe in, then it means nothing."

Sources

Calio, Jim. "If You Knew Oprah Like I Knew Oprah . . . " *Redbook,* February 1998, pp. 62 ff.

James, Caryn. "Oprah Book Club: Adding Power of TV to Power of the Page." *The New York Times,* November 21, 1996.

Johnson, Marilyn. "Oprah Winfrey, A Life in Books." *Life,* September 1997, pp. 44 ff.

Lynch, Lorrie. "Oprah's new mission." *USA Weekend,* October 9-11, 1998, pp. 4-6.

Maslin, Janet. "*Beloved:* No Peace From a Brutal Legacy." *The New York Times,* October 16, 1998.

"Oprah Winfrey." *People Weekly,* December 28, 1998-January 4, 1999, p. 86.

"Oprah Winfrey Biography," "Oprah Winfrey wins beef suit." Mr. Showbiz, February 26, 1998. [Online] Available http://mrshowbiz.go.com/ (March 8, 1999).

"Oprah Winfrey named most powerful person in entertainment industry."
     Jet, November 9, 1998, p. 11.

"The Oprah Winfrey Show Goes Beyond Paradise to The Atlantis" (February 1,
     1999); "Oprah Winfrey to Continue to Host and Produce The Oprah
     Winfrey Show for an Additional Two Years Through the Year 2002!"
     (September 24, 1998); "A New Era of Oprah Begins Live On Tuesday,
     September 8, 1998" (September 3, 1998). OPRAH.COM Press Releases.
     [Online] Available www.oprah.com. (March 8, 1999).

Powell, Joanna. "Oprah's awakening." *Good Housekeeping,* December 1998,
     pp. 112 ff.

Sutton, Larry et al. "Beloved, alas, by too few." *People Weekly,* November 9,
     1998, p. 13.

Cumulative Index
to Volumes 1–4

Italic type indicates volume numbers (*1–3:* refers to entries in the 3-volume *Performing Artists* base set); **boldface** type indicates Volume 4 entries and their page numbers; (ill.) indicates illustrations.

Italic type indicates volume numbers (*1–3:* refers to entries in the 3-volume *Performing Artists* base set); **boldface** type indicates Volume 4 entries and their page numbers; (ill.) indicates illustrations.

265 | **Cumulative Index**

F

The Fabulous Baker Boys 1–3: 542

The Faculty 4: 184, 254

Fame 1–3: 12–13, 285, 348

Family Business 1–3: 322

Family Ties 1–3: 220, 222–223, 225

Far and Away 1–3: 143

Farewell My Concubine 4: 31

Farley, Chris *4:* 213

Fast Times at Ridgemont High 4: 109

Fat Albert and the Cosby Kids 1–3: 126, 128

Fatal Beauty 1–3: 69

Father of the Bride 1–3: 425, 430

Father's Day 4: 245

Fear 4: 239

Fearless 1–3: 535

Feel My Power 1–3: 297

Feeling Minnesota 4: 47

Female Health Foundation (FHF), *4:* 8

Ferrell, Will *4:* 112

A Few Good Men 1–3: 144

Field of Dreams 1–3: 136

Fifth Element 4: 227

54 4: 21

Figaro 1–3: 494

"Fight the Power" *1–3:* 564

A Fine Mess 1–3: 34

Firebird 1–3: 649, 651

Firefox 1–3: 186

Firestarter 4: 3

The Firm 1–3: 144

First Blood 1–3: 639

Fishburne, Laurence *1–3:* 201–207, 201 (ill.)

The Fisher King 1–3: 679

Fist of Fury 4: 31

A Fistful of Dollars 1–3: 184–185

Five Corners 1–3: 218

The Five Heartbeats 1–3: 660

Flatley, Michael *4: 59–65,* 59 (ill.)

Flatliners 1–3: 589

Flockhart, Calista *4:* 244

Flubber 4: 245

Folksingers 'Round Harvard Square 1–3: 42

Fonda, Bridget *1–3:* 208–211, 208 (ill.)

For the Boys 1–3: 440

For a Few Dollars More 1–3: 185

For Love or Money 1–3: 224

For Me and My Gal 1–3: 370, 372

Forever Your Girl 1–3: 1–3

Forrest Gump 1–3: 303; *4:* 100

Foster, Jodie *1–3:* 212–219, 212 (ill.), 327, 535

461 Ocean Blvd 1–3: 117

Four Rooms 4: 182

The Four Seasons 1–3: 455

Fox, Michael J. *1–3:* 210, 220–225, 220 (ill.)

Foxes 1–3: 215

Foxx, Jamie *4: 66–71,* 66 (ill.)

Foxy Lady 1–3: 109

Frankie and Johnny 1–3: 542

Freak 4: 146

Freaky Friday 1–3: 214

Freaky Styley 1–3: 582

Freeman, Morgan *1–3:* 226–231, 226 (ill.), 294, 666 (ill.)

The Fresh Prince of Bel-Air 1–3: 624, 626; *4:* 205

Friday 4: 227

From Dusk Till Dawn 4: 183

From Earth to the Moon 4: 102

From Russia With Love 1–3: 123

The Funky Headhunter 1–3: 298

Happy Birthday, Gemini 1–3: 455

Happy Days 1–3: 460

Happy Gilmore 4: 188

A Hard Day's Night 1–3: 56

Harlem Nights 1–3: 287

Harris, Neil Patrick *1–3:* 306–308, 306 (ill.)

Harrison, George *1–3:* 53–54

Hart, Melissa Joan *4:* **104–08,** 104 (ill.)

Harvey 4: 223

The Harvey Girls 1–3: 254

Havana 1–3: 577

Hazme Sentir 1–3: 32

Heart in Motion 1–3: 273–274

Heart of Stone 1–3: 111

"Heartbreak Hotel" *1–3:* 553

Heckerling, Amy *4:* **109–14,** 109 (ill.), 112 (ill.)

Help 1–3: 56

Henry V 1–3: 510

Hepburn, Katharine *1–3:* 277, 309–313, 309 (ill.), 548; *4:* 221

Hercules 4: 137

Hercules and the Amazon Women 4: 137

"Here You Come Again" *1–3:* 521

Hero 1–3: 251

He's the DJ, I'm the Rapper 1–3: 625

Hewitt, Jennifer Love *4:* 15 (ill.), **115–21,** 115 (ill.), 117 (ill.)

High Plains Drifter 1–3: 186

Hindman, Earl *1–3:* 19

Hines, Gregory *1–3:* 150, 314–318, 314 (ill.)

His Girl Friday 1–3: 277

History of the World, Part I 1–3: 316

Hitchcock, Alfred *1–3:* 278; *4:* 253

Hocus Pocus 1–3: 440

Hoffman, Dustin *1–3:* 143, 319–322, 319 (ill.)

Holiday 1–3: 277, 311

Hollywood Shuffle 1–3: 658-660

Home Alone 1–3: 152–155

Home Alone: Lost in New York 1–3: 154

Home Fries 4: 7

Home Improvement 1–3: 15, 18, 20

Home Invasion 1–3: 345

Honkytonk Man 1–3: 186–187

Hook 1–3: 322, 589, 679

Hope Chest 1–3: 655

Hopkins, Anthony *1–3:* 105, 323–329, 323 (ill.), 507

Horton, Lester *1–3:* 6, 8

Hotel New Hampshire 1–3: 217

"Hound Dog" *1–3:* 553

House Arrest 4: 118

House of Buggin' 4: 145

House Party III 4: 226

Houston, Whitney *1–3:* 80, 330–334, 330 (ill.); *4:* **122–25,** 122 (ill.), 124 (ill.)

How the Grinch Stole Christmas 4: 26

How Will the Wolf Survive? 1–3: 402

Hughes, Albert *4:* 199, 227

Hughes, Allen *4:* 199, 227

Humanitas International *1–3:* 44

Hung, Sammo *4:* 33

The Hunt for Red October 1–3: 124

Hurston, Zora Neale *4:* 14

Huston, Anjelica *1–3:* 335–340, 335 (ill.)

I

I Do Not Want What I Haven't Got 1–3: 504

"I Got You, Babe" *1–3:* 107, 111

Italic type indicates volume numbers (*1–3:* refers to entries in the 3-volume *Performing Artists* base set); **boldface** type indicates Volume 4 entries and their page numbers; (ill.) indicates illustrations.

275 | Cumulative Index

Weaver, Sigourney *1–3:* 668–674, 668 (ill.)

Webber, Andrew Lloyd *4:* 19

The Wedding Singer 4: 6, 190, 190 (ill.)

West Side Story 1–3: 12, 451, 453, 455

The Whales of August 1–3: 166

What Dreams May Come 4: 246

What the Hell Happened to Me? 4: 189

What's Eating Gilbert Grape? 1–3: 176; *4:* 54

What's Love Got to Do With It? 1–3: 206

What's Your Name? 4: 190

Whatever Happened to Baby Jane? 1–3: 165, 166 (ill.)

Whedon, Joss *4:* 88

When Harry Met Sally 1–3: 146, 150

When a Man Loves a Woman 1–3: 251

Where Are You Now, My Son? 1–3: 44

Where in the World Is Carmen Santiago? 1–3: 456

The White Album 1–3: 58

White Men Can't Jump 1–3: 535, 633

White Nights 1–3: 317

White Oak Dance Project *1–3:* 47, 51

Whitney 1–3: 332

Whitney Houston 1–3: 331

Whoopi Goldberg 1–3: 267

Wild at Heart 1–3: 84

Wild Things 4: 21

Wild, Wild West 4: 208

Williams, Robin *1–3:* 267, 322, 367, 675–680, 675 (ill.); *4:* **243–47,** 243 (ill.), 246 (ill.)

Williams, Vanessa *1–3:* 681–686, 681 (ill.)

Williamson, Kevin *4:* **248–55,** 248 (ill.)

Willis, Bruce *4:* 236 (ill.)

Winfrey, Oprah *1–3:* 687–694, 687 (ill.), 693 (ill.); *4:* **256–61,** 256 (ill.), 259 (ill.)

Winslet, Kate *4:* 56

Wisdom 1–3: 198

The Wishing Chair 1–3: 654

The Witches of Eastwick 1–3: 111, 539–541

With a Song in My Heart 1–3: 496

Witness 1–3: 258, 260

The Wizard of Oz 1–3: 252, 254

Wolf, Scott *4:* 117

Wolf 1–3: 542–543

Wolfen 1–3: 316, 514

Woman of the Year 1–3: 312

"Wonderful Tonight" *1–3:* 117

Woo 4: 202

Woodstock 1–3: 40, 43

Working Girl 1–3: 673

The World According to Garp 1–3: 676–677

Wuthering Heights 1–3: 509

Wyatt Earp 1–3: 136

X

Xena: Warrior Princess 4: 137

Y

The Year of Living Dangerously 1–3: 671

Yellow Submarine 1–3: 58

Yo! Bum Rush the Show 1–3: 563

You Can't Hurry Love 1–3: 209

You Gotta Believe 1–3: 414

You Only Live Twice 1–3: 123

You've Got Mail 4: 102

Z

Zoot Suit 1–3: 513, 514